ONE WEEK LOAN

Renew Books on PHONE-it: 01443 654456
Help Desk: 01443 482625
Media Services Reception: 01443 482610

Books are to be returned on or before the last date below

Treforest Learning Resources Centre
University of Glamorgan CF37 1DL

Problems at the Roots of Law

Problems at the Roots of Law

Essays in Legal and Political Theory

Joel Feinberg

OXFORD

UNIVERSITY PRESS

2003

OXFORD
UNIVERSITY PRESS

Oxford   New York
Auckland   Bangkok   Buenos Aires   Cape Town   Chennai
Dar es Salaam   Delhi   Hong Kong   Istanbul   Karachi   Kolkata
Kuala Lumpur   Madrid   Melbourne   Mexico City   Mumbai
Nairobi   São Paulo   Shanghai   Taipei   Tokyo   Toronto

Published by Oxford University Press, Inc.
198 Madison Avenue, New York, New York 10016

www.oup.com

Oxford is a registered trademark of Oxford University Press

Library of Congress Cataloging-in-Publication Data
Feinberg, Joel, 1926–
Problems at the roots of law : essays in legal and political theory / Joel Feinberg.
    p. cm.
Includes index.
ISBN 0-19-515526-2
1. Law—Philosophy.   2. Law and politics.   I. Title.
K230.F44 A2   2002
340'.1—dc21   2002025753

9 8 7 6 5 4 3 2 1

Printed in the United States of America
on acid-free paper

To
James M. Dunn-Smith
and
Ron Milo

PREFACE

This fourth collection of my essays, like its predecessors, has sufficient unity to be construed as a book and not merely as a collection of independent articles. What these essays have in common is a genuinely philosophical concern with basic questions. The first chapter, for example, on judicial interpretation, deals with what might be called the "Nuremberg problem." Was the punishment of the Nazi war criminals a departure from law or the use of an implicit norm within the laws of all nations, "a law of nature"? The primary example in my essay of the conflicting positions on this issue is the American fugitive slave cases in the decades preceding the Civil War. Surely no question in the philosophy of law is more fundamental than whether valid law can give the right of ownership of a person to another.

The essays that follow this one turn from the nature of law to the nature of individual responsibility. The second chapter in this collection examines the relation between law and morality, just as the opening chapter does, but in this case the emphasis is on one particular concept, that of a right. Here I defend the very idea of moral rights against the theory that only institutionally conferred rights really count as rights. The view that I prefer is that even when a person has a legal right to this or that, such a right is not necessarily preemptive. It can make clear sense to maintain, for example, that certain classes of persons can have a right to certain classes of goods even though such rights are not recognized by the normal right-conferring agencies.

The next essay (chapter 3) examines critically some conflicting analyses of criminal entrapment. When government agents arrange the circumstances so that a person freely chooses to do a criminal act that he would otherwise not have done, are not the police "creating the crime" that ensues, and are they not therefore the true instigators of the crime? Is it conceptually possible for one person to cause another person to act voluntarily? Finally, what moral judgments (as opposed to legal judgments) are we entitled to make about the wrongdoer who would have lived out his days in perfect innocence but for the manipulative intervention of police agents?

One of the most debated questions of legal philosophy, one that troubled Plato and still engages legal theorists today, is the question of whether a failed attempt to achieve a criminal objective should be punished as severely as a completed crime. A thorough attempt to resolve the problem soon involves one in further problems about desert, guilt, remorse, and the aims and grounds of legal punishment. In chapter 4, I try to straighten out confusions about these concepts while avoiding failures in my own "attempt."

One of the sources of interest in my essay on government subsidies of the arts (chapter 5) is the way it dovetails with my earlier work (*The Moral Limits of the Criminal Law*) on governmental restraints on liberty. One of the functions of government is to *take*, as for example in taxation, and another is to *give*, as for example in subsidies. Could the ultimate theories of justification on both sides be the same? Can a theory of governmental subsidies hope to proceed without a corresponding theory of political liberties? Here we reach again a fundamental question, this time a question of political theory.

The chapter on evil attempts to cast light on the concepts that are probably the most troublesome to ordinary citizens. My original interest in crime was stimulated by the reported frequency with which cruel and apparently senseless crimes are committed. These criminals are often interpreted as mentally ill, in which case, one would think, they ought not to be held responsible, or they are said to be cases of plain, old-fashioned, pure evil (or equivalently, sheer wickedness). Opponents of the medical model find it obscure. Hence they turn to the "pure evil" notion. But defenders of the medical model find "sheer evil" and the like even more obscure. And behold! We have in this conflict of obscurities a philosophical conundrum formed right before our eyes, nourished by the abundant newspaper accounts of crimes that are "sick! sick! sick!" Newspaper columnists and popular magazine writers seem to divide into two groups, according to how they understand these criminals. "Senseless" murderers, those who have no apparent reason for their grotesque atrocities, are thought by some to be "sick! sick! sick!" and thus excused from culpability. Other commentators reject the medical model and think of atrocious criminals as "pure evil, plain and simple." It soon becomes apparent to the investigating philosopher, however, that neither of these major theories is "plain" or "simple." And further complication is produced by the fusion of moral and psychiatric norms, a process that began with Plato and that I explore in the concluding chapter of this volume.

ACKNOWLEDGMENTS

Most of the essays in this book have been previously published. The second section of chapter 6 was first published as "Wickedness or Sickness? New Conceptions and New Paradoxes" in the *Journal of the American Academy of Psychiatry and Law* (1999). "Pure Wickedness, Plain and Simple," the third section of the same chapter, has not been previously published. It is continued here by "Further Studies in Evil," the final section of chapter 6, which studies fictitious evil beings, such as Satan, and some real historic persons, such as Nero and Hitler.

"Criminal Attempts: Equal Punishments for Failed Attempts" is an expansion of the lecture I gave at the colloquium celebrating my retirement from the University of Arizona in October 1994. It was published subsequently in the *Arizona Law Review* 37, no. 1 (1995).

"The Dilemmas of Judges Who Must Interpret Immoral Laws" was drawn from my unpublished manuscript "Natural Law Theory: A Critical Exposition." The section of that manuscript included here amounts to approximately 50 percent of the whole. The shorter version was printed in Jules Coleman and Joel Feinberg, eds., *Philosophy of Law* (Belmont, Calif.: Wadsworth, 1999).

" 'Not With My Tax Money': The Problem (for Liberals) of Justifying Government Subsidies for the Arts" was presented at the fiftieth annual meeting of the American Society for Aesthetics in 1998 and in 1999 at the Pacific Division of the American Philosophical Association in San Francisco.

"In Defense of Moral Rights" was the fifth annual Herbert Hart Lecture in Jurisprudence and Moral Philosophy at University College, Oxford, in May 1991. It was originally published in *Oxford Studies in Law* 12, no. 2 (summer 1992).

I am indebted to Pamela Murphy, whose skill at turning a handwritten manuscript into a book is unsurpassed in my experience. My gratitude also to my wife Betty for her essential help in editing the manuscript.

CONTENTS

Problems at the Roots of Law

1

NATURAL LAW

*The Dilemmas of Judges Who Must
Interpret Immoral Laws*

Filling in the Gaps in Human Law
with Precepts of the Natural Law

Perhaps the most distinctive tenet of natural law theory is that morality—or some sector of morality, notably, justice—is not simply a useful criterion for evaluating any given system of human law nor simply a desirable feature to import into law. In natural law theory, morality is an essential part of law as it is. Some reference to morality (that is, to critical, objective, natural morality, not simply to the conventional morality that happens to prevail in one place or another) must be made as part of the very analysis of what human law is as well as what substantive rules it contains. According to natural law theorists, this connection is a necessary one, derived from conceptual analysis, or definition, of the terms involved. It is not, therefore, a merely contingent connection that could vanish in time as human institutions change.

Legal positivists have been especially puzzled by this claim. What are the ways, they ask, in which human law could be thought to connect with a moral law that is only discovered by human beings, not invented or created by them? One natural law reply is that judges must appeal to natural justice in those "hard cases," as they are called, where the law seems somehow incomplete or indeterminate, yet judgment is required anyway. There are at least three types of hard cases. First, the case before the court may be one in which a statute's wording is vague, and the court must decide, by eliminating the linguistic indeterminacy, whether a defendant is properly convicted of violating it. Suppose a person is charged with violating a local ordinance against "reckless" or "drunk" driving, because while drunk he was discovered riding a horse along the side of a public road. Suppose the facts are not contested. He was drunk; he was on horseback; he was moving along a public road. What is at issue is whether horseback riding is a form of driving. Suppose that because of vagueness the legal issue cannot be settled on linguistic

3

grounds alone. Suppose further that conscientious efforts by the judge to determine the intentions of the original legislators one hundred years earlier are totally frustrated. It is commonly said that, in circumstances like this, where there is a gap in the positive law, the judge is free to legislate on her own and decide the culpability of the horseman on grounds of public policy, including effects on the economic interests of local businesses. At this point, a somewhat cautious natural law theorist might agree, though his misgivings might lead him to add that, if any principle of natural justice is applicable to the issues in the gap of the positive law, they take instant priority over considerations of any other kind. In fact, insofar as justice does apply in the gap, it is no real gap at all, because natural justice brings with itself a kind of automatic legal relevance. This is especially true when the judge's reasonings in the gap lead to results that conflict with principles of fairness that are only implicit in the written part of the law or that can be presumed to apply in the gap simply because it goes without saying that at least some minimal reasonableness is an essential element of law. Minimal reasonableness is, after all, part of the very concept of law, whether put explicitly in the language of a statute or not.

In other words, a vaguely written statute might leave out any mention of fairness or unfairness, in which case, natural justice, though unstated, must be assumed to cover the omission. Or the statute might, in a way, be overwritten, making explicit judgments of fairness that are incorrect, since they conflict with the models of fairness that are a part of natural law. One principle of justice thought to derive from natural law, for example, maintains that justice consists in the exclusion of arbitrary inequalities in the allocation of the benefits or burdens of citizenship. As Aristotle put it, relevantly similar cases are to be treated in similar ways and relevantly dissimilar cases in dissimilar ways and in direct proportion to the degree of dissimilarity between them.[1] Interpreting relevance can be a difficult matter, but some of the irrelevant dissimilarities, at least, can be easily spotted. In deciding which of two persons, A or B, is to be taxed more heavily, conscripted into military service, awarded the starring role in a stage play,[2] or appointed to an appellate court, skin color, as such, is self-evidently irrelevant. So any rule for settling such matters that treats skin color as relevant has not excluded the arbitrary. There may or may not exist some cases in which gender *is* relevant. But that there exist *any* such cases at all is controversial and a reason for reserving special scrutiny (as our constitutional tradition puts it) for claims that the dissimilarities between men and women are *ever* relevant. Perhaps women's relative muscular weakness renders them less suitable for heavy physical labor than men, or more vulnerable to harm, say, in military combat. Or perhaps their greater biological fitness for the care of infants gives them a priority for work in maternity wards. The point is that some such reason must be offered, defended, and then examined with very careful scrutiny if discriminatory treatment based on gender is to pass the test of natural justice. This test is presumed to be implicit in all substantive legal rules but should be especially visible where there is an interstice (gap) in the written law.

Natural law theorists are especially persuasive when they point to examples of a kind of unreasonableness that undermines fairness in a perfectly transparent fashion. In these cases the unreasonable claims are in a statute's language when that language is interpreted with almost childish literalness; natural justice, on the other hand, lingers in the interstices, unspoken.

A specimen example is *People v. Johnson*,[3] a New York case from 1967:

> The defendant was charged with the violation of a statute designed to regulate the resale of theater tickets, in that she did sell two tickets to an opera for $40 each, which tickets were originally priced at $20 each. The court found the defendant not guilty. It appeared that the defendant had purchased the tickets for $20 each in the hope of making them the key to a reunion with her estranged husband. When her husband refused to accompany her, she decided not to attend the opera, and placed an ad in a local newspaper inviting offers to purchase the tickets. In response to the ad a city police inspector telephoned the defendant. He and a policewoman went to the defendant's apartment, agreed upon a price of $40 a ticket, and after the exchange was made the officers disclosed their identity and placed the defendant under arrest, charged with the resale of tickets of admission. . . . The court could not believe that it was the legislative intent to embrace a case such as the one at bar within the ambit of the statute. Rather, the court said, the statute was designed to apply to those engaged in the business of reselling tickets, and the court observed that "business" has been described as a word of large import, rather than a mere isolated transaction. . . . The court found that the prosecution's contention that any sale, even to a relative or friend, of a ticket . . . with or without profit, constituted a violation of the law, was unacceptable, and a reductio ad absurdum [of the prosecution's case].[4]

There was not even an apparent gap in this case. The conflict with justice was located entirely in what was said in the statute and its interpretation by the prosecution. Here the prosecution provided its own interpretation of the imprecise words in the statute in such a way that the words applying to the case at bar were utterly unreasonable and unfair. No statute could be that arbitrary and still be valid law. So, if this statute is valid law, it must be interpreted in such a way that it does not conflict with the minimal rationality and fairness that natural law contributes to all valid human law.

The judge in *People v. Johnson* never mentions natural justice or natural law, but it is not far off the mark to take his decision for acquittal to be an appeal to natural justice. Its main argument is not a survey of relevant precedents nor does it depend on the exact language or plain meaning of a statute. There is no insistence on the fact that explicit exceptions do not appear in the wording of the statute. Rather, the judge relies on the conviction that neither valid law nor legislative intent could be as crazy as this statute is when it is not understood to contain tacit exceptions. And when the exceptions are made explicit by sensible judicial interpretation, the statute is seen to be reasonable.

I trust that it is not too misleading to characterize an argument as an appeal to "natural justice" if it appeals to a fairness or reasonableness that is based upon considerations other than or in addition to "the letter of the law." Some will appeal to standard rational principles of justice, like the Aristotelian exclusion of arbitrary inequalities or the principle of fair opportunity. Tacit appeals to natural justice then can be used to support either an interpretation of a legal judgment or rule or a declaration of its validity or invalidity. Typically, such appeals are used, as in *People v. Johnson*, to support both an interpretation and, in an intertwined fashion, a judgment of validity or invalidity. The interpretation of this statute must be this way because otherwise the statute would be laughably unreasonable and sadly unfair, hence invalid, even though we did not think of it as invalid in the beginning. That is one way the argument might go. Alternatively, we might concede that the statute is properly interpreted in this other way and then judge it invalid because it leads to extreme unfairness, as properly interpreted, and valid law cannot be that unjust.

How severely unfair must a statute be if it is properly to be declared invalid on the ground of conflict with natural justice? The difficulty of this question is perhaps the chief impediment in the way of accepting the natural law doctrine as a theory of legal validity. Cicero, Augustine, and Aquinas all espoused the doctrine (or at least gave lip service to it) that *lex iniusta non est lex* (an unjust law is no law at all). When we think of cases like *People v. Johnson*—or, better, those actual or hypothetical cases like *People v. Johnson* except that interpretations like the prosecution's in that case are explicitly endorsed in the statute itself—we can be easily tempted by the *non est lex* position. But it is a sobering thought that many or most statutes accepted as valid by the courts, partly because of the legitimacy of their origins (the procedures by which they were enacted), are at least to some degree unfair to someone or other. Some are extremely unfair to whole classes of people. Sales taxes, for example, since they are regressive, hurt the poor more than the wealthy. As a result, they are unfair, but even the thousands of citizens who share that opinion recognize, nevertheless, that the statutes imposing the taxes are valid laws creating moral obligations to comply. It is almost impossible to imagine the chaos that would result if everyone honestly believed that unjust laws are not laws at all, but only acts of force obliging compliance without morally obligating anyone to comply.

In addition to statutes whose key words (like "drive") are vague, there are at least two other types of situation that can seem to present judges with gaps, or interstices, in the law. A second type of hard case results from another class of words used in the formulation of legal rules and principles, those that express what have come to be known as essentially contested concepts. In an example of Ronald Dworkin's,[5] a statute may render void all "sacrilegious" contracts, requiring a judge to decide in a particular case whether a contract signed on a Sunday is truly sacrilegious. Similarly, a court may have to decide whether a lower judge's sentencing of a convicted criminal is truly "cruel"; whether a given price is "just compensation"; or whether some behavior was "due," "reasonable," or "appropriate" in the circumstances. According to some theories at least, the judge is on her own in these cases too; she must apply her own moral standards—that is, what she honestly believes are the objectively correct moral standards—to the case at issue. Insofar as the law requires the judge to speak first as a moralist and only then as a jurist, these are hard cases too.

Finally, there are cases that are hard because they are "cases of first impression" with no binding precedent nor even a close analogy to any prior cases in the judge's jurisdiction. The lack of precedent may be because the facts are novel or it may be because, though the facts are familiar, the bringing of a suit under those facts is unprecedented. In the former category are recent suits for the custody of frozen embryos or for the removal of feeding tubes from patients in persistent vegetative states. In the second category, to select just one example, was the first tort suit for emotional damage to a relative of the direct victim of a negligently caused accident.

In both of these types of hard cases, the judge appears to be required not only to legislate, but to legislate in a special way, not appealing to general policy considerations as a genuine legislature might do nor guessing about "legislative intentions" or a dictionary's description of the common usage of words like "drive," "death" (in the feeding tube case), or "damage." Rather, the judge is called upon to decide the case—if it is to be decided at all—by affirming and defending a substantive moral judgment and thus engaging in a type of reasoning for which the written law provides little guidance. Is it *fair* to make a negligent motorist pay for a purely psychological kind of suffering, with no physical basis, of the direct victim's aunt who learns in a telephone call of injury to her nephew? Is it fair to a husband filing for divorce from his wife for the wife to preserve, over his protest, the embryo that they had earlier agreed to create by the fertilization in vitro of her ovum by his sperm, for implantation in her womb? Which is the more important interest here: the wife's interest at the age of forty in bearing a child of her own (this may be her last chance) or her ex-husband's desire not to have a child of his raised by a biological mother he despises? Is a contract signed on the Sabbath truly sacrilegious? All of these questions are issues some judge once had to decide, with clear guidance from neither statute nor precedent, only by the application of some commonly acknowledged or rationally certified principle of natural justice to an unusual-fact situation. Critics of "judicial activism" often say that this construal of the situation suffers the fatal flaw of permitting the judge to apply *her own* values or appeal to *her own* moral convictions, as if it would be better if she appealed to someone else's moral principles that she might not personally share. Of course the principles she uses must be "her own"—that is, principles in which she genuinely believes. Otherwise, her opinion in the case would lack conviction, and she would lack sincerity and integrity. Those principles, however, are relevant and proper not because they are hers. Rather, they are hers because she thinks they are cogent for quite independent reasons, because the reasoning that leads her to them is sound, and because the principle of natural justice that she invokes is correct. There can be no certainty about that, of course, but practical certainty is hard to come by even in those complex legal decisions that confront no gap, involve no purely moral reasoning, and require no leap across the chasm to natural justice.

Natural Law as a Handful of Partly Uninterpreted Abstract Principles

If any of the propositions of the natural law are in some sense a part of the human law too, it must be the more abstract ones. The natural law itself should be thought of as more like a constitution than a municipal code and not at all like the complete set of particularized rules both procedural and substantive—that is, statutes, judgments, and judicial precedents. Some collections of books of rules require whole buildings for their storage. The natural law may be a collection of principles, precepts, and very general rules; if so, it is a collection of only the most general of them, before they are actually applied to factual situations. The result of their application will be particularized rules about safety precautions in boiler factories; hours during which the drivers of ice cream trucks are permitted to ring bells; the maximum percentage of alcohol permitted in the blood of car drivers, but perhaps not horse and mule drivers; distinctions between grades of burglary; and so on. I deliberately make this list as miscellaneous as possible. I do not think that Aquinas, for example, conceived of the natural law as even mentioning alcohol, ice cream, gasoline combustion vehicles, or boiler factories. It is more likely, I think, that the natural law resembles the Ten Commandments or perhaps a small, very small, list of maxims of justice, all put in the abstract, like Aristotle's formulas for distinguishing between genuine equality of treatment and invidious discrimination. The U.S. Constitution, with its Bill of Rights and its Fourteenth Amendment, come to think of it, might make a better model than even the Ten Commandments and the conclusions of Aristotle's theory of distributive justice. In short, if we wrote down the "natural law," it might appear as a list of ten or twelve moral judgments of a very abstract kind, and the whole printed document might be no more than two or three pages long. Perhaps there would be a single ultimate principle, or two or three. Indeed, John Rawls sums everything up in two principles of

justice; his utilitarian opponents, in one.[6] Blackstone wrote that we should
live honestly, should hurt nobody, and should render to everybody his due,
"to which three general precepts Justinian has reduced the whole doctrine of
law."[7] Less abstract but more thorough philosophers might formulate the requirements of equal justice; several more, principles of liberty; and still a few
others, spelling out the principles of autonomy (what is now misleadingly
called "privacy").[8] Absolute orders of priority among the principles, in order
to guide judges to decisions in cases where principles seem to conflict, would
probably be impossible. No mechanical decision procedure in these cases could
substitute for moral sensibility, analogical reasoning, and Solomonic wisdom.[9]
A statement of the full content of natural law would not only contain the
principles that protect citizens from their governments, but also the principles
that protect them from each other. Those principles might include the most
general—responsibility, justification, and excuse—as well as the first principles
of tort and contract liability, child custodianship, and property rights. Perhaps
our full statement of the natural law at this point would come to seven or
eight printed pages, a statement longer than the Ten Commandments but
approximately the same length as the Constitution with its amendments. In
fact, a system of human law that consisted of no more than that brief statement of natural law would be much like one that could lead judges to leap
to the constitutional level immediately in every case, a system that could cut
the rest of the law adrift.

We can think of the abstract natural law precepts, in this model, as related
in one or both of two ways to the more particular judgments and rules of
the human law with which they exist. Natural law functions both as a pro-
genitor of human law rules and as a standard of legitimacy by which the
complex and particularized rules are judged valid or not. Typically, I should
think, the general (natural) and particular (positive) rules are not allowed to
conflict because the natural rules have themselves been used to produce the
positive ones, by application to ever-more-complex factual circumstances and
ever-more-refined restatements of the generating rules themselves as they
spin off exceptive clauses and the like. If a generating rule seems to conflict
with some of its offspring, it is understandable that, other things being equal,
the more concrete derived judgments should be the ones that are invalidated,
since they are inconsistent with the rational precepts that produced them in
the first place.

Consequently, a town ordinance that permits blacks to sit only in the back
row of a public bus is flatly inconsistent with a precept of natural law requiring that laws not be used to enforce arbitrary inequalities. In that case
the ordinance, in contradicting a principle of justice, is itself shown to be
unjust and, therefore (the difficult step), legally invalid. As Cicero and Augustine would have said, it is as if there were no law (governing the distribution of bus seats by race) at all. It is instead just a blunt and forcible way
of putting blacks in their place, as guns or clubs might do. The U.S. Supreme

Court came to the same result (*non est lex*) not explicitly via natural law, but in virtue of the supreme authority of the U.S. Constitution, whose Fourteenth Amendment is itself subject to a kind of natural law interpretation, especially when it invites its judicial interpreters to apply moral standards of what is fitting, appropriate, due, reasonable, unreasonable, cruel, excessive, impartial, equal, private, and so on. Where can the judge turn to find answers to subtle moral questions if not to the objective moral judgments discovered by reason rather than merely invented to serve one's pleasure? That zone, the argument concludes, is the realm of natural law.

Some natural law theorists, of whom Blackstone is perhaps the most typical example, give more than a routine respectful nod to positive law. They believe that positive law rightfully prevails *except* where it contains "flat absurdity or injustice."[10] Only when it is extremely unfair and downright irrational is an otherwise legitimate positive law invalidated by its content. This seems to be simply another way of saying that positive law is to prevail except where it contains a gap but that, within the gap and until it is closed by the enactment of new positive law, natural law is to prevail. If the natural law in the gap conflicts with the positive law that surrounds the gap, then positive law wins out. In these respects, this interstitial theory of natural law is the very opposite of the "higher law" version of the natural law theory associated with Ghandi and Martin Luther King, Jr.

From examples like this, we can see that positivists often differ only in degree and emphasis from other positivists, just as natural law partisans often differ only in such ways from other natural law advocates. Each group of philosophers contains people who respect both established law and its duties of fidelity and obedience, on the one hand, and precepts of justice with their duties of reasonable fairness, on the other. Given the conflicting claims to superior authority of these positive and natural rules, it is not surprising that some nominal positivists bend over backward to accommodate natural rules, some nominal positivists bend over backward to accommodate natural justice,[11] and some natural law theorists in their writings make at least a respectful nod to such positivist precepts as that expressed by *stare decisis*.[12]

Even pure positivists, who insist that law is one thing and morality another, and never shall the one concept be reduced to the other, are likely, as we have seen, to interpret what their rivals call natural law as a set of objective criteria for evaluating a given statute or a given set of established positive rules as good or bad, just or unjust, efficient or cumbersome. They agree with their natural law friends that positive law *ought* to be just and that the criteria of justice are themselves objective truths accessible to reason, denying only that these standards of evaluation are themselves actually part of the law. The positivist writers, on the other hand, who are most respectful of natural law are those who would let enacted or judicially established law prevail except where there are gaps in the positive law itself. These gaps are a consequence of the open texture of language, the unavoidability of essentially contested concepts in the wording of statutes and constitutions, and the legal vacuums produced by unprecedented factual circumstances. Such vacuums are often the consequence of new technology or sometimes simply a reflection of the fact that every precedent in the law is a link in a chain of cases that goes back to an original precedent that was itself decided in the absence of still earlier relevant precedent. Some otherwise positivist judges would insist that courts always decide these cases of first impression on moral grounds by appealing directly to natural justice, for example. Antislavery judges in the nineteenth century, torn apart by the conflict between their antislavery consciences and their sworn duty as judges to uphold the established law, tried hard to reinterpret some laws regarded by their colleagues as established. These judges tried to show that the laws were not really established, because gaps existed in them. In some of these instances it was difficult to know whether to classify the judge as a positivist or a natural law theorist, since he tried so hard to find gaps in the positive law into which he could cram as much natural law as possible.

Most of the theories about how morality or natural law is related to positive or human law are compromises between two distinct and often conflicting kinds of value. At one extreme, we have the higher law version of natural law theory, which pays little respect to positive law as such. (The fact that segregation statutes in the South were properly enacted by legitimate rule-making bodies held very little weight with them.) At the other extreme, pure positivism, even when sympathetic to the goal of suffusing more justice into the law, had no sympathy for the view that *lex iniusta non est lex*, that unjust requirements are already excluded from law by definition. Apart from these groups, the other theories can be understood as efforts somehow to have it both ways, to be a natural law theorist who respects the moral importance of established law or a positivist with a tender sense of justice, particularly pertaining to the operations of her country's legal system. These matters may seem at first to be merely problems for scholars and philosophers trying to achieve consistency, but when we turn to the moral obligation of our obedience to the law, we soon discover that they mask conflicts of practical commitment, sometimes with matters of life or death riding on their outcome.

Fuller, Radbruch, and Hart: The German Experience with Nazism

Perhaps the most influential of the non-Thomist natural law theories in the twentieth century was that of Lon Fuller. Fuller insisted on the essential connection between law and morality, but his secularized version of legal naturalism hd no theological grounding. Moreover, morality provides criteria, in Fuller's view, for the existence of a legal system, not criteria for the validity of a single rule or statute. It is possible then, according to Fuller, for an unjust law to be a valid law. But if the whole network of rules and rule-making powers, or a substantial subsection thereof, is antithetical to morality, then it is no longer a functioning legal system; it is, at best, another method of social control based on arbitrary power.

The morality that Fuller held essential to the existence of a legal system is wholly procedural and does not apply directly to the substantive content of regulations and statutes. Fuller denied that there is some higher law, external to established law, to which the latter must correspond if it is to exist. The morality that is essential to law Fuller calls "the internal morality of law" or "the morality that makes law possible." In his book *The Morality of Law*, he sketches the principles of this internal morality:

1. The rules must be general and not mere ad hoc commands.
2. There can be no secret (unpromulgated) rules.
3. There can be no retroactive rules.
4. The rules must be understandable to those to whom they apply.
5. The rules must not be either self-contradictory or contradictory as a group.
6. The rules must not demand actions that are beyond their subjects' powers to perform.
7. The rules must not be constantly changing.
8. There must be some minimal correspondence between what the rules say and how they are administered or interpreted by the courts.[13]

A total failure in respect to any one of these principles, or a partial failure in respect to most or all of them, implies not simply that there is a bad legal system, but that there is not a legal system at all.

One consequence of Fuller's conception is that the existence of a legal system is always a matter of degree, since the degree of conformity to the internal morality of law can itself be a matter of degree. Some critics of Fuller found degrees of existence to be an odd notion. Other critics, including even some who could make sense of it, objected to Fuller's use of the word "morality" for the principles of order that make a legal system, whether just or not, workable. "Why not call them the conditions for effective lawmaking, or the maxims of legal craftsmanship?" they asked. A traditional legal naturalist might say of some particular positive law of the Nazi era, "This is so evil, it cannot be a law." In most of these cases, Fuller claims, one could usually have said instead: "This thing is a product of a system so oblivious to the (inner) morality of law that it is not entitled to be called a law."

In their famous debate in the *Harvard Law Review* in 1958 and 1959, Fuller and H. L. A. Hart differed over the legal consequences in the postwar period of actions performed under the laws (pseudolaws?) of the Nazi regime. Fuller staunchly defended, and Hart respectfully criticized, the position of Gustav Radbruch. Radbruch, once a leading German legal positivist, had converted to a traditional natural law theory in his efforts to deal with the claims of German citizens in response to moral outrages against them during the Nazi era by acts that were considered perfectly legal at the time committed. Despite their philosophical differences over the relations between law and morality, Radbruch, Hart, and Fuller came to similar practical conclusions. German citizens had been under no overriding moral obligation to obey the Nazi statutes, they all concluded. Fuller held this view because the statutes were the product of a system that could not claim to be a legal system; Radbruch, because the individual statutes were too evil to be legally valid; and Hart, because the statutes, though legally valid, were too morally evil to be obeyed, since there are moral obligations that can, in given cases, outweigh the moral obligation to obey valid law.

These differences were so subtle that some commentators suspected that they were theoretically insignificant. Lloyd L. Weinreb, for example, asked, "Can it possibly make so much difference whether we say, 'This enactment is too immoral to obligate us; therefore it is not law' or 'This law is too immoral to obligate us; therefore it ought not to be obeyed' "?[14] It is easy to sympathize with Weinreb's complaint, but here I shall try to clarify the controversy and reformulate the obedience problem in a way that recaptures its importance and its poignancy.

Most but by no means all legal philosophers believe that there is a moral obligation to obey the valid laws of one's community, especially in a country that is genuinely democratic and by and large just. In the past I have had some difficulty accepting the arguments usually made in support of this belief, but since it has almost a commonsense status for the great majority of people who hold it, I am willing to assume it here for the sake of argument. To affirm it, after all, is much like saying that there is a moral obligation to keep one's promises or to tell the truth. Notoriously, life is capable of creating circumstances in which these moral obligations conflict so that, whatever one does, one will be violating at least one of them. So, for example, there may be circumstances such that, if I tell the truth, I will be breaking a promise and, if I keep my promise, I will be telling a lie. Instead of concluding that whatever we do in those circumstances will be wrong, philosophers have reinterpreted the moral principles, imposing the duties as conditional. We have a general moral obligation to tell the truth, for example, except when we are under another moral obligation that is even more stringent in the circumstances, and there may indeed be such a conflicting obligation. Moral obligations, then, do differ in degrees of stringency, or weight, and vary in such a way that it is impossible in the abstract to formulate a hierarchy of weightiness on the moral scales, a hierarchy that will hold whatever the circumstances may be. In some circumstances the duty to tell the truth takes priority; in others, the duty to keep a promise. It all depends on the circumstances.

According to H. L. A. Hart, we do have a moral obligation to obey any valid law, even an unjust or evil one. But we also have a moral obligation to oppose injustice and, when a valid law reaches a certain degree of evil, the obligation to obey is outweighed by an even more stringent moral obligation to resist. Insofar as the statute in question is a valid one, we are tugged one way; insofar as it is immoral, it tugs us the other—sometimes, it tugs even harder. The moral obligation to obey the law is an example, therefore, of what some writers call a prima facie obligation (abbreviated henceforth as PFO).

Not in every case is a PFO a decisive moral reason, but it is always a relevant supporting reason and one that would be conclusive if no other relevant reason of greater strength applied to the situation. Hart's account is "candid," he says, because it allows us to say both of these things: that the validity of an applicable rule is always a reason, and a powerful one, for obeying it (or if one is a judge, for applying it), but that it is not necessarily a decisive reason when it comes into conflict with moral PFOs of other kinds. This account, Hart maintains, explains exactly and truly what we are doing when we conscientiously disobey the law. We are acting illegally, and we know it. Fidelity to enacted law is morally required of us, but it is not the whole of what is morally required of us. Some things, at some times, may be even more important morally, and it is disingenuous to label these things as law too. That would be to disguise even from ourselves what we are really doing, namely, deliberately disobeying the law for the sake of something we deem more important.

Duty versus Conscience: The American Experience with Slavery

Some of the moral duties generally believed to be created by laws are private duties—for example, the negative duties not to harm others nor to be rude or tactless to them, and the positive duties to be sociable and cooperative. Some of the private duties can be interpreted as the duties of a *citizen*: to stay informed, to vote, to pay one's bills and taxes. Still others are the duties of a *neighbor*: to maintain the exterior appearances of one's property and to be prepared to help one's neighbors in emergencies or to do minor favors, like taking in a neighbor's mail when she is on vacation. Examples of these kinds might tempt us to the view that all duties are in a sense public, that is, derived from one's occupancy of an office in some institution. The temptation is re-inforced by our ability, usually, to add the words *as an office holder* to our description of our own duties. I have duties not only as a citizen and as a neighbor, but also as a father and as a husband, and some of my duties are as a teacher or policeman (or whatever my job happens to be). A family is a relatively private sort of institution—compared, say, to a corporation or a jury—but it is some sort of institution. And there are still other duties that are more private still, deriving from no institutional office at all, public or private, but rather from my status as a human being among other mostly unrelated human beings. Our duties to strangers encountered in lonely places (our duties not to beat and rob them, for example) are duties we have simply as human beings, not as institutional office holders of any kind—not private, like the family, nor more public, like the employer/corporation.

On the other hand, many of our more important and determinate duties are near the public end of the spectrum. A so-called public official is a person with a specific set of duties derived from his job. These public duties are added to those moral duties that the official shares with everyone. Some public officials, like tenured judges, hold their offices for extended periods of time. Others occupy temporary offices created for specific tasks. A good example of the latter would be the office of juror in a public trial in a criminal court. To understand what it is to be a judge or a juror is just to know what the duties are that define the job. Those duties then descend on a person when she is actually sworn in as a judge or juror. What creates the special duties of the job is often an oath in which the designate swears to discharge the job-defining duties to the best of his personal ability.

The juror solemnly promises to obey the judge's instructions, chief among which is to base one's verdict strictly on the evidence and find the defendant guilty only if the presented evidence establishes that beyond a reasonable doubt. It is also the juror's duty to vote for the defendant's acquittal if and only if the evidence leaves a reasonable doubt of guilt. From a solemn promise, sworn as a public oath, derives the juror's clear duty not to acquit unless the evidence does leave the required residue of doubt. Yet the court, in a number of ways, seems almost to encourage juries to cheat! The jury members, for example, have both a *moral duty* to honor their oath and (let us imagine) to convict the accused and a *legal power* to acquit without answering to anyone. Jury deliberations are secret and are not subject to review after the trial; jurors may not be subjected to any penalty for bad judgment or for dereliction of official duty; and acquittal verdicts may not be appealed or overturned because of the constitutional protection against double jeopardy. It is evident that there is no way to prevent a jury from acquitting a clearly guilty defendant when conviction would offend their consciences—when, for example, the jurors must pass judgment on a clearly guilty eight-year-old child charged with stealing a turnip during the early Victorian period, when such a petty theft was a capital crime. In such cases the jury knows that it can set the child free by "voting its conscience" instead of doing its duty. Yet juries are instructed that they have, individually and collectively, an unqualified duty to follow the judge's instructions and put their consciences aside as they decide on guilt or innocence according to the evidence alone. Each juror takes a solemn oath to do just that. So it appears that the law, in a perfectly explicit way, confers a power on juries to do what they have an equally explicit duty not to do.

As things now stand, conscientious jurors in morally difficult cases are in an unenviable position. From the purely legal standpoint, their position is not so difficult. Their duty is to decide according to the evidence only. If the evidence leaves no reasonable doubt of guilt, their duty is to convict. But human beings are more than the sum of the duties of their stations, and the morally right way to act may violate any given one of their official duties or even the sum total of their duties on balance. What morality requires of a person, in morally difficult circumstances, is not something to be mechanically determined by an examination of the person's office or role-centered duties. An individual must on rare occasions have the courage to rise above all that and obey the dictates of conscience. One's conscience may be wholly convincing, considered only on its own terms. But its conflict with duty will nevertheless make the occasion for decision morally complex and difficult. It is no laughing matter, morally speaking, deliberately to violate one's own privately acknowledged duties, and our public institutions would be gravely endangered if our officials as a matter of routine were prepared to do that. The circumstances must be extreme and the emphasis on duty strong and unremitting if an official is even to consider such a drastic course. A juror has no moral right to violate the solemn oath on the ground that there would probably be some unfairness in punishing the defendant, even though he is plainly guilty, or because the juror disapproves of the statute the defendant is charged with breaking. Rather, the juror must place a substantial surcharge on departures from her official obligations. Conviction must seem more than unfair; it must seem unconscionable, a gross injustice given the defendant's undeniable moral right to do what he did. A single juror who makes these moral judgments can nullify the judge's instructions quite surreptitiously, so that no one will ever know what has happened. Sometimes, in morally desperate circumstances, that is what a juror should do, since secret nullification does less damage to a just institution (jury trials as currently constituted) than would open and clear nullification. But departures from duty—any duty—should never be taken lightly.

The Moral Duties of Judges

When we discuss disobedience of ordinary citizens, either to the validly enacted statutes of their communities or to the rules defining their own official roles, if any, in their community's legal system, the quarrels between positivists and natural law theorists are likely to seem arid and picky. What difference does it make, we might ask in our impatience, whether this extremely unjust statute is too wicked really to be a statute at all (despite its impeccable pedigree), as the natural law theorist might maintain, or that it is a legal statute all right, but one that is too wicked to obey, as the positivist would have it? The positivist would admit that, insofar as it is a valid statute, he has a moral obligation to obey it, but he would also argue that that prima facie obligation has little weight when placed on the scales against stronger PFOS that will outweigh it in these circumstances. In any event, the positivist and the natural law theorist will be allies against any wicked dictatorship that tries to disguise its unjust commands by representing them as valid laws (as they may or may not be). Neither will they have any respect for the egregiously unjust content of the law, or pseudolaw, that they disobey. So what practical difference can there be between them, and between the legal philosophies they espouse?

The conscientious judge's situation is quite different, especially when he is a judge in the nation's highest appellate court. This judge will have a conscience that could on occasion be in conflict with the duties of his office, duties the judge has solemnly sworn to discharge. But the judge does not have legal power of the same degree of effectiveness as that of the ordinary citizen or the juror. Paradoxically, the higher we climb in the court system, the less effective power to breach official duties do we find. I suspect that is because the duties themselves, at that level, are regarded with awe and thought to be of maximum or supreme stringency. After all, the Supreme Court justice has solemnly, and with great publicity, sworn to uphold the highest source of law in the land, the Constitution itself. No justice can take that duty lightly. Moreover, the Supreme Court judge is not protected by the same degree of secrecy as the mere juror. Nor can she so easily escape sanctions afterward. The Supreme Court justice is subject to impeachment and subject to great social pressure to give an accounting of each judicial decision and mode of argument. Such a judge is not truly free to be candid and confess that she knowingly violated a most sacred promise to the public and did so in order to satisfy personal conscience. Very likely the critics will respond that a willingness to break so important a promise betrays not so much a sensitive conscience as a conscience insensitive to the moral bindingness of voluntary commitments.

It is puzzling to know how to exercise our terminological options in this situation. Most of us, I think, would be made uncomfortable by talk of a conflict between duty and conscience. After all, our ordinary role- or job-connected duties also have a voice in the chorus that is conscience. Moreover, a person could say without being incoherent that conscience forbids him from being derelict in (other) duties, or that he has a duty to obey conscience. Yet there *is* an intuitive distinction between, say, my duty as a teacher and all or most of my other duties combined. The collective voice of the other duties may have the timbre and tone that we attribute to conscience.

The best historical example of an intractable struggle within the forum of a judge's mind between the duties of public office and the duties of private conscience is that which tormented large sections of the American judiciary in the decades preceding the Civil War. A number of distinguished judges of profound and genuine abolitionist convictions, men who hated slavery with an intense moral passion, struggled to reconcile their consciences with what looked like a plain constitutional duty: the duty to order the return of escaped slaves to their southern masters. On one side of these intrapersonal conflicts

was a role-duty as stringent and weighty on the moral scales as role-duties
ever are, partly because it derived from the most basic source of law in our
legal system, the Constitution itself, and partly because it was so undeniably
explicit, precise, and unambiguous. On the other side was a moral consensus
against human slavery. This consensus dates back to the early Christians,
Stoic philosophers, and even Roman jurists, and includes the leading political
philosophers of the seventeenth and eighteenth centuries—Locke, Puffendorf,
Montesquieu—and the ideological fathers of the French and American rev-
olutions. Every schoolchild could recite passages from the Declaration of Independence, the constitutional preamble, and the speeches of Patrick Henry,
James Madison, and Thomas Jefferson (ironically, all from the southern slaveholding state of Virginia). These works affirmed the natural rights of *all*
people, whatever the positive laws of their governments might say or leave
unsaid to the contrary. Moreover, these rights were said to be noncontroversial
because their existence was *self-evident*. Taken together, all this authority constituted as powerful a display of intellectual reinforcement for a consensus of
conscience for which anyone could ever hope even though much of its support under pressure would turn out to be mere lip service and political rhetoric.

By 1850, most of the American judiciary had joined most of the educated
public in thinking of the Constitution, in critical part, as a compromise over
slavery.[15] The compromise consisted of the agreement of the slaveholding
states to join the union, provided that the new nation's Constitution recognized and promised to preserve the legal legitimacy of slavery in those states
that wanted to keep the practice. Those who were impressed by this interpretation could point to five provisions in the original Articles of Confederation
that were evidence for it, chief of which was "the bloody clause," as Wendell
Phillips called it.[16] This clause was the original fugitive slave provision, the
price paid by the free states, according to the Great Compromise theory, for
having the benefits of an enlarged union from the beginning of national
independence. The fugitive slave clause in the original federal Constitution
(superseded after the Civil War by the Thirteenth Amendment) declared, "No
person held to service or labor in one state, under the law thereof, escaping
into another, shall, in consequence of any law or regulation therein, be discharged from such service or labor, but shall be delivered up on claim of the
party to whom such service or labor may be due." Thus, if Massachusetts
enacted a statute requiring that fugitive slaves be fully liberated upon crossing
its border and permitted to stay on, as free persons in permanent residence
there, the statute would be clearly unconstitutional; it would be void *ab initio*
in virtue of this clause. Slave owners from the escaped slave's state could then
dispatch slave hunters to Massachusetts to capture the escapee, certify with
the local authorities that the hunter was reclaiming his employer's property,
and return the wretched slave, in shackles, to servitude. Periodically, the slave
would be intercepted by local citizens and rescued, at least for a time. Often

these conflicts got into the courts, as would-be rescuers and their aiders and abettors appealed convictions for interfering with property, or the slave owners petitioned for return of their property. Almost invariably the slavers triumphed in court, in virtue of that inescapable barrier to justice and humanity, the bloody clause. It cannot have been a pleasant experience for the judges, particularly those of abolitionist conviction and natural law philosophy.

In his penetrating history of the legal struggles against slavery in the first half of the nineteenth century, Robert Cover distinguishes four possible responses of a judge caught in the grip of a duty-versus-conscience struggle:

1. He may apply the law against his conscience.
2. He may apply conscience and be faithless to the law.
3. He may resign.
4. He may cheat, and state that the law is not what he believes it to be, and thus preserve an appearance (to others) of conformity to the law and morality.[17]

Finally, there is a fifth possibility. The judge may adopt an ameliorist solution. He "may introduce his own sense of what 'ought to be' interstitially, where no hard law yet exists."[18]

All five of these choices were actually made or advocated by abolitionist judges. Most of them stopped resisting the clear language of the bloody clause. There it was, in plain English, a clear constitutional recognition of slavery. Clearly, a given judge's duty as a judge was to obey the explicit dictates of a Constitution that could no longer be respected and morally embraced. It was of course a literal bloody shame that thousands of human beings were oppressed and, at best, treated as animals. But it must be remembered that such results are not the personal responsibility of the judge but, rather, commands of the impersonal voice of the law. The judge's job is to discover the law and then be its voice, totally uninfluenced by his personal opinions, even by his moral convictions. He can say, "Not I, directly or indirectly . . . but the law, which is given to me and is my master, says thus."[19]

At first that kind of political eloquence functioned primarily as a line of defense for the judge. As such, it was an argument from humility, more a self-minimizing apology than a full-blooded justification. But the fuller justification, usually forthcoming, was simply to opt for legal positivism, except perhaps in respect to those gaps in the positive law, where some judges hoped to introduce natural law interstitially in virtue of "a sort of bend-over-backward principle . . . an obligation to achieve a pro-freedom [antislavery] result unless there [was] a very specific, concrete positive law that prevent[ed] it."[20] Perhaps it was possible at the time of the Constitutional Convention to deny that the fugitive slave clause was specific or concrete. But the fugitive slave clause was a kind of invitation to Congress and to state legislatures to provide their own detailed implementation language. The Fugitive Slave Acts of 1793 and 1850 enjoined very specific procedures to be used in capturing and returning fugitive slaves—none of which were at all advantageous to the fugitive. Northern abolitionists loudly accused Congress of interfering with (more irony) states' rights, in particular the constitutional rights of the states to establish their own rules providing more due process for the prisoner and his rescuers both (including a jury trial guaranteed elsewhere in the Constitution). By 1850 few interstices were left in those statutes that further restricted the rights of the escaped slave. By then the bend-over-backward principle was rarely used and was often explicitly rejected. Ameliorist natural law theories intended only for that diminishing interstitial area of the positive law tended to be absorbed by the "legal duty" option and the legal positivism that was its foundation.

The second option was for the judge to abandon the very law he was sworn to apply and to apply instead the dictates of his own conscience. It is difficult to understand, of course, how such reasonings could be explained by the judge in presenting his conclusions to the public. Could he write an opinion affirming his conscientious conviction that slavery is monumental injustice and cruelty, rejected almost everywhere as contrary to the laws of nature (morality) and therefore impossible for a right-thinking person to promote? Could he continue by pointing out that his clear legal duty would require that he contribute to the strengthening of slavery and that, therefore, he had decided to reject his legal duty (his duty as a judge) and vote instead for the position recommended by his conscience? It would be acceptable to the public if he affirmed those premises but drew a different conclusion from them, namely, that he resign his appointment as a judge immediately and not take part at all in the legal proceedings already under way. That third option, resignation, was a choice that was popular with abolitionist judges. But that is altogether different from saying, "I know my duty but I am not going to do it. I will do what is contrary to my duty instead." I can imagine that universal condemnation and impeachment would await the judge at the end of that line. And his colleagues would hector him repeatedly about what the legal system would be like if every judge felt free to renounce his duty whenever it conflicted with one of his own moral beliefs.

The third option was chosen by Wendell Phillips, who not only resigned his own judgeship, but wrote a book advocating resignation by public officials and the organizing of a political party encouraging withdrawal and noncooperation. In his book Phillips quotes from the letter of resignation of Francis Jackson, who wrote:

> "The oath to support the Constitution of the United States is a solemn promise to do that which is a violation of the natural rights of man, and a sin in the sight of God. . . . I withdraw all profession of allegiance to it [the Constitution] and all my voluntary efforts to sustain it." . . . More and more, it appeared that the question ought not to be put, "How should a

judge of integrity decide these cases?" but rather "How can a man of integrity judge these cases [at all]?"[21]

The making of dramatic resignations conjures up pictures of heroic resistance, but in some instances there is a suspicion that self-indulgence might be the better term. If a judge's resignation is motivated entirely by his desire to preserve his own moral purity, so that his hands will not be soiled with the blood of others, then he makes a poor hero, though his action on his own behalf might have required considerable courage. But would not a more fruitful use of his courage and a craftier use of the power of his office, if any, be more commendable? What help does he give the suffering slaves by concentrating his efforts on his own integrity? I suspect that efforts to preserve integrity in situations like these will inevitably be self-defeating, because true integrity requires more effective resistance and less narcissistic self-concern. "It is a waste to refuse to use accessible power for a good purpose."[22]

Few did, and few would now, embrace the fourth choice, which requires the conscientious but frustrated judge to cheat. That can hardly be the kind of advice that one would expect to find in a law manual, text, or casebook. The advice to violate legal norms in order to avoid morally unacceptable results cannot itself be a legal norm; an enumeration of the duties of a judge can hardly include the duty to cheat when there is no other way to produce a just result. Still, we should note that the moral situation of an abolitionist judge at a hearing concerning the fate of an escaped slave is basically no different from that of a juror in a trial of an eight-year-old child for the capital offense of stealing a turnip from a neighbor's field. The main relevant differences are that the juror's cheating is secret and may never be known; the judge's opportunities are not as great. Moreover, the judge speaks officially on behalf of the nation's legal system; the juror speaks only to a question of fact. The juror's "cheating" consists simply in lying about those facts in order to prevent suffering and injustice. Both the juror and the judge must pay a price for the nullification they achieve by their untruthfulness. But we are all threatened more by the judge, who because of greater visibility and greater impact generally, has a greater potential for harming the system if the scheme goes awry. In both cases great emphasis must be put on the importance of legal duty, and its strict bindingness, if we are to ensure that misrepresentation happens only rarely, in the most extreme cases, and not as a general rule.

The chief opponent of the resignation school, Lysander Spooner, was also the chief spokesman for the cheating alternative. He did not convince many judges, so far as we know, but one cannot but smile at his ingenuity:

Spooner was willing to treat the problem *arguendo* as one of a judge who had sworn to uphold an unjust constitution (even though he, Spooner, believed that the U.S. Constitution is properly interpreted as a just nonslavery instrument). Spooner acknowledged that the dominant position seemed to be that such a judge should resign. But he thought that the proper analogy was one of a man given a weapon on condition that he kill an innocent and helpless victim. In such a situation, Spooner argued, it is proper to make the promise, keep the weapon, and use it to defend rather than attack the victim. To give up the sword, to resign the judicial office, is "only a specimen of the honor that is said to prevail among thieves."[23]

In both cases, that of the judge torn between morality (conscience) and law (duty) and that of the party who accepts his neighbor's weapon, the cheating consists of breaking a promise to uphold the law even when it conflicts with morality or, in Spooner's example, breaking the "promise" to kill the innocent third party. The receiver of his friend's weapon could certainly not ever justify *keeping* his promise to his neighbor to kill the third party. Suppose, neverthe-less, that he does keep his promise and shoots the third party dead with the weapon given him for that purpose by his neighbor. "I hated having to kill him," he might say, "but if I had saved him instead, that would have been to break my promise, and couldn't do *that*!" The abiding message of this analogy is that duties to keep one's promises do not *always and necessarily* take pre-cedence over the PFOs with which they may conflict.

In Closing: A Friendly Philosophical Dialogue

Do we need a conception of natural law to do justice to the claims that morality makes on legislators and judges? William James once wrote, "Every difference must make a difference."[24] That is to say that, if two theories are distinct in meaning, it must be because there is at least some conceivable difference it would make to our experience if one, but not the other, were true. Alternatively, if some single theory has a sense to it, that sense must be the difference we can imagine for our experience if the theory happened to be true. Whether that pragmatic theory of meaning is correct is a technical question well beyond the scope of this essay. But its full adequacy aside, the theory can provide useful assistance to our understanding of a philosophical proposition. It advises us simply to look for the difference it would make in our lives if the proposition were true and creates a presumption at least that, if its truth would make no practical difference, then there is really no theo-retical difference either, between its being true and its being false.

More precisely, our questions are these: Does morality have to pretend to be literally a part of law in order for it to perform its function as protector of human interests and ground of political obligations? Does it really matter to any of our practical purposes and values whether we think of morality as inside, or outside, or both inside and outside our legal codes? We saw earlier that we expect jural laws of a variety of kinds to impose moral obligations on the citizens who are subject to them. The criminal code, for example, imposes obligations of obedience on everybody, whereas the rules defining public offices—either relatively permanent, like the office of judge, or relatively temporary, like the office of juror—impose moral obligations only on their occupants. In addition, the making of promises and the swearing of oaths are legal mechanisms for generating official duties. In the same way, ordinary promises between citizens generate ordinary moral obligations between them, whether enforceable by the state or not. Likewise, social roles, both when filled voluntarily (like that of husband or wife) and even when filled nonvoluntarily (like that of daughter or son), are recognized generators of moral obligation. Our classification approaches completeness when we add mention of informal social roles (like that of neighbor) and private institutional roles, offices, or jobs (like that defined by the duties of a janitor or the duties of a chief executive officer in a private corporation). All of these duties are or can be moral duties—both those generated by private rules and procedures, informal or institutional, and those derived from legal rules, both those that apply to all citizens alike and those that impose the moral obligations of public officials and are peculiar to them.

Earlier I discussed the moral obligations normally imposed by a legal system, at least in a democratic, more or less just country, on all citizens. Sometimes particular statutes in such a system are extremely unjust or even irrational ("crazy," as we say), and questions arise whether our normal obligation to obey *any* valid law is weakened or even dissolved in this case. For a judge presiding over a trial of a citizen for violating such a law, the problem to be dealt with is one of judicial *duty*. Does the normal duty as a judge, to apply the law as it is written, get weakened or suspended in the case at bar because of the immoral content of the governing statute? For the defendant, a private citizen occupying no judicial office, the problem is, or was, one of private conscience. The statute that the defendant deliberately violated was so utterly wicked, she did not think it could possibly have any obligatory force. Moreover, she could not act as the law seemed to enjoin her to act, without a severe crisis of conscience.

Suppose, for example, that the statute defines a capital offense—perhaps not an act so utterly trivial as stealing a turnip, but close. It forbids any derogatory oral statement about the country's political leader, on pain of death, and requires the persons overhearing such a statement to inform the police. If they fail to do so, they are subject to life imprisonment at hard labor. Moreover, the conscience-stricken citizen has learned that the law was not debated in her country's parliament but only given a unanimous rubber-stamp approval, which was ordered secretly by the country's leader. The parliamentary approval was intended to place an ex post facto veneer of legality over the punishment of a dissident, which had occurred a few days earlier. The legal system is now obviously breaking down and has reached the point where Lon Fuller is prepared to pronounce it nearly dead.

The positivistic H. L. A. Hart concluded about this only partly fictitious case that the law deliberately broken by the conscientious citizen was indeed a valid statute in the legal system (if that system still existed), having been duly enacted by an elected legislature in accordance with the procedure prescribed by the country's unamended ancient constitution. Nevertheless, he found it so extremely wicked that his conscience too would forbid him from obeying it. As a legal philosopher, he would admit that the offending law was valid; as a moral philosopher, he would deny that he was under a moral obligation, all things considered, to obey it, since the moral obligation of obedience normally generated by a valid law was not produced in this case.

On the other side, Fuller, in the position of the conscientious citizen, would also have disobeyed, but he would have denied that he had broken a valid law in any operative legal system. When the content of a rule is that wicked, cruel, and unjust, and the methods of generating it so corrupt, then it is no legal rule at all, but only a pretender to legal status. Since it was not a valid legal rule and the legal system of which it might have been a part hardly exists any more, of course it does not generate a duty derived from the general capacity of valid law to generate moral obligations of obedience. Therefore, Fuller would conclude, he was under no obligation to obey.

So Hart and Fuller, for all their philosophical quarreling, would be allies in the political arena and perhaps cellmates in the same prison. Is there any actual difference between their philosophies then? Do we have an answer to Lloyd Weinreb, who wonders what possible difference it makes whether we describe the moral situation in Nazi Germany as Fuller did (no legal system, no obligation of obedience) or as Hart did (a valid law but too evil to obey)?

I think we can say that, if there is an important theoretical difference between these two positions, it is not because of any important practical difference they yield. The ruthless dictator, after all, would have them both butchered. As we have seen, Hart did claim a small advantage for his position in what he called the merit of candor. As he reconstructs the practical reasoning of two dissidents, one a legal positivist and the other a natural law theorist, the positivist would tally up the score in such a way that disobedience would have a huge balance over obedience but not a complete shutout. The score might be 9–1 (these numbers, of course, are not to be taken seriously), but that one point would register on any sensitive conscience, since it is the minimal force that comes from the recognition of a valid law. For the positivist there is a conflict of prima facie obligations: the PFO of obedience to valid law (here represented as weakly as possible) versus the PFOs (all of them here at maximum strength) to oppose injustice, to prevent suffering, to speak truth, and more. It is a one-sided conflict, Hart would say, but a conflict for all that, and to characterize it in that fashion is to exercise the virtue of candor. Fuller, on the other side, would tally the score as 10–0 against obedience. For him there was no conflict at all, since all the relevant PFOs spoke with one voice, and there was no valid law involved that might bring the moral duty of fidelity to law into play.

I conclude, then, that the famous differences between the positivist and the natural law theorist on the question of the private citizen's moral obligation to obey the law do not amount to much. But I am reluctant to draw the further inference, without some caution, that the difference between legal positivism and natural law theory, as general accounts of the relation between law and morality, do not come to much. I do not wish to be hasty and skeptical about that, not after studying the way those called positivists and those called natural law theorists divided over the vital political issue of fugitive slave laws that, in the end, split the country and exploded into a bloody conflagration.

There is at least one possibly significant way in which the Hart-Fuller problem, inspired by the historical record of the Nazi government of Germany and the fugitive slave issue of the shaky American union between the Revolution and the Civil War, can be shown to make a difference. In our example from Fuller and Hart, we are concerned with the moral obligations people had *as private citizens* to obey the law. In the example from the Civil War period, we are dealing with the moral obligations that one class of public officials (appellate judges) had to interpret and apply laws that others had written. Let us explore, then, how the *judge's* moral obligations might be importantly different depending on whether he is a positivist or a natural law theorist.

This time, let us consider how a fictitious Supreme Court judge, who happens to be a theorist of natural law (NL), might have debated that matter with a time-traveling judge from the twentieth century, who happens to be a legal positivist (LP).

LP: Surely it is as clear as it ever is in law that the Fugitive Slave Acts are valid law, whatever reservations we have about their content. The question of legal validity in America is settled by reference to the Constitution, and that document, our ultimate "rule of recognition," goes out of its way, in Article IV, to recognize the legitimacy of human slavery, and it explicitly requires that escaped slaves "shall be delivered up" on claim of their masters.

NL: We both know that the reason why this statement was included in the Constitution is that it was part of the original bargain that induced the slave states to join the union in the first place. But, in any complete and accurate consideration of a judge's moral obligations when an appeal of the fugitive or his rescuer comes before him, that can hardly be the end of the matter. You and your colleagues have within your collective power the fate not just of this one wretched human being—sick, undernourished, devastated psychologically, and subject to who knows how many fierce beatings upon his return—but also, in virtue of precedents, thousands more who will follow.

LP: I sincerely and deeply regret that my actions may have those terrible results. You know that I hate the institution of human chattel slavery just as much as you do, and I have opposed it just as long and just as strenuously as you have. But I don't see how I have any choice in the matter. I didn't make that loathsome law nor do I have the power to change it. My job is simply to apply the law as it is, indeed, as others have written it. I may have political convictions *as a private citizen* about the moral merits or demerits of the laws I am to apply, but my duty *as a judge* is to determine what the law is, not what it ought to be. In short, I am here to make strictly legal judgments. Moral judgments are for others, and I am sworn to put them aside.

NL: I insist, however, that you cannot separate law and morality in that facile and complacent fashion. Certain minimal conditions of reasonableness and fairness must be presumed to be a part, usually an unwritten implicit part, of any valid law. Cicero said that and so did Augustine, Aquinas, and the leading writers of our own revolutionary period. And surely our own Constitution is full of testimony to the natural rights of man and the moral foundation of all legitimate government. The fugitive slave clause flies in the teeth of all of that. Its presence in the Constitution renders that document incoherent and contradictory. There cannot be an ultimate source of positive law, as our Constitution claims to be, whose parts are mutually contradictory. When all but one part of the document affirms human rights to freedom, equality, autonomy, and the means to happiness, and one specific part explicitly denies those rights, then clearly the only reasonable way to restore coherence is to invalidate that one clashing part.

LP: Good heavens, look at what you are saying! You say that the fugitive slave clause conflicts with morality, human rights, and justice. But even if that were so, it would not follow that it is not valid law! Are you suggesting that a part of the Constitution itself could be unconstitutional? Look who is talking about inconsistency and contradiction!

NL: No, it makes no sense to say that the Constitution, or one of its parts, could be unconstitutional. But the Constitution could suffer a kind of disability analogous to unconstitutionality. It could conflict sharply with a basic principle of morality, a principle of justice, or equality, or humaneness, or autonomy.

LP: I agree that there are certain abstract principles of morality that, despite their appearance as vacuous and imprecise—or perhaps because of it— are objective truths endorsed by a large and confident consensus. Justice, for example, excludes arbitrary inequalities. We can all agree on that precept, provided it is kept abstract. There will be more disagreements when we try to decide whether a given inequality is arbitrary or whether a dissimilarity—say, in skin color—is relevant as a ground for dissimilar or unequal treatment. I concede further that there is some reason to be optimistic about the possibility of strong consensus even about those more determinate, derivative moral judgments. But my main point is that my duty as a judge, to which I was solemnly sworn, is to interpret and apply only what is internal to the law. We both have the highest respect for morality, even perhaps as much as for law. But morality is something outside of law, and I am only to consider what is inside law, so to speak.

NL: That seems to be the nub of the disagreement between us. I am strongly inclined to say that the basic principles of justice, for example, have a home within every actual legal system, or a kind of implicit presence in the interstices of every legal statute, in effect putting a limit on how far that statute can drift away from justice without losing the character of legality. The Fugitive Slave Acts, I should say, are about as far from conformity with that internal justice requirement as it is possible to get. You need not fear violating your judicial duty by declaring them, because of their extreme immorality, null and void as law.

LP: Would that it were that simple! What can it mean for a moral principle to be "part" of a legal rule? Or for morality to be "implicit in the interstices" of law? This smacks of obscurantism. Normally, law and morality are understood as contrasting. Law is law and morality is morality. You would convert a generic distinction into one between a genus and one of its own species. Instead of morality having a character different enough from law's to disqualify it as something properly called law, you juggle the terms about so that morality suddenly become a species of law rather than a contrasting genus. And not only is morality itself a kind of law, even a part of a system of positive law, it now becomes a *higher* kind of law, or a test of what else can be or not be law. Why don't we simply say, with Bishop Butler, that "a thing is what it is and not another thing" and add that a system of law that fails to measure up to the standards of morality is a pretty lousy system of law?[25]

NL: But still law?

LP: Yes, still law.

NL: Would you then have decided cases in 1850 in such a way that certain northern states would be prevented from declaring a fugitive slave to be a free citizen and from welcoming him to permanent residence?

LP: I couldn't say now. Your question is too hypothetical.

NL: But can you think of *any* circumstances in which your legal philosophy would permit you to decide a case in accordance with the abstract principles of justice instead of the plain meaning of the terms in which the governing rule is stated?

LP: Maybe my legal philosophy is not where we should turn. Try my moral philosophy instead. I might have no doubt at all what my duty as a judge requires of me. But as a full human being, not simply a judge, I may be so appalled morally at what my legal duty requires that my conscience will tell me not to do my judicial duty.

NL: Give me an example other than the fugitive slave example.

LP: Well, this is a bit fanciful, but suppose that back in the days before women had the franchise (back in your time) somebody introduced a bill, in the usual way, on the floor of a state legislature. Imagine that a quorum of legislators was in attendance, in accordance with the state's constitutional requirement for valid lawmaking, and they astonish the world by passing the bill into law. The bill legalizes rape in that state. I would not hesitate to judge that a valid law had just been created, but I would be prepared, as the morally sensitive human being I am, to throttle personally any young scoundrel I would see who was attempting a legal rape. I wouldn't care that his behavior was legal. I would beat the hell out of him anyway.

NL: But judge, you are now talking about your duties, liberties, and liabilities as an ordinary private citizen. What I want to know is whether you would discharge your judicial duty, as you see it, to uphold this law the first time the question of its constitutionality arose or whether, in the same spirit as that manifested in your attack on the scoundrel in the other example, you would vote to invalidate the statute because of its conflict with justice and morality?

LP: Well, maybe I would declare it invalid for the reason you mention, but if I did that I might want to conceal what my real reason was. I wouldn't want the world to think that I would shrink from my duty for the wrong kind of reason. There would probably be something in the state constitution I could cite as conflicting with the statute, thus entailing its unconstitutionality. Its injustice and immorality needn't be mentioned.

NL: If you *were* to refer to the statute's injustice or inhumanity, would you be going outside of the law for your justification?

LP: Yes, I would. I think the conceptual distinction between law and morality is too useful to undermine as you keep trying to do. But as I said before, I might nevertheless choose to go outside the law in violation of my legal duty, because when I take into account all the prima facie obligations to which I am subject as a human being, my judicial duty (which is also one of my moral duties) may be outbalanced by the other PFOs that have a bearing in those circumstances on my decision.

NL: Your reasoning, then, is precisely parallel to that of H. L. A. Hart in his discussion of the moral duties of ordinary citizens when confronted with extremely unjust laws that they know, in addition, to be the work of thoroughly corrupt legislatures. In both examples, we are dealing with the problem of determining our resultant bottom-line duties as human beings when there is conflict among the various PFOs to which we are subject, including the special and stringent PFOs of a public official generated in part by the solemn promises of her office. Does the fact that the deliberating individual in the second example is a *judge*, with an additional kind of duty to throw on the deliberative scales, make no difference then? Or is there no real difference between the positions of the natural law theorist and the legal positivist in respect to their judgments about the duties of judges?

LP: I would say that there is some difference but perhaps not as much as I thought before this discussion. What confuses or troubles me most is the abundance of distinctions among types of duty that this discussion generates. Assume that we are discussing purely moral philosophy and our question is of quite the same kind as if we asked whether in some hypothetical case a person should do his or her moral duty (PFO) to tell the truth and thereby violate in those unusual circumstances the duty (PFO) to keep a promise. In that event, we may be talking about moral duties that do not come from the definition of some role, station, or office. The conflicting PFOs are PFOs to which the person is subject simply as a human being. In deciding, he will have to weigh, so to speak, these PFOs against one another and then be moved in the direction of the weightier one. One PFO may outweigh (or outscore, to use our earlier sports metaphor) the other by an overwhelming amount (a score of 10–0 or 9–1, as in the earlier examples) or the score may be close— perhaps 5–4 or 4–5, as in the fugitive slave dilemma.

Perhaps, in the majority of cases where the decision to be made has this form, at least one of the contending PFOs will derive from the definition of a social role, job assignment, or office occupied by the decision maker, but even then the role- or office-duty will be just one among the several that have relevance to the decision. Some PFOs will derive from the general and ill-defined roles we all have, for example, the role of citizen. In the Nazi example debated by Fuller and Hart, these two eminent legal philosophers agreed that the PFOs they had *as citizens* to obey the law were outweighed by far by other PFOs they had, perhaps also as citizens, to oppose social injustice. The bottom-line duty, as you called it, is by definition the PFO that carries the day. Adjusting this terminology to fit our moral priorities is a difficult and even dangerous thing. It is dangerous because it may lead us to overlook the way our terminology can commit us to positions that we do not hold, positions whose truth or falsity, before argument, should be open questions. Thus we can think of the duty that carries the day as being identical by definition with a duty we have as human beings, not merely as role players or job or office holders. But that begs the question in favor of a controversial substantive position, namely, that when role- and office-duties clash with more general nonrole- and nonoffice-duties, the latter must *always* win out. A person's duty as a judge, for example, can never be as weighty as a clashing duty that she has quite apart from any role, relation, or job or any promise already made. More confusion can result if we think of the winning duty as the one we will *call* our duty as human beings. Then, if on argumentative or intuitive grounds, we find that a competing PFO, which we have as role or office occupants, seems weightier, we will have to call *that* duty the duty we have as human beings. This result undermines our original distinction.

We also have available, as a way of referring to the bottom-line duty, the term *conscientious duty*. That is a term commonly reserved, I suspect, for the bottom-line winner, because it seems odd that a lesser PFO could outweigh a PFO of conscience. After all, it is conscience that "sits on the throne." But if in fact a role-duty *can* outweigh a stringent nonrole-duty in certain circumstances, and that is at least a genuine possibility, then I suppose, we should have to say, "Ignore your conscience and do your role-duty instead." But that sounds so cynical, even if inadvertently so, that we should probably avoid that usage. But suppose we define *conscientious duty* as the duty that is the weightiest of the competing duties before us. Then, when the duty that seems intuitively to win out is a role-duty, we would have to call *it* the voice of conscience, and the distinction between conscientious duties and role-duties is undermined. It would be better in advance of argument not to identify the bottom-line duty (the one that carries the day), by definition, with any other category.

[Pausing for breath] Wow, these things are complicated! Am I still on the right track?

NL: Yes, I think so. You have already made enough distinctions to cover the Hart-Fuller case. There the personal moral decision of the citizen was to overrule the individual's PFO to obey the valid laws of the community and fulfill instead the PFO (also as a citizen? more likely, simply as a human being) to oppose injustice, particularly political injustice. Now what further distinction must we apply; I wonder, to the PFOs of the *judge* in our two examples? Consider (1) the historical example of the fugitive slave cases and (2) your strange example of the legalization of rape.

LP: In the judicial cases, we simply have the possibility of new PFOs that are present only when the moral deliberator is a judge. The judge must deliberate on two levels. The first is entirely legal. He must look inside the law for rules, statutes, precedents, and the other appropriate legal data that might enable a judicial decision. But the judge is not a mere computer. First of all, before a judge is ever a judge, he is a human being made of flesh and blood, who is subject to many more PFOs than simply that of the job of judge. Normally his PFOs as judge are extremely stringent and the opposing PFOs on the scale are greatly outweighed, so that deliberation is quick and easy. Normally, the judge doesn't have to put the evils of human slavery or rape on the scales at all. But in this case the comparative "weight measurement" is extremely close. After hours of weighing and reweighing, the judge sees that the more stringent PFO is not his duty as a judge but instead his duty as a human being.

NL: Now we are precisely at the point where a difference will appear, if it is to appear at all. What should the human being/judge do at this point, and how can he do it? His counterpart in the private citizen example at this point omits legal duty, the legal duty, say, to inform on a neighbor or a spouse. The private citizen leaves town without an exit permit. She writes a farewell letter that condemns the country's political leader, then sends a copy to a newspaper for publication as a letter to the editor. The citizen fires shots at police officers when they are trying to arrest a known dissident, joins the underground resistance, and renounces once and for all, as in a declaration of war, the PFO to obey the laws of the government. The judge could well be a natural law theorist (like me or Lon Fuller) who denies that the citizen is breaking a law at all through all these rebellious activities, since there are no laws to break. That makes it extremely easy. But a colleague of this judge could just as well be a legal positivist, like you or H. L. A. Hart, in disagreement with the judge over whether the citizen is breaking a law but morally bound to behavior no different from that of the other judge. So far, their philosophical differences make no difference to their conduct.

When the human being/judge decides that his PFO to resist injustice, which he has as a human being, outweighs the PFO that derives from the definition of his job, even when the latter is reinforced by his PFO to keep his promises and honor his oaths, what does he do? Here the parallel with the case of the private citizen begins to break down. The judge can over-rule the actions of a lower court in judging the appeal before him, even though the opposite course appeared clearly to be the legally correct one. But the judge cannot do that secretly, so that nobody notices it, and then sneak out of town like a common criminal. He must stand up in a public forum and declare his conclusion and the legal reasons supporting it. In effect, he will be either presenting arguments that support a conclusion other than the one he declares to be correct or (equivalently) arguing, not really for the course that it is his duty as judge to certify, but rather for the course that it is his moral duty as citizen perhaps, but more likely as human being, to do. After that, he can avoid the hubbub by resigning his judgeship, but that would probably be a self-defeating thing to do, since he would be replaced by a more reliably "dutiful" judge, who in time would find a way to undo whatever his predecessor had achieved.

Now if the judge were a legal positivist, he would find it impossible to give a straightforward legal argument for the conclusion his conscience would have him declare. He would have to admit that a judge can only refer to matters internal to the law in arguing for a legal conclusion and that, by his lights, questions about justice and injustice are external to the law and therefore may not be considered. That leaves him only the option of giving all of the arguments that support his bottom-line duty as a human being and violating his duty as a judge. If he is candid, then, he must in effect tell the world that he did not reach the judgment that it was his duty as a judge to reach, but rather the judgment imposed on him by his conscience. That would be almost as shocking as a confession of a crime. Your fellow legal positivists would lead the chase, denouncing as usurpation any judge's claim that he has discretion to appeal to wider considerations to settle a question of law. In the period before the American Civil War, Great Britain's Lord Camden was often quoted: "The discretion of a judge is the law of tyrants. . . . [At] its best it is often-times caprice—[at] its worst, it is every vice, folly, and passion to which human nature is liable."[26] I think that, if the positivists knew more people like *you*, they would be less unwilling to confer on a judge the discretion to appeal to natural justice in arguments. But as this quotation shows, it was not that most of them disparaged justice. It was rather that most of them distrusted *people*, especially people in positions of power, like judges.

LP: Perhaps the only legitimate course for the judge in hard cases of the sort we have been considering, in effect, is to cheat, paradoxical though that would be. If I were a judge in one of the fugitive slave appeals, I would try to present as plausible an argument as I could find for invalidating the bloody clause without once mentioning such external factors as its natural injustice, arbitrariness, inhumanity, and so on. I could say that the recognition of slavery was at odds with the whole drift of the Constitution and the other foundational documents of our government. I could show the banner of states' rights (a huge irony in 1860) and deny the power of the federal government to prevent individual (northern) states from holding fugitives until their lot could be determined by the state's own rules of due process, including the trial by jury guaranteed by the federal Constitution. I could try all those gambits, but it would be a heroic, uphill, losing fight. After all, good friend, the damned bloody clause in Article IV came right out and said that fugitive slaves must be "delivered up" as soon as an authenticated representative of their owner made claim to them. There is simply no way around that, even for so wily a lawyer as me.

Anyway, even if my cleverness enabled me to make some sort of standard argument for the morally preferable outcome, albeit a hopelessly unpersuasive one, that would simply help to gum up the law and create tricky precedents of the kind that any self-respecting positivist would abhor. So the position of the morally conscientious legal positivist judge in these examples is an unenviable one. Would the morally conscientious judge who is an advocate of natural law theory be in any better a position?

NL: Well, I for one, would be much better off. In my theory, when I appeal to natural justice, I am appealing to something internal to the law. I do not have to concede, as you would, that contrary to my oath I am going outside the law for considerations that will support my legal conclusions. In response to those who would accuse me of substituting merely my own opinions about morality and justice, subjective and ungrounded as they are thought to be, for the straightforward and objective dictates of the law, I can cite a dazzling array of authorities—from Cicero, Aquinas, and Blackstone down to Jefferson and, in our own time, Lincoln—for the proposition that the principles of justice are objective and rooted securely in the nature of things, independent of anyone's mere opinion. It would be hard to pin the label "moral crackpot" on me or my mere opinions, so long as I am in *that* company.

LP: There is a subtle point, I think, about a source of discomfort that would apply as well to the natural law theorist as to the positivist in their roles as judges. There is something essentially *public* about the judge's reasons for acting. The judge's reasons, even those that he might give for what is essentially an act of judicial nullification, become a part of the official record, where they remain forever in a position to influence the future course of the law. The judge is an official spokesperson for the state; there is something impersonal about that arrangement that makes it peculiarly jolting for a judge to introduce predominantly autobiographical materials into his reasonings about the validity of laws, for example. And that is just what is done by the judge, whether he be a positivist or a natural law partisan, when he states and defends a position about his own duties, not as a judge, but as a human being.

In this respect the judge's dilemmas that we have been considering differ both from the moral dilemmas of the ordinary citizen as citizen or as human being and from that of other officials, like jurors. The juror, for example, makes nothing public but her verdict. She is not required to give her reasons even for that. Her defiant act of jury nullification, if any, is done in secret, and its reasons and supporting arguments become part of no record. Moreover, the juror, in theory, decides only about the facts. She is in no position, therefore, to influence the future course of law. And in no sense does she speak for the state.

I must admit at this point that the only place where one's stand on the positivism–natural law controversy seems to have practical effects is the situation in which the philosophers are also judges and they have good reason to find their personal, moral duties as human beings even more stringent than their sworn duties as judges when those duties are weighed on the scales of conscience, all things considered. The main practical difference made in these circumstances by one's philosophical stance seems to be to the disadvantage of my allies, the legal positivists. Their position, as we said, is more uncomfortable than that of their natural law counterparts. Comfort, to be sure, is much preferred over discomfort. But isn't there a limit to the relevance of such a consideration when we come to evaluate theories as true or false? Is there not even a limit to the relevance of discomfort to a determination of whether the two theories really have *differences* in their morally important consequences?

I am glad that we had this chat, even though we are a long way from a resolution of the problems that engage us. I must confess that you have made natural law theory a good deal more plausible than I ever believed it was. But I can hardly accept it at this stage of our discussions, for I must first be led to understand one of the tenets that is both obscure and central to natural law theory, namely, the notion that moral principles are a part of, identical with, or essentially connected to legal rules or are themselves legal rules of a special implicit kind, or that as "higher law" they are part and parcel of every legal system, capable of invalidating any other legal rules whose content conflicts with their own, or that they fill the interstices of all legal systems, and similar claims. If you could explain how morality got into the law in the first place or what it can mean to say that its necessary presence within every legal system is conceptually entailed by the very idea of law, I would be more friendly to your view. The consequences of natural law theory in courts of law have often been benign, but until these notions are clarified, I am unwilling to accept the theory as true.

NL: I too have enjoyed our philosophic exchange, and we must get together again soon to continue our discussion right where you left it. In the meantime, permit me also a moment of politeness. You have succeeded in puzzling me about my own theory and, if only to that extent, leading me to have more respect for legal positivism. But if I too am a bit uncertain what it means to assert that deep and fundamental moral principles are implicitly a part of every legal system, simply as a definitional truth, like "All true laws are promulgated" or "Secret laws are not true laws," I am much less puzzled about what it means to advocate or recommend that some moral precepts be acknowledged as part of *our* legal system, not because of some alleged conceptual truth that ties *all* legal systems to certain moral precepts necessarily, but rather because such a measure would promote both justice and efficiency, and that is reason enough. You ask how morality got into the law. Part of the answer to that question, especially in respect to the minimal requirements of fairness and reasonableness, is that *we put it there*. If it seems not to be there at all in our legal system, then our legislators ought to put it there.

LP: But I'm not sure that our suspicious legislators would be very enthusiastic about that suggestion! They are happy to give lip service to such glittering ideas as justice and morality, but when it comes to practical action, they would probably let us down.

NL: We would have a better chance if we emphasized that it is only a bare minimal morality that we would put into law. We ask only that they agree that there is (or should be) a limit to how crazy, mean, cruel, or senseless a law (or legal interpretation) can be. To my mind, the natural law theory, which assures us that morality is already in law, is most persuasive when it is the relatively noncontroversial minimal morality we are talking about. Then I can say something that strikes your ear as obscure and rhapsodical—that morality is just naturally there, growing like flowers on a bed of law—and say this while confident that I can get even good legal positivists like yourself to join our efforts to *make* this true, even if it is not already true by nature.

LP: What, then, do you propose, you compromised former natural law theorist?

NL: It's very simple. I would have moral principles (at first, very abstract and not very controversial ones) made quite explicit, perhaps in an asterisked endnote at the bottom of the page on which every bill of legislation and every enacted statute is printed, just as the phrase "We are an equal opportunity employer," or words to that effect, now appear on the official stationery of many universities. At first, the explicit statement should be quite minimal, ruling out only extremely unjust and irrational rules, judgments, verdicts, and sentences. Once it is understood that there *is* such a superrule, or higher law, in our system, the way is open for courts to find some laws to be invalid for no other reason than their conflict with those principles of justice. It would have to be heavily emphasized, of course, that simple unfairness and commonplace unreasonableness are not enough, that only transparently flawed legislation could be invalidated in this fashion: flagrant, gross, and outrageous injustice and utterly crazy, pointless unreasonableness. Anyone who has made even a casual perusal of casebooks knows, however, that such flagrant flaws are frequently found in the arguments of prosecutors, judges, and others. And to the objection that this procedure would give too much power to judges, who in turn would use their new discretion in capricious ways, I would reply by pointing to the other places in the law where judges are invited to apply their own standards to determine what is substantial, reasonable, excessive, cruel, fitting, appropriate, due, and other such predicates. A legal system in the modern world could hardly get along without such open-textured and essentially contested terms and the discretion they bring with them. My proposal would only empower courts to filter out the most extreme unreasonableness and unfairness from our laws, without giving discretion to judges to enter into the deeper questions of justice on their own, without controls. And legal philosophers would no longer be puzzled about what it means to say that moral precepts are a part of our legal system (if not all other legal systems).

2

IN DEFENSE OF MORAL RIGHTS

In Great Britain and the United States women have the right to vote. But there was a time, of course, when women did not have the right to vote in the United States, and even now (1992) women do not have the right to vote in Kuwait and some other countries. These appear to be empirical judgments supported by the factual evidence. On the other hand, we are inclined to say that even in the United States of 1890, and even in Kuwait at present, women *really* had the right to vote, but that this right was wrongfully withheld from them by their legislators and constitution makers. This second kind of judgment, which by now is familiar to us, is one that has raised philosophical problems. The existence of rights in this category is said to be prior to and independent of their enactment by legislatures or their declarations, explicit or implicit, by constitution makers. We need not and cannot confirm them, as in the first class of rights, by gathering empirical facts as evidence of their actual acknowledgment or enforcement in the political societies in question, because their existence is not said to depend in any way upon their recognition in those societies, but has some independent source that can establish them even where they are not generally valued or even wanted. In positing the existence of rights in this second class, we do not act as impartial social scientists describing the facts of actual practice for better or worse; rather we jump into the moral arena, and take a stand ourselves. All adult human beings, we might say, have a right to participate in the political decisions that govern their affairs, and of course, this holds for women too. Even where women as a class do not have a *legal* right to vote, they clearly have a moral right, derived from their humanity and the moral principle of equality, to vote along with men. The philosophical problems, not all of which I can address here, is to explain what such moral rights are and where they come from, how we can recognize them and resolve disagreements about their existence, and what practical consequence, if any, follows from their possession, especially when they are not given legal protection.

When we assert our own rights or the rights of others, very often the rights we affirm are of the sort I am calling "moral rights." An abundance of examples will illustrate how ordinary and familiar is this category of rights. In addition to Kuwaiti women's right to vote, one can mention the right to breathe clean air claimed by enemies of tobacco smoking prior to any legal rules that might have been adopted to protect it; the right of a married couple to use contraceptives in the privacy of their own bedroom, first affirmed by the U.S. Supreme Court in *Griswold v. Connecticut* decades after the practice had become both prevalent and illegal;[1] the right of legally competent adults voluntarily to get married even though the man and woman are of different races, a right first vindicated by the U.S. Supreme Court in *Loving v. Virginia* in 1967;[2] the right to organize into trade unions, claimed by British agricultural laborers before legal recognition was first forthcoming;[3] the right to picket peacefully which, until this century, was honored mainly in the breach; the right to know one's own medical prognosis ("Tell me the truth, doctor," we say, "I have a right to know"); the child's right to a voice in family decisions, which is not and could not be a *legal* right,[4] and similarly, a parent's right to be spoken to civilly by his children; a student's right to be graded without prejudice; a terminal patient's right (whatever legal rules or hospital codes may say about the matter) to the termination of treatment designed simply to keep him alive as long as possible; a young girl's right, even among peoples whose traditional practice requires it of everyone, not to have a ceremonial clitorectomy imposed on her as a precondition of the wedding ceremony;[5] the Indian widow's right, even before 1829, when the practice of suttee was banned throughout British India, *not* to immolate herself on her husband's funeral pyre, despite social, religious, and even political pressure to do so;[6] the right to the free exercise of one's religion, which was systematically violated, for example, by the legal authorities of Iran in the case of the Bahai religion, whose temples were destroyed and leaders executed; and, finally, the right to freedom from arbitrary arrests and incarceration, as in the standard Gestapo practice of raiding the homes of Jews and dissidents at four in the morning, pounding peremptorily on the door, and then carting away the terrified residents, who were often never heard from again. Surely if we have any rights at all, we have rights not to be treated like that!

These examples are designed to show that moral rights are not some esoteric construction of otherworldly philosophers, but common parts of the conceptual apparatus of most if not all of us when we come to make moral and political judgments. One of the best definitions of moral rights in the present sense comes, ironically, from a philosopher who is an avowed skeptic about their existence. Raymond Frey defines a moral right as "a right which is not the product of community legislation or social practice, which persists even in the face of contrary legislation or practice, and which prescribes the boundary beyond which neither individuals nor the community may go in pursuit of their overall ends."[7]

Several further distinctions must now be made in order to clarify this definition. First of all, obviously, the categories of moral and legal rights overlap, so that a given moral right can also be a legal right if a rule calling for its recognition and enforcement has been duly enacted into law. The right of women to vote, long a moral right, has since 1920 also been in the United States a legal right. Second, a distinction must be drawn between moral rights in the sense I have been assigning to that term and moral rights in a much weaker sense, namely, the rights conferred on people by the rules of the conventional morality—or the "moral code," as we say—of their communities. These are the rights that Frey's definition attributes to "social practice" in contrast to genuinely moral rights which, coming from some objective and universal principles of morality, exist as independently of social practice as they do of legislative enactment. Conventional morality varies from group to group; we speak of "bourgeois morality," "socialist morality," "Nazi morality" (which was an immoral morality indeed), Catholic morality, Eskimo morality, Hottentot morality, and the morality of the ancient Spartans or Babylonians. These various systems of norms for the most part contain many proscriptions and injunctions in common, but they also differ in some striking ways. Infanticide, for example, was permissible in Spartan and Hottentot morality; it is a dreadful sin in Catholic morality.

In contrast, what is sometimes called "true morality" is thought to be immune to such fluctuations, being at least to some degree "part of the nature of things," critical, rational, and correct. True morality, so understood, provides the standards and principles by which to judge the actual institutions of any given society, *including* its conventional morality—the rules and principles actually established in that society, for better or worse. Rights conferred by a universal true morality may also be a part of the conventional moralities of many societies, as the right not to be killed or the right to have what was promised to one, for example. Furthermore, a moral right in the objective sense may be conferred by a given code of conventional morality and a system of positive law *both*, in which case it is a true moral right, a conventional moral right, and a legal right, all at once; or it may be unrecognized by both a country's conventional morality and its legal system, in which case it remains a true moral right anyway. This latter point is well illustrated, I think, by the Gestapo arrests, the right to the free exercise of religion in Iran, the right of Indian widows not to incinerate themselves, and the right of the daughters of Cairo not to be subject to sexual mutilations before marriage. Arguably, in each of these cases, critical morality confers a genuine moral right that is unrecognized, indeed explicitly denied both by the conventional morality of the group and by its legal system, insofar as it has one.

Third, there is a distinction between those moral rights that are *exercisable* even prior to legal recognition and those that cannot be exercised before being enacted into law. There is no way, for example, in which women can exercise their moral right to vote in a country where that right has not been given legal recognition, whereas one can exercise the moral right to picket peace-fully before legal recognition, at least until the police arrive to haul one away. Better examples of exercisable moral rights are the right to practice one's religion (even secretly) and the right to commit suicide in order to hurry a death that would otherwise be painful. This distinction is of no deep theoret-ical importance, but a fourth distinction, related to it, may be of greater interest. Women campaigning for the right to vote may say, "We demand our rights." This suggests that what they want is to be granted rights—legal rights—which they do not yet have, since in the example the only rights they have in respect to voting are moral rights, which being nonexercisable are not in themselves operative "voting rights." What good is it then to have nonexercisable moral rights? Are the women in the example merely demand-ing the recognition of rights they already have when they demand their rights, like the followers of Martin Luther King, Jr., who assumed that they already had certain constitutional rights whose benefits were being wrongfully withheld from them? King's followers were not asking for new rights but for enforcement of actual legal rights they were confident they already had. But in the women's case, valid laws on the books and in effect explicitly denied them what they were after.

The women's demand for their rights should be interpreted as a demand for new legal rights, which they did not at the time possess. When they said that they "want their rights," they meant to put in a claim, based on their actual possession of a moral right, to be given the corresponding legal right. What they were asserting is that they have a right to be granted a right, a moral right against the state to be given a new legal right. The moral right functions as the basis of their entitlement to the legal right analogous to the way in which a title establishes a claim to property. Without the moral right, the women could still *demand* the new legal right and fight for it effectively, but they could not make claim to it as rightfully theirs, and push that claim against the consciences of legislators. What the women wanted was not sim-ply something that would be good to have, but something *that they had coming anyway as their due*, and this is an idea that the language of rights with its tone of urgency and righteousness is uniquely suited to convey.

Another word about terminology. Sometimes the term "natural right" means nothing more than "moral right" as we have defined it. In eighteenth-century terminology in particular, the natural was contrasted with the arti-ficial. The natural is what is "there" to be discovered, quite apart from human design or construction, as opposed to that which owes its existence to human invention and design. If that is all we mean by "natural," then the terms "natural right" and "moral right" are perfectly interchangeable. Natural rights are part of the nature of things to be discovered by human reason, whereas conventional and institutional rights, including legal ones, are the products of human draftsmanship and general compliance and acceptance. But some-times the term "natural right" means more than critical moral right. In this further sense, a natural right is a moral right derived from "the nature of man," conferred on human beings as parts of their original constitutions, like their biological organs, bones, and muscles. And, like their biological counterparts, natural rights in this conception are conferred by natural laws—the laws of our being. Here the idea of scientific laws reporting invariant regularities in experience and that of jural laws of the sort made by human legislatures, only here discovered not made, blend together to the irritation of many thinkers who would otherwise be sympathetic to the generic idea of a natural, that is, moral right. That is why I prefer the language of "moral rights" over the language of "natural rights" even when the terms are synonyms.[8]

Finally, we should distinguish between the moral rights that some human beings have because of their special properties, offices, or relations to others— the special rights of children, the aged, students, criminal defendants, promisees, and citizens—and the more abstract rights said to belong to all human beings as such, simply by virtue of their humanity. The former group can be called special rights, and the latter are commonly called "human rights." Both are equally moral rights, or natural rights in the generic sense, and both are frequently included in conventional moral codes and systems of jural law.

There was a time some fifty years ago when treatises and textbooks in moral philosophy were overwhelmingly concerned with our duties and what we ought generally to do (these were usually taken as equivalent). Typically, moral rights were addressed, in an appendix[9] or a late chapter,[10] as a kind of afterthought. Unlike duties, which were recognized as commonplace and foundational in the moral life, moral rights were suspect and often thought to be mysterious or strange. The commonly heard question was "Where do they come from?" (We know where legal and other conventional rights "come from.") This difference is especially puzzling when one remembers that statements of rights are often logically connected to statements of duties. There are, to be sure, more consistent skeptics who have equally severe doubts about moral rights and moral duties, and indeed about all allegedly objective moral rules and principles. That kind of consistent skepticism poses a serious challenge to the theory of moral rights, if only because its doubts apply to rights and duties both. The more selective skepticism that singles out moral rights may be somewhat easier to cope with.

More commonly the token chapters on rights were dismissive in another way. Moral rights, instead of being odd or exotic, were thought to be commonplace, derivative, and trivial. To be sure, they are logically correlative with duties, but duties were the fundamental notion, and rights were merely an alternative way of speaking of other people's duties.[11] In theory, the moralist could say everything he needed to say in the language of duties (perhaps supplemented by talk of "values"); statements of rights were thought of as mere convenient shorthand ways of talking about duties and their logical consequences. Professor Raymond Frey is a recent representative of this mode of dismissiveness. Rights talk, in his view, is not merely derivative and secondary; it is in principle and in fact totally *superfluous*. "As far as I can see," he writes, "not even a practical advantage is gained by positing some moral duties based upon agreed moral principles, since I, as a moral man implementing and following my principles will behave the way you want me to even without [your having] the right."[12] Rights, in short, add nothing; they are dispensable entities with no further function than to confuse philosophers. If we list all of the duties that people have, then we need no further list of anybody's rights, for the universal discharge of duties would fully satisfy anything that might be claimed as a right.

The quick answer to Frey is that what one person's rights add to another person's duties is some measure of control by the right holder over those duties.[13] He can release the other from his duty if he pleases, for example, thus exercising a kind of "moral power" analogous to legal powers to bind or release.[14] Moreover, the right holder's right often provides the whole grounding for the other party's duty; it is for his sake that the other has his duty. If *B* has a right that *A* do (or omit doing) *X* for him, then *B* can claim *X* from *A* as his due. He is, morally speaking, in a position to say to *A*, "You owe me *X* as my due." Moreover, if *A* violates *B*'s valid claim, *B* can voice a grievance against *A*, now being in a position to charge not only that "you acted wrongly" but also that "you wronged me" in so acting. If the wrongful act or omission of *A*'s were a mere dereliction of his own duty instead of being also an infringement of *B*'s right, then *B* would have no personal grievance, and *A* could reply to his complaint by saying, "What business is it of yours whether I perform my duties? That is a matter between me and my conscience, or between me and God. It is no proper concern of yours, so stay out of it." At the very least this reply is a misreading of the moral situation, and if it were correct, then *B* having no claim, no grievance, no proper business or concern, no representation in the grounds of *A*'s duty, and no control over the content of that duty, would have less dignity in the eyes of others, and, if he himself believed Frey's superfluity thesis, less respect for himself as a maker of moral claims against others, as a person whose own basic interests matter.[15]

If rights really seem superfluous to Frey, it may be because his "principles," which tell him in advance what he morally ought to do in every situation, themselves have respect for the rights of others already built into them. It is difficult to imagine how one could know what one ought to do (generally) without first determining what rights various persons are likely to have against one, and which of these rights are likely to be waived. There is, I think, considerable plausibility in the view that your rights have a moral priority over my duties, in the sense that the duties are derived from them rather than the other way around. It is because I have a claim-right not to be punched in the nose by you, for example, that you have a duty not to punch me in the nose. It does not seem to work the other way. That is, it is not the case that my right not to be punched in the nose by you exists only because you have a prior duty not to punch people in the nose. My claim and your duty both derive from the interest that I have in the physical integrity of my nose. To make your duty basic and controlling is to misrepresent the way rights of this sort are grounded and to give no plausible grounding at all for your duty.

Consider, as an analogy to Frey's superfluity thesis, a blind man who is incapable of reading the "Private Property. Stay Out" signs along his path, but who has memorized a set of instructions on how to get to his destination: "one hundred steps straight ahead, two hundred to the right, three hundred to the left," and so on. These instructions are at least partially analogous to Frey's "principles"; both are morally reliable directives that do not make references to rights. But in each case, part of the method for determining what the contents of the directives are is first to determine what rights various persons have against one. Once these rights are given their due, further explicit reference to them, supplementary to the principles they have generated, will be "superfluous."

Frey does not maintain that rights claims are gibberish, communicating no sense. He generously concedes that rights talk is a somewhat confused way of focusing attention on the interests of the party or parties said to have the right or of asserting the moral wrongness of harming those interests. These functions, he admits, can be forensically useful, provided no one is tempted to believe that there actually are such entities as moral rights.

Frey's most interesting suggestion for preserving the intuitive meaningfulness of rights talk puts him squarely in a tradition that goes back at least to Jeremy Bentham. One can get rid of the mysterious element in moral rights talk, Frey suggests, by interpreting it as a confused and indirect way of referring to *legal* rights, which, being plain matters of fact, are *not* themselves mysterious. (Moral philosophers who assume that their subject matter is more mysterious than that of law have obviously never studied law with any seriousness.) I call this the "there ought to be a law" theory of moral rights, for it holds that the sentence "*A* has a moral right to do (have or be) *X*" is to be understood, insofar as it makes any sense at all, to be saying, "*A* *ought* to have a *legal* right to *X*."

I agree that sometimes the "ought to be a law" analysis does seem to provide a sensible interpretation for moral rights talk. It may, for example, be a plausible interpretation of the United Nations Declaration of Human Rights that the *welfare rights* it ascribes are proposed objects of legislative aspiration merely, in no sense existent and in effect everywhere *now*. If every human being has a moral right to "periodic holidays with pay," as the United Nations' statement declares,[16] this can only mean that commercial and industrial organizations everywhere ought to put in place now plans to increase production to the point where universal employment is possible, and paid holidays are routinely affordable. *Now, of course,* the economic conditions of much of the world make the idea of mandated paid vacations a utopian dream, nothing that starving Ethiopian farmers, for example, are in a position to claim as their due, quite unlike the moral rights that Kuwaiti women have to vote in their national elections. The best analysis of the periodic paid vacation right, perhaps, is that it describes something that ought to be a legal or other conventional right when or if the time ever comes when the whole world can afford it.[17]

It may then be a reasonable interpretation of the welfare rights that manifestos assign so generously that they merely describe an arrangement of human affairs that is desirable and worth aiming at, but nothing yet existent as a true moral right at this instant. It is, however, quite unconvincing to say that the eventual fitness to be legal rights explains what we *normally* mean by the expression "moral rights," for this account cannot be reconciled with some familiar uses of the language of moral rights. It cannot plausibly explain what is meant, for example, by talk of persons *exercising* their moral rights before those rights were legally recognized, as in the case of demonstrators arrested for illegal picketing, or religious worshipers conducting secret services in a country where they are persecuted. On the "there ought to be a law" model, what these people are "exercising" is no kind of actual right at all, but rather what *ought* to be a right, a kind of ideal right, which they do not yet have and may never have, though they ought to. There is, in short, no actual right of any kind in these circumstances to be exercised, but rather only a suitability to be a right—and how does one exercise a suitability? Moreover, when the state prevents one from doing what *would* be an exercise of legal rights one ought to have, then on the "ought to be a law" theory, the state violates no right that one actually has at the time.

To be sure, many, even most, of the moral rights on our initial list of examples are *also* such that they ought to be legal rights. But that suitability is not what we mean when we call them moral rights. Their fitness to be legislated is something extra. The reason why we think that they ought to be legal rights is that we recoil at their violation now. The sexual mutilation of a young girl with unsterilized razor blades is a wrong to her. It is also true that it ought not to be permitted by law or by convention, but what we condemn here and now is not merely that the law does not prohibit it, but that it is done at all. The girl in our example would be wronged whether the act that wrongs her is legal or not, and *that* is why it ought not to be legal.

A second difficulty of the theory that a moral right is simply what ought to be a legal right is its apparent inability to provide a plausible account of what it could be to have a moral right to *rebel* against a tyrannical government. Since the right to revolt against established authority could not be a legal right conferred by the government in power, it could not very well be true that it ought to be so conferred. Yet it does make good sense to say, with Jefferson, that the right to rebel against tyranny is a genuine right which we all have *now* along with (or side by side with) our various legal rights.

The key premise in this simple valid argument, of course, is that the right to revolt cannot be made a legal right, not at least without serious, even insurmountable, practical difficulties. Independent arguments for the truth of this key premise have been made by various writers, of whom perhaps, the most typical is Joseph Story, the virtual founder of the Harvard Law School and a U.S. Supreme Court justice during the turbulent 1840s. According to Professor Robert Cover, in Story's book *Commentaries on the Constitution*, Story

> hypothesizes a state of affairs in which the various departments of government instead of checking on one another, "concur in a gross usurpation." He [Story] hypothesized that the normal remedies would be unavailing should the oppressed group be a minority. In such a case, asserts Story, [quoted by cover] "If there be any remedy at all . . . it is a remedy never provided for by human institutions. It is by resort to the ultimate right of all human beings in extreme cases to resist oppression, and to apply force against ruinous injustice." The moral right was asserted here, side by side with denial of the possibility of institutional reflection of that right.[18]

The acts of "gross usurpation" that Story had in mind are acts of government officials contrary to law, violations of rules defining offices and limiting their powers, and acts of corruption, bribery, and legally unwarranted coercion. When office holders conspire to act improperly, and their crimes are covered up by their colleagues or vindicated by members of the judiciary, all of them parties to the conspiracy, then it is hard to imagine what further institutional remedy, beyond the definitions of the crimes actually committed, could become available. An institutional right to take up arms whenever one believes that rules have been violated to one's disadvantage would be chaotic. It is hard even to recognize a *moral* right, for example, to attack the nation's military forces in an attempt to overthrow the entire authority of the government, in response to one particular set of abuses by corrupt officials.

The argument, however, does not have to involve gross usurpation in Story's sense, and in fact can make its point more clearly without it. Imagine then the following unlikely scenario. Suppose that a neo-fascist "Purple Shirt party" grows ever more powerful in an economically stricken United States. A parallel example can be provided, of course, for the United Kingdom. The central element in their program, let us imagine, is what they call "the final solution of the Ruritanian problem": All citizens of Ruritanian descent are to be rounded up and shipped to slave labor camps to be worked to death, or killed as part of some scientific experiment in the public interest. At first, there is no success in passing this program into law, as all the state legislatures and the national Congress have non–Purple Shirt majorities, but after a number of years, as economic conditions worsen, and citizens become more bitter and irrational, Purple Shirt majorities are established in all of the legislatures, and the White House itself is occupied by a Purple Shirt president. Quickly the Purple Shirt program is enacted in the Congress and signed into law by the president. Ruritanian Americans begin to be arrested, at first only in small numbers. One of them appeals to the highest court to overturn the legislation under which he has lost his liberty. The court decides, nine votes to nil, that the anti-Ruritanian legislation is unconstitutional, being in flagrant contradiction to most of the first fifteen amendments to the Constitution, including virtually the entire Bill of Rights. All Ruritanian prisoners are ordered released, and the laws under which they were captured pronounced null and void.

The peculiar characteristic of the Purple Shirt leaders, however, is their devotion to acquiring political power by means of democratic support. They always resort to political persuasion by legitimate means. They are so confident of their political skills that they are able to maintain an untarnished record of respect for law and legitimacy, assuring that every move they make in the pursuit of political power is strictly in accordance with the laws of the land and the constitutionally specified rules of proper procedure. Accordingly, they introduce a bill to Congress, and simultaneously to the fifty state legislatures, to amend the U.S. Constitution. Article V of that document specifies how the Constitution is to be amended: Two-thirds majorities are required in both houses of Congress and simple majorities in three-quarters of the state legislatures. So powerful have the Purple Shirts become that they have no trouble in finding the requisite votes. We can imagine then that the relevant prior amendments to the Constitution are themselves amended by ad hoc exceptive clauses excluding persons with at least three Ruritanian grandparents from their protection, or simply abrogated altogether. The Purple Shirts, having acted in accordance with proper procedures and respect for constitutional law at every step, are now free to implement their entire program. The original legislation is reintroduced, quickly passed, and signed into law. An appeal to the Supreme Court this time is promptly rejected by a unanimous vote. At this point the Ruritanians are all shipped to death camps; the Purple Shirt leadership goes to celebrate; the rest of us, confident of our moral position, prepare to go to war.

How could this military insurrection have been legitimized in advance by a legal rule conferring a right to rebel against tyranny? Even if it is coherent to grant a legal right to overturn by force a government that has committed no infractions, overt or covert, of legal rights—a tyrannical government of impeccable fidelity to proper procedure—could not the Purple Shirt legislative majorities in due time ratify the appointment of new Supreme Court justices known to be partial to the Purple Shirt program? Could not such a court, without conspiratorial "usurpation," find, after the fact, that the Purple Shirt government was not tyrannical within the meaning of the law? (If, instead, the would-be revolutionaries petition the court in advance to judge whether just cause for rebellion exists, how could the court decide affirmatively without joining the insurrection itself?) Returning to the problem of judicial judgment *after* a failed rebellion, is it possible to imagine that the losing side in a morally justified insurrection would be found by a magnanimous court of the very government that has just defeated them in a bloody civil war to be not guilty of treason or any other crime, that is, to have been legally justified in their failed insurrection? If it is inconceivable that this should happen, then what point would a "legal right to rebel" have? Yet, for all of that, I submit that there is a moral right to rebel against tyranny even though it would be pointless to attempt to write it into law in a "tyrannical democracy."

A stronger but less certain version of the argument might claim that a legal rule permitting rebellion against tyranny would be not only pointless but positively pernicious. It would surely be difficult to formulate such a right-conferring rule so as not to encourage misguided violence or to increase political instability generally. If we permit rebellion against tyranny, oppression, or injustice, how will we prevent people from rebelling over an inequitable tax law, or a particular instance of excessive criminal sentencing, or similar specific injustices? How could we possibly spell out the domain of the right in detail? How oppressive must oppression be to warrant rebellion? We *could* avoid these problems of legislative draftsmanship by producing a deliberately vague statement as a piece of "harmless rhetoric" of the sort characteristic of revolutionary manifestos, a spare moral tribute to an abstract idea. But this is just what Bentham hated, and with good reason: the idea that moral grievances automatically ground revolutionary violence. Bentham attributes to those Enlightenment revolutionaries who promoted the theory of natural rights the following attitude: "Whenever I find a man who will not let me put myself on a par with him in every respect [e.g., a nobleman or a rich man with unearned and undeserved advantages], it is right and proper and becoming that I should knock him down, if I have a mind to do so, and if that will not do, knock him on the head, and so forth."[19] It is a dangerous habit of mind indeed to shout, "To the barricades!" automatically whenever one encounters an injustice, whatever the extent, whatever the availability of a remedy, whatever the gravity of the evil. Rebellion is too costly a remedy for minor ills, and even abstract rhetorical tributes to morally justified rebellion included among a set of institutional rules probably do more harm than good.[20]

A final argument against the "ought to be a law" theory of moral rights might now seem anticlimactic. There is, however, an argument much closer to everyday things than the imaginary "right to rebellion" scenarios we have been considering. The analysis of moral rights as properly legal rights cannot make sense out of many homely examples of moral rights on our earlier list of familiar specimens. One might well acknowledge, for example, a parent's right to be spoken to civilly by her children, and a student's right to be graded without prejudice by his teachers, while denying that those undoubted rights ought to be legal rights at all. At least these and similar moral rights, then, cannot plausibly be construed as ideally legal or properly legal rights. We think of them as rights against private parties, not necessarily against legislators,[21] and as rights that can be exercised, stood upon, waived, or infringed, quite apart from what the law might say about the matter.

But could not Frey, Bentham, and their colleagues reply that these examples are cases of *conventional* moral rights only? They are resistant to the "ought to be a law" analysis, they might say, only because they already exist as part of the community's conventional moral code. Perhaps then a small modification in the "there ought to be a law" analysis is in order. Its defenders could retreat to the position that an assertion of moral right is a judgment that a given norm ought to be part of a conventional system of operative norms, *either legal or merely conventional*, for example, part of our prevailing moral code. Since the rights in question are already part of our conventional morality, to call them "moral rights" may simply be to judge that they ought to be maintained and strengthened as conventional rights. Their presence on our list of sample moral rights then can be accounted for by the amended theory.

A better example from our list would be the right of a suffering terminal patient to active euthanasia from his doctor or friend. This right may *not* yet be part of our conventional code, but it is plausibly claimed to be a moral right by Professor Yale Kamisar, for example, who proceeds to argue in his famous article that it ought *not* to become a legal right because of the possibility of mistake and abuse.[22] One might, on the same grounds, argue that it ought not even be a conventional moral right. Yet it is arguably a critical moral right for all of that.[23]

Bentham's use of the "there ought to be a law" gambit is somewhat different from that discussed so far. Unlike Frey, he does not argue "generously" that although ascriptions and claims of moral rights make no sense, people *seem* to be making sense when they ascribe or claim them, so what they must mean (or what perhaps they do mean) by "moral right" is simply "what ought to be a legal right," the latter notion making perfectly good sense. Rather, Bentham argues in the opposite direction. If people mean by a moral right simply "what ought to be a legal right," they ought to say so. That would be unobjectionable.[24] But when they fall into the language of moral rights, they inevitably are led to assume that what ought to be a legal right in our system of laws already is a right actually in force in some ghostly cosmic system of laws, parallel but superior to our own, and this is both muddled and pernicious. "All such language is at any rate false . . . or at the best an improper and fallacious way of indicating what is true."[25] Bentham then concludes with characteristic rhetorical overkill: "Reasons for wishing there were such things as rights are not rights; a reason for wishing that a certain right were established is not that right; a want is not supply; hunger is not bread."[26]

To be sure, a reason for wishing to have a right is not the same thing as a right, but it taxes credulity to represent the couple cowering in bed as the Gestapo boots are pounding up their stairs as having no greater moral claim in that situation than a reason for wishing that they had a protective legal right! That is all the moral standing Bentham will allow them, all the content he will grudgingly concede to their moral right. At least Bentham understands, unlike the generous Professor Frey, that the genuine belief of moral rights advocates, no matter how muddled or pernicious it might be, is that moral rights are actual rights, existent and in effect, and not merely what ought to be contained in our legal or other conventional norms.

L. W. Sumner, in his excellent work on the theory of rights, sympathizes with Bentham's contempt for the muddled idea of a ghostly cosmic system of legal-like rules from which actual moral rights are derived. He tries to avoid that conception in his own account of moral rights, to which I shall soon turn, but his accurate understanding of Bentham's motives is well expressed in the following passage.[27]

> Although a skeptical argument like Bentham's cannot show conclusively that the very idea of a natural [i.e., moral] right is incoherent, it would be strengthened if some alternative explanation could be given for the persistent belief in the existence of natural rights. Suppose that the legal system governing us has denied us some legal right which we believe we ought to have, and that we wish to make a case for being accorded that right. Since we believe that we ought to have the right then we believe that in an ideal legal system we would have it. It is then but a short and tempting step to claiming that an ideal legal system exists in which we *do* have the right, and then to saying that the right conferred on us by this ideal system constitutes our case for having the same right conferred on us by our *actual* system. The mechanism at work here is projection. As a corrective to the [moral] imperfections of the actual world we invent a [morally] perfect world in which individuals possess just those rights which, morally speaking, they ought to have, and then we treat this invention as though it were real.[28]

Positing moral rights then turns out to be an instance of wishful thinking, and that is what Bentham thinks explains the widespread and persistent belief in them.

How does Sumner himself manage to defend belief in the existence of moral rights without projecting his "wishes" into some ghostly cosmic system? He defines a moral right as "a morally justified conventional right."[29] "I have a moral right," he says, "just in case my possession of the corresponding conventional right is morally justified."[30] At times he suggests that a moral right is a species of a conventional right, so that I cannot have a moral right unless I already have the conventional right with the same content, that conventional right itself amounting to a moral right if its inclusion in a conventional code or legal system is morally justified. But on the whole, I think that the best interpretation of his intentions is to say that a moral right is either an actual conventional right that is morally justified or that *it would be morally justified*, in the strongest sense, to adopt as a conventional right, in case it is not a conventional right already. Either the conventional rule system in question already recognizes the moral right or it does not. "If it does," says Sumner, "then what must be justified is the continued recognition of the right. ... If it does not, then what must be justified is altering the system so that it comes to recognize the right. . . . We may call each of these options—either maintaining an already existing conventional right or creating a new one— a social *policy*. A moral right exists when a policy of either sort is [morally] justified for the relevant rule system"[31]—usually a system of laws.

The major advantage Sumner claims for this analysis is that it explains what the moral credentials of a moral right are and why it has moral force, the answer being, of course, that it includes the requirement of moral justification. What is to be justified, however, is not a moral claim made by the right holder in the face of some threatened infringement, but rather the social policy of introducing or maintaining a rule in a conventional system. This feature, Sumner contends, has the added advantage of making "no references to a ghostly realm of natural moral rules," since "the only rules referred to are conventional."[32]

Sumner's definition of "moral right" seems to be a more refined version of what I have called the "there ought to be a law" analysis. His version is stronger than most, in that it does not restrict the relevant class of justified conventional rules to legal rules. By virtue of this enlargement, his version of the theory preserves the possibility that some moral rights exist because it would be justified to maintain or introduce them into a system of conventional moral rules even though it would not be justified to include them as elements of a legal system. This move renders the theory immune to such counterexamples as the child's right to a voice in family decisions, a parent's right to be spoken to civilly, and so on. Moral rights of this class would not be justified as legal rights, but they might well be justified as rights conferred by conventional morality, and thus would qualify as genuine moral rights in Sumner's view.

Moreover, Sumner's analysis would please Bentham by its avoidance of any apparent commitment to a ghostly realm of legal-like rules. (I too share Bentham's ontological squeamishness in this matter.) The weakness of Sumner's account, however, lies in its failure to capture a central feature of moral rights, the fact that they are taken to be actual rights at the moment they are asserted, in place, or in effect, generating other people's moral duties, capable in many cases of being exercised, and in all cases capable of being either respected or violated. The indicative claim that I have a right to use contraceptives or to marry a woman of another race is not fully translated into any number of subjunctive claims that certain social policies would be justified if . . . If it is a claim about justification at all, it is the straightforward, nonconjectural claim that interference or noncooperation with me in certain specifiable ways is not justified, that others have a real duty subject to my control not to interfere in those ways.

It would appear then that an adequate definition of moral rights should satisfy at least two tests: (1) it should not be committed to a ghostly realm of legal-like rules ripped from their normal connection to actual legal institutions, and (2) it should preserve the directness and matter-of-factness, the immediate, nonsuppositional actuality of moral rights that is part of their normal conception. The way to do this, I submit, is to bypass an intermediate step in Sumner's derivation of moral rights. What is to be morally justified in Sumner's theory is a kind of legislative act of creating institutional or other conventional rules. I would substitute a simpler account in which what is to be directly justified is not a hypothetical legislative act or policy, but rather the claim of present moral right itself.

There are as many as six elements in Sumner's more complicated analysis:

1. The candidate for the status of moral right.
2. The rule purporting to confer that right.
3. A system of conventional rules requiring, permitting, or prohibiting certain kinds of conduct, for example, a legal system or a conventional moral code.
4. A legislative context, that is, the actual circumstances in which the candidate rule would operate at the time at which it would be maintained or introduced into the system (i.e., right now). ("Moral rights which exist under some social conditions may fail to exist under others.") That is, they may acquire or lose their justifications, as historical circumstances change. This leads, Sumner says, to "a certain relativity in the concept of a moral right."[33]
5. An imagined act/policy of maintaining or introducing the candidate rule into the conventional rule system.
6. The correct principles of moral justification, whatever they may be (e.g., the principle of utility, a contractarian principle, the principle of autonomy, Thomist natural law theory, Kantian universalizability, or Marxist historicism).

The candidate moral right turns out to be a genuine moral right if and only if the act/policy of maintaining or introducing it into the system of conventional rules is, in the actual present social circumstances, justified by the correct principles of moral justification, whichever they are.

The simpler account I propose would make reference only to two of the elements in Sumner's test: a statement of the purported moral right and the correct principles of moral justification, whatever they may be. On this simpler and more natural reconstruction, a purported moral right is a genuine moral right if and only if it is validated as such by correct moral principles. More precisely, it is a genuine moral right if and only if its truth follows from true premises, at least one of which is a moral principle. In a parallel way, a purported moral duty (like the duties not to act cruelly or deceitfully) is a genuine moral duty if it is certified as such by correct moral principles. If this simple derivation of duties is untroublesome, conjuring up no visions of a spooky cosmic legal system, why should not the correspondingly simple derivation of rights be equally untroublesome? The advantage of this simple form for a derivation of moral rights is that it explains how we can have moral rights in the same direct and immediate way we have moral duties, how the two come from the same source, and why they are called "moral" whether or not they are recognized by the conventional rule systems of particular communities. If a correct moral principle, conjoined with some factual premises, logically implies that I have a right to be free from arbitrary arrest and detention, then that right exists as a moral claim binding on the public and on private individuals.

But where do the "correct moral principles" themselves come from if not from some ghostly realm? I cannot here attempt to give a complete metaethical grounding or even an identification of ultimate moral principles, but I can urge that they not be understood on the model of legal rules. They are not the legal-like statutes of some cosmic legal system nor some partial analogue of a legal system without its own charter or constitution, without its own offices and office holders, without its own procedural requirements, without its own secondary rules for changing the primary ones, without its own legislature with its own store of sanctions, without the means to effective public promulgation, without its own trial courts and courts of appeal, and so on. This obscure conception is "spooky" because it posits a legal system that is not quite a real legal system like our earthly exemplars; it is the same perhaps in some quite essential respects as a legal system, but different in other equally essential respects.

Note that a ghost in folklore and fiction is the *same* as a human being in some respects—identifiable form and features—but totally different in other equally essential respects: no flesh and blood, no weight, no physical substance, no tangibility. For that reason "ghostly" is an apt term for a special cosmic legal system different in some essential respects from all mundane legal systems. Gilbert Ryle found a similar use for the ghost analogy when he lampooned the Cartesian conception of the mind as "a ghost in the machine," a person conceived as essentially nonmaterial, but one whose function it is to pull the mechanical gears and levers, and connect or disconnect the electrical circuits of the body it operates. Yet the immaterial ghost is treated by the Cartesians as itself a kind of machine, a special *ghostly* machine, which initiates bodily action by "flexing an occult non-muscle," in Ryle's wonderful satirical phrase, in just the sort of way that causes the flexing of a nonoccult real muscle. A ghost among the gears is supposed to be essentially different from a material object, and yet every property and function the Cartesians assigned to it suggests that they understood it as if it were a special kind of material object—an occult nonmuscle flexer. Similarly, we have a tendency to treat moral principles, which we normally distinguish in some ways from institutional rules, as if they were themselves the rules of an essentially institutional noninstitution (an analogy with the essentially mechanical nonmachines of the Cartesian philosophers).

The parallels between the so-called paramechanical hypothesis Ryle ascribes to Descartes and what we might call the "paralegal hypothesis" scorned by Bentham are striking. "The differences between the physical and the mental," says Ryle, "were . . . represented as differences inside the common framework of the categories of 'thing,' 'stuff,' 'attribute,' 'state,' 'process,' 'change,' 'cause, and effect,' " so that minds were thought of in Ryle's words as "rather like machines but also considerably different from them."[34] Similarly, the differences between legal (or other institutional) rights and moral rights are represented as differences inside the common framework of the categories of enactment, adjudication, amendment, jurisdiction, sanction, and so on, so that moral rights, for example, are thought of as rather like legal (or other institutional) rights "but also considerably different," in fact, essentially different, from them. Again, Ryle comments:

> The logical mold into which Descartes pressed his theory of the mind . . . was the self-same mold into which he and Galileo set their mechanics. Still unwittingly adhering to the grammar of mechanics, he tried to avert disaster by describing minds in what was merely an obverse vocabulary. The workings of minds had to be described by the mere negatives of the specific descriptions given to bodies; they are *not* in space, they are *not* motions, they are *not* modifications of matter, they are *not* accessible to public observation. Minds are not bits of clockwork, they are just bits of not-clockwork.[35]

In a quite parallel manner, some philosophers may have spoken of the moral as if it were both in essential contrast to the legal and yet set in the same logical mold. Still unwittingly adhering to the vocabulary of law, they try to avert disaster by describing morality in a merely obverse vocabulary. Moral rights are *not* enacted, *not* in force, *not* adjudicable, *not* amendable, *not* enforceable, and so on. Moral principles are not just standards applicable to legal rules; they are themselves spectral-legaloid rules of an essentially noninstitutional institution. No wonder Bentham was so scornful.

There is no necessity, however, that we think of moral principles in that way. Rather, we should think of them as in essential contrast to legal rules of all kinds, both those of human institutions and those of their fancied celestial counterparts. Professor Sumner joins Bentham in assuming that if we are to make room for the concept of an existing moral right actually in place now, but not part of any system of laws or other created rules, then we must invent a special spectral realm for it as its own home jurisdiction, so to speak. They look about them and see rights conferred by rules designed by human rule makers to apply in clubs, churches, and corporations, in games and commercial transactions, in systems of civil and criminal positive law, even in the informal norms of conventional morality. When natural rights advocates claim that in addition to these institutional and other conventional rights, there are actually existent moral rights, their critics mistakenly infer that these rights too would have to attach to an institutional base, a special kind of institution to be sure, one not located anywhere in particular—well, not exactly an institution at all. And this quasi institution becomes more "ghostly" the more one thinks about it.

It is interesting to note how the Bentham-Sumner argument turns the argument of the naive believer in moral rights on its head, and commits an equal and opposite mistake. The naive rights believer, whose faith in moral rights, according to Bentham and Sumner, is a kind of wishful thinking, argues as follows:

1. There can be no rights except as attached to an institutional base, for example, to a legal system.
2. There *are* actual moral rights. Therefore,
3. There is an actually existing "ideal legal system" (albeit in a ghostly realm).

Bentham and Sumner argue, on the other hand:

1. There can be no rights without an institutional base.
2. There is no institutional basis for "actual moral rights" (except in some "ghostly realm," an idea which is confused and incoherent). Therefore,
3. So-called actual moral rights do not exist.

Both Bentham, as represented by Sumner, and their naive opponents thus share a common premise, namely, that there can be *no* rights without an institutional base for them, and this is the premise, I have been arguing, that is false. If I am right about that, one may logically elude both Bentham's case for rights skepticism and the spooky realm to which his early opponents were reluctantly committed.

The truth of this matter was perhaps too simple for these authors (Bentham and Sumner) to notice. Ultimate moral principles, as both Bentham and Sumner agree, are rational principles, and reason neither has nor needs some special institutional home of its own.[36] When we affirm that some person has a moral right to something, whatever the local institutions, positive laws, and established conventions may say, we are endorsing reasons derived (we think) from wider principles that are applicable in other contexts, in support of that person's claim. Those reasons themselves are addressed to the consciences of second and third parties, and place the right holder in a moral position to assert her claims, whether she knows it or not. No mention of spooky institutions is required, only reference to broader principles providing cogent reasons in support of individual claims.

I cannot forbear from concluding this essay with a kind of *tu quoque*. If Sumner's appeal to moral principles in justification of legislative acts and policies does not implicate him in the ghostly domain so scorned by Bentham, why should my appeal to such principles (possibly even the very same principles) implicate my account? The only difference in our appeals to critical morality is that he invokes moral principles to justify legislative acts or policies toward maintaining and introducing conventional rules, whereas I invoke them to establish truth claims on behalf of some statements of rights that have nothing necessarily to do with the rules of human institutions. I think we are both innocent of the common error of reinterpreting essentially non-institutional moral principles as if they were special institutional rules. But my simpler account has the added advantage of preserving the direct and indicative character of rights claims, which is assumed, at least in our time and in our culture, by good moral sense.

3

CRIMINAL ENTRAPMENT

Instigating the Unpredisposed

Causing Another Person's Voluntary
Behavior

There are many different ways of getting a person to act as you want him to act. Aristotle quite plausibly argued that only some of these ways, those employing force or a certain kind of deception, provide the actor with an excuse for his action when what he did was wrong. Among the forceful techniques, we can list ordinary compulsion, in which the instigator, for example, pushes or kicks the other, or fastens a chain around him and drags him along the ground. More likely, the forceful instigator will threaten the second party with harm to himself or others to be inflicted if he fails to do what the threatening party wants him to do. This technique, which resorts to force only indirectly as a backup to a threat, is commonly called coercion or duress.

Similarly we can defeat a charge of wrongdoing by showing that another person got us to do the wrongful act by providing us with false information so that the act we believed we were doing, the act we intended to do, was not in fact the act we did. I may think that a nun in her habit is soliciting funds for a church charity, as she says, when in fact she is no nun at all, but a man masquerading as a nun in order to raise funds for himself. In that case, I can argue that even though what I did (put a dollar on his plate) was under one description voluntary, under another it was not. I did not voluntarily contribute money to the private bank account of a criminal, and therefore I cannot be held responsible after the fact for any act under *that* description. Similar techniques, however, lose their exculpatory effect when the deceiver is a police officer baiting her hook to catch a criminal who has a known readiness to commit a certain kind of crime. If B offers to buy a packet of cocaine from A, apparently a willing and eager drug dealer but actually a police agent in civilian dress, B is deceived about no element of the crime he is bent on committing, but only about the identity of the dealer and his chance of getting away with it. It is no excuse to the charge of buying illegal drugs that the buyer believed his dealer was not a police officer.[1]

On the other hand, there are various other techniques of manipulation that are quite consistent with the manipulated party's responsibility. Some of these can be as effective as compulsion and coercion in getting him to do what his manipulator wants him to do, and yet they are not themselves uses of force or coercive threats. A may goad or prod B, persistently coax or implore him, scold or berate him, importune or cajole him, all to a degree that amounts to pestering him. For convenience we can label this somewhat miscellaneous category *goading* techniques. A's conduct in all of these examples falls short of using force or violence and makes no explicit threat of harm. If B lets it "get to him" and does A's bidding, he cannot escape at least shared responsibility for his actions, even though it is unlikely that he would ever have performed those actions if A had not got him to do so.

Entrapment in the Criminal Law

Police officers have frequently used agents provocateurs and similar techniques to get people to commit crimes so that they can be caught in the criminal act, arrested, convicted, and incarcerated, their dangerous propensities no longer likely to produce harm to the people who would otherwise be their victims. Sometimes the disguised police officer has little to do but make known to the criminal that he has an opportunity to commit the crime, and the eager criminal, already predisposed to take advantage of such chances, leaps to the bait. Thus, a secret agent may offer to purchase a prohibited drug from a suspected drug dealer, who immediately agrees, asks a certain price, hands over the drug, and pockets the agent's cash. Even before the dealer can say, "Thank you, have a nice day," the agent identifies himself, announces that the vendor is under arrest, and puts him in handcuffs. In other cases, however, the police plot is more complicated, and its target is an unwary criminal or merely an "unwary innocent" tricked or lured into committing a crime she probably would not otherwise ever have done.

"Entrapment" then has become a derogatory term, referring to governmental abuse of power, so that for a defendant in a criminal trial to prove police entrapment now is for him to use a defense that can get him off the hook of criminal liability. The classic definition comes from the first Supreme Court decision to recognize and formulate an entrapment defense, *Sorrells v. United States*,[2] in 1930: "Entrapment is the conception and planning of an offense by an officer and his procurement of its commission by one who would not have perpetrated it except for the persuasion of the officer."[3] This defense is obviously not available to the drug dealer who quite willingly agrees to sell a prohibited drug to a secret agent. He was ready and willing to engage in that criminal behavior whenever he had the opportunity. Similarly, the defense is not available to the purse snatcher who takes the handbag of a secret "lady cop" who carries it strapped over her shoulder in the common manner, in a crowded department store, and makes no special effort to lure or encourage him. In other cases, however, it may seem clear that but for "repeated and persistent solicitation," the defendant would not have done anything illegal then and there, and probably would have spent the rest of his days as a respectable law-abiding citizen. That kind of defendant needs an entrapment defense and gets one in virtue of the decision in *Sorrells v. United States.* The Supreme Court in that landmark case overturned Sorrells's conviction for the illegal sale of an alcoholic beverage during the Prohibition era. Leo Katz tells the story:

> Sorrells, who lived in a small town in North Carolina, received a visit from several of his friends. They brought with them a stranger named Martin, who introduced himself as a furniture dealer from Charlotte, just passing through the town. When Sorrells discovered to his great pleasure that Martin and he shared a common background—both having served in the Thirtieth Division of the American Expeditionary Forces during World War I— the two became fast friends. Martin, Sorrells, and another friend of Sorrells . . . then began to reminisce about their war experience. After a little while Martin asked Sorrells for some liquor. Sorrells apologized because he didn't have any. Some more time passed, and the conversation was taking an increasing nostalgic turn. Martin again asked Sorrells for some liquor. He explained that he was anxious to buy a half gallon for a friend back home. Sorrells replied that he did not "fool with whiskey." As time went on Martin reiterated his request for liquor some six or seven times. Finally Sorrells got up, excused himself for about twenty minutes, and returned with the requested half gallon. Martin gratefully accepted and paid him five dollars. Alas, Martin turned out to be a prohibition agent posing as a tourist.[4]

The Supreme Court considered carefully just how Sorrells's conduct was instigated by the Prohibition agent. The criminal act, it said, was "a creature of *his* [the agent's] purpose." Sorrells, it seemed clear, was both pestered by repeated and persistent solicitations, and lured by nostalgic sentiments of camaraderie, in the absence of either of which he would surely not have sold liquor to the agent. Perhaps the Court spoke a bit carelessly when it asserted that Sorrells had "*no* previous disposition" to do what he did, and that the agent "implanted in his mind" the disposition to commit the offense. Since Sorrells did what he did voluntarily, he must have had *some* prior disposition to act as he did in the sort of circumstances, rare and contrived as they were, that obtained. But *that* disposition—the tendency to act against one's own principles or interests when pestered, deceived, and lured in just the manner in which he *was* pestered, deceived, and lured by his instigators—should not have been inculpatory. The Prohibition agent did not so much *implant* the disposition as (to switch to a better metaphor) *trigger* the weak disposition that was already there.[5]

Usually, factors of two kinds, the police inducement and the defendant's predisposition, are debated at a criminal trial in which the entrapment defense has become the chief issue. It is normally up to the trial judge to decide whether the police inducement had been so inordinate that the trial must be terminated and the police reprimanded, no matter how telling the evidence of the defendant's readiness to commit the crime would have been had it been admissible. If the trial is permitted to proceed, then the defendant's prior readiness to commit the crime that was then encouraged by secret police inducers must be proved to the jury, along with the elements that define the crime.

Generally, the weaker the police inducement, the more "ready" or "predisposed" the defendant must have been to commit the crime anyway, even without the inducement. Similarly, the stronger the police inducement, the less likely it is that the defendant was prepared to commit the crime, and the less stringent the independent evidence must be that he was in fact so predisposed. In the limiting case where police agents are involved only minimally in the creation of the crime, say, by merely providing the defendant with an opportunity, hardly any evidence at all is required of the prisoner's criminal predisposition. If as little influence as *that* could produce his immediate criminal response, he must have been predisposed. The case for the weakness of the inducement itself implies or produces the case for a strong predisposition, just as a case for the weakness of the predisposition would itself imply a case for a strong, possibly "inordinate," inducement. In such ways the arguments against the inordinate inducement and for the criminal predisposition become intertwined, each a part of the other.

Scams and Stings

The most publicized examples in recent years of prima facie improper governmental inducements and blameworthy predispositions have been elaborately designed Federal Bureau of Investigation scams by which the government cast its nets widely in the hopes of convicting large numbers of corrupt officials, including such powerful persons as members of the U.S. Congress. The most interesting aspect of these cases, I think, is that the entrapment arrangement employed by the defense did not prevent juries from convicting the celebrity defendants. Since it appeared, in the leading case at least,[6] that there was something approaching inordinate inducement from the FBI and only a very weak degree of readiness on the part of the defendant representatives, it may well have been the jury's view, and a plausible view it is, that the office of a member of Congress is so elevated and powerful that a representative must be held to a higher standard of probity than that which is customarily applied to ordinary citizens. She must be more than relatively difficult to corrupt; she must be as close to absolutely incorruptible as human nature will permit.

This conception of the responsibility of Congress members was shared by the law enforcement officers who were motivated by it to establish the so-called ABSCAM (short for "Arab Scam") program in 1981 to test the integrity of high government officials. Toward this end, the FBI hired a professional con man with a long criminal record of extortion and fraud, Melvin Weinberg, who posed as an Arab sheik, caftan and all, and assumed an Arabic name. Leo Katz tells the story from that point:

> Weinberg let it be known that the sheiks were concerned that a change in government in their homeland might force them to emigrate to the United States. To insure against any problems they might have should the occasion arise, Weinberg indicated, the sheiks wanted to "sign up" as many congressmen and other pubic officials as possible. The congressmen could expect, in return, sizable investments in their districts and payments of cash to them personally. The first of those baits was, of course, entirely legitimate; it was the second only that constituted a bribe.[7]

Weinberg's "prodding" of Representative Richard Kelly, as Katz puts it, was at times "relentless"—similar to that of Martin in the *Sorrells* case, but more powerfully alluring and more persistently pursued. Weinberg, posing as an Arab sheik, made an appointment with Kelly. He found the congressman interested in the offered investment in his district (as indeed he should have been, according to Katz), but determined to reject the personal payoffs out of hand. He wanted "no part in that." Through a number of subsequent meetings, Kelly remained adamant. Then, like Sorrells (but from quite different motives), he gave in "when $25,000 was displayed for him spread out in packets of $100 bills. He stuffed the bills into his pocket and left."[8]

Some readers may feel no sympathy for Kelly whatever. But I find that my reaction is both confused and ambivalent. On the one hand, Kelly betrayed his trust as a high government official. He did not *have* to give in to the temptation. Neither compulsive pressure nor coercive threat was used against him. Even the FBI deception was not of the sort that would diminish the voluntariness of his conduct. He did not voluntarily walk into an FBI trap, to be sure, but he did voluntarily commit what appeared even to him to be a crime. On the other hand, Kelly was induced to act as he did by police agents; his criminal conduct was their idea and their initiative. Without their instigation, certainly Kelly would not have acted as he did then and there, and the probability of his *ever* acting in that fashion was very low. Kelly was a middle-aged man who had never even been *accused* of a crime. His character was thought by all who knew him to be impeccable. But for the deliberate trickery of the government in artificially creating the opportunity for his crime, his perfect record would probably have remained forever untarnished.

Perhaps a case can be made that Kelly has been treated unfairly. But there is something unseemly about *his* being the one to voice that grievance. Gerald Dworkin has a point when he says that the trapper should be treated as a "tester of virtue not a detector of crime,"[9] and even Kelly will have to admit that he flunked the virtue test. There is no way in which his wrongful action can be justified or excused, wherever the original initiative for that action is located. The combination of these points seems to yield a moral paradox. Kelly was treated unjustly, as "a means only," yet his behavior, though initiated by the unjust parties, was nevertheless his own, somehow expressive of his own character, and therefore his own responsibility. After all, the government did not force him to take the bribe money. Neither compulsion nor duress was used. Rather the instigators lured, goaded, coaxed, and implored; they urged and encouraged, and in the end, given their success, perhaps it can be said that they *seduced* him into doing it. But these verbs are not the names of legal defenses. The law rightly refuses to accept as an excuse the claim that another party made a criminal act seem so attractive an idea that a person could not resist its appeal. It seems clear that the FBI in the Kelly case "got" their man to do what is criminal and to do it voluntarily, on his own responsibility.

Are We All Criminals—More or Less?

Why do we find the idea of entrapment so disturbing? Leo Katz suggests that our moral discomfort with entrapment stems from our belief or fear that there are criminal dispositions in all of us. For each forbidden act, we suspect that there is some set of circumstances, however rare and unlikely, in which you, the reader, would voluntarily commit that crime, and similarly for all the rest of us. It is more plausible, of course, to think of everyone as capable of committing *some* kinds of forbidden acts (e.g., overtime parking) but not others (e.g., first-degree murder). Nevertheless, one can learn some alarming facts about what one would be likely to do in certain extraordinary circumstances if one has a sufficiently resourceful imagination, or better still if one reads many books by imaginative and insightful novelists. I remember how shocked I was to learn that I could—indeed, that I probably would—commit murder with a more or less clear conscience in circumstances like those that enveloped the protagonist in Ludwig Lewisohn's horrifying novel, *The Case of Mr. Crump*. That novel, written in 1926, is the story of a woman who manipulates a gifted and sensitive man, twenty years her junior, into a marriage and then exploits his weakness and inexperience, as well as the stupidities of the old New York state divorce laws, to keep him in a hellish relationship that ruins his career, renders impossible his ambitions, and finally steals from him his last and only chance of love. In the end the man has no alternative but to destroy this ruthless virago. He does, and so probably would I if *mirabile dictu* I were in his shoes. In short, I have a disposition even now, as I write, to commit murder if I were in the extraordinary and highly improbable circumstances of the fictitious Mr. Crump. Fortunately, no one has anything to fear from me, given how rare and unlikely such circumstances are. It is important to note, however, that it is not so much the character of my dispositions themselves that give reassurance as the improbability of the circumstances that could activate them, and the occurrence or nonoccurrence of such circumstances is, in a sense, a matter of luck, beyond my control.

Tests of Strength

It is the existence of a predisposition, according to the Supreme Court, that determines the guilt of an entrapped person when the entrapment is legitimate. This upsets and alarms people, as we have seen, when they come to suspect that all of us have predispositions to various crimes if only in the very dilute sense that there are wildly remote and unlikely circumstances in which, acting in character, we would perform a forbidden act. There cannot be much blameworthiness attached to *that* kind of disposition, surely. But dispositions differ in strength; one person may be *more disposed* to do something than another person. Correspondingly, we would expect the stronger dispositions to be the more blameworthy ones, other things being equal. We have already encountered some of the ways in which there can be a "more" or a "less" human disposition along some relevant quantitative dimension. A disposition is expressed in the form of one or more hypothetical sentences predicting how the possessor of the disposition would act in various kinds of circumstances. Our first quantitative measure then might be to determine how likely or unlikely the precipitating circumstances are to occur. If the United States were to drift into a form of government similar to that of Germany under the Nazis, then John Doe, a very ordinary sort of guy, might find himself employed as a prison guard in a concentration camp, and highly recommended for his stern measures against prisoners, his businesslike efficiency, and his sincere desire to please his superiors. Right now, in the real world, Doe lives an unnoteworthy life. He works as a security guard at an office building, earns a moderately good salary, is faithful to his wife and kind to his children. But if the changes in his external circumstances are like those that occurred in the 1930s in Germany, then without any further change in the dispositions that collectively constitute his moral character, he might routinely perform acts of great cruelty. But in the real world, as opposed to the hypothetical world so easily created by philosophers, he does not appear to be a cruel man. His circumstances give him no reason for it.

Richard Roe shares some of John Doe's dispositions of character, but cruel behavior is often elicited from him even in the actual circumstances in which we all live now. He is, in one rather unfamiliar sense, more "cruel" than John Doe simply because his immoral behavior is more readily produced by his actual circumstances. The more remote and unlikely the circumstances that can trigger acts of cruelty from the person who is predisposed to be cruel, the less cruel, in this sense, that person is. Similarly, my disposition to be a wife murderer would call for circumstances so extraordinary and unlikely that I can hardly imagine, without the help of a novelist, what they might be. For that reason it is clear that I am much less disposed to be a wife murderer than, say, Bluebeard or Henry VIII.

Of course, the larger number of actual circumstances in which their uxor-icidal dispositions would be activated is not the only respect in which these murderous scoundrels differ morally from me, to my advantage. More impor-tant, perhaps, is the fact that Bluebeard has dispositions to kill people in circumstances in which I would not kill, but that there are no circumstances, or many fewer of them, in which I would kill but he would not. This clear respect in which Bluebeard and King Henry are *more* savage, ruthless, and cruel than I is not just their bad luck or my good luck in stumbling into, or away from, activating circumstances. Rather that difference, I hope it is clear, reflects a comparison of our separate dispositions to be cruel, namely, that their dispositions surface on occasions when mine do not, and theirs are therefore, in that sense, stronger than mine. The important difference between me and Bluebeard (as Walter Sinnott-Armstrong has pointed out to me in his helpful commentary) is not just that Bluebeard "faced actual circumstances which would also have triggered my dispositions" but rather that "he com-mitted murder in circumstances in which [I] would not have done so." Thus my disposition to murder, appraised in this somewhat more familiar way, is less *inclusive*, and therefore not of the same "strength," by that test, as his.

Situational (or "circumstantial") tests of dispositional strength are those that hold the intrinsic aspects of a person's character constant and vary the circumstances in which that person might find himself. The more it is the case that circumstances (total circumstances in some tests, probable ones only in other tests) trigger the disposition, the stronger the disposition must be. The inclusiveness test discussed previously is a way of applying situational tests to the direct comparison of two or more individuals in respect to the strengths of dispositions they may have in common. Now we come to a second type of criterion, the kind that employs what we can call "intrinsic indicator tests." These criteria supplement the situational tests by holding the circum-stances in which a person finds himself constant, and alternating in various ways the character traits themselves. They measure strength by considering how difficult it would be right here and now to trigger the disposition, how resistant to inducement it is.[10] The metaphor of the "trigger pull" of a gun, measured in pounds, is useful here if not taken too seriously. According to our first (situational) test of dispositional strength, the more remote and improbable the circumstances in which one is disposed to commit a given crime, the weaker that disposition is, and in most cases a weak disposition to commit a given kind of crime can be treated in the same way as a strong disposition *not* to commit that crime. The second kind of measure of dispositional strength (the intrinsic test) determines how easily manipulable the disposition is, and may yield the result that although a person has a strong disposition not to commit a given crime (by the situational criteria), that disposition is rather easily overcome by manipulative inducements, in which case it may continue to be appraised as strong by the first criterion, but weak by the second.

It may be less misleading to suggest that there are two senses of the word "strength" involved here, rather than two criteria of strength in the same sense of the word "strength." In any case, the greater the amount of pressure required to move a person's trigger to the firing point, the stronger must have been her disposition *not* to commit the crime, and of course, the stronger the disposition not to perform the criminal act, the greater the mitigation of guilt for performing it at another party's initiative. This test, formulated in terms of the triggering metaphor, may be the same measure of dispositional strength and weakness that Aristotle expressed in botanical (not mechanical) metaphors. The more "deeply rooted" and resistant to weakening a given disposition is, the stronger it is. So if my disposition *not* to perform acts of the kind you want me to perform is deeply rooted (perhaps through continual "cultivation" over a long period of time), then my affirmative disposition to perform it is weak, and the mitigation of my guilt considerable. Finally, we can measure the *comparative strength* of a disposition by evaluating empirically whether it determines my behavior in more types of situations than do other people's dispositions to the same conduct. This is the inclusiveness test discussed earlier. In conclusion, a disposition that is *bad but weak* by any of these quantitative measures is less guilty than a disposition that is *bad and strong*.

It is useful to have the distinction between intrinsic variations in the strength of dispositions and situational variations, because it can happen, and in unusual cases does happen, that a person acts totally out of character in doing some bizarre or wicked deed, when in fact the dispositions that constitute his character have *not* vanished or changed, but remain precisely the same as they have always been, while the unusual circumstances that led him voluntarily to act in so uncharacteristic a way have come into his situation for the first time in his life.

Moral Luck

Sting victims like Representative Kelly are unlucky in that they have become properly subject to adverse moral judgment. Such victims of police entrapment have been revealed as seriously defective morally, even though the circumstances in which they acted immorally are so rare that they would almost certainly not have occurred without being elaborately contrived by police who meant to discredit them. In fact the circumstances that led to their immoral conduct were so unlikely to occur that their dispositions to behave as they did in those circumstances might have been unknown even to them, coming as a surprise and a disappointment.[11] Philosophers in recent years, stimulated by the exchange on the subject between Bernard Williams and Thomas Nagel,[12] have rediscovered what they call "moral luck," but that is not the kind of luck, I think, that characterizes the Kelly episode. Therefore, I shall reopen the matter here and, taking the ABSCAM traps as my example and Nagel's essay as my foil, attempt to explain in what way deserving adverse moral judgment can, and in what way it cannot, be a matter of luck.

Nagel's basic mistake, it seems to me, is to begin with an unrepresentative set of examples. He seems to focus his attention on a relatively narrow and somewhat unrepresentative class of moral judgments, namely, ascriptions of blame *for* some unfortunate happening or result. These judgments are analogous to, and probably derived from, judgments of civil and criminal liability in courts of law. But even in the noninstitutional settings of ordinary life we have many occasions to make judgments of the form: *B*'s injury was *A*'s fault, or (equivalently) *A* is to blame for the harm done to *B*, or (still equivalently) *A* is responsible (properly subject to adverse criticism, pressure to make compensation, or even punishment) for *B*'s losses. Responsibility judgments of this type, when made informally outside of a legally structured context like a courtroom, can be labeled "moral judgments," but they hardly exhaust the whole miscellaneous class of judgments we call "moral." It is equally a moral judgment to say that *A* was morally at fault in his conduct but fortunately no one was harmed by it. There may be no harm to be compensated, and no clearly evidenced behavior to be punished for, yet *A* is properly subject (liable) to adverse criticism for what he did. A traditional moralist might even say of some other person that he is "morally guilty," or blameworthy, for entertaining, say, lascivious thoughts, even though they are not reflected in his conduct, much less implicated in the causation of some specific harm.

Nagel points out that what we are properly held responsible *for* is often in large part a matter of luck. Standard legal examples clearly bear out that claim. A driver who speeds down a residential street at sixty miles per hour will be found guilty of reckless driving and sentenced (perhaps) to forgo his driver's license for one year. But if another driver, differing in no relevant respect from the first, inadvertently runs over a drunken pedestrian who steps carelessly into her path, the driver may be punished for manslaughter and in some places imprisoned for several years. Similarly, we can judge two hypothetical tales of bank robbery in the same way. In one version of the story, the robber aims his gun at a guard and squeezes the trigger with the intent to kill or seriously injure him, and he is successful in his undertaking—the guard dies. In the other version, the robber has exactly the same conscious objective, the same intention, and the same motive, and therefore the same degree of "moral guilt,"[13] but the guard moves at the last moment so that the robber misses his target. The first armed robber can be found guilty of first-degree murder and in some places executed, whereas the second robber can be convicted only of attempted murder, which is punished much less severely. Nagel is right in pointing out that the difference in severity of punishment in the two cases is entirely a matter of luck, good luck for the first reckless driver and the second bank robber, bad luck for the second reckless driver and the first bank robber.

The reason why luck has so large a role in the law is clear. In cases like these, the pronouncements made by courts are judgments of *responsibility for some result*, and the actions of the defendants make only partial causal contributions to that unhappy result. Crucial contributions are also made by other causal factors for which the defendant can take neither blame nor credit because they were beyond his control, such as whether or not the targeted bank guard moves at the last moment, or the drunken pedestrian lurches into the street.

Clearly criminal liability, like civil liability in torts, is partly a matter of luck. But this does not show that all moral judgments are matters of luck, which in some places seems to be Nagel's view. Only "blame-for" judgments assigning responsibility for harmful results have been shown thus far to fit the luck model. I do not see how it is a matter of luck whether certain other types of moral judgment correctly apply to one's conduct. It is bad luck that a pedestrian happened to appear in the path of the reckless driver, but it is not bad luck that she was at fault in driving sixty miles per hour. That is, it is not a matter of luck that the latter moral judgment is true of her, at least for any reason we have thus far considered.

There are roughly four ways, according to Nagel, in which "the natural objects of moral assessment" are disturbingly subject to luck, but only two of them are relevant to the theme of this essay, namely, those he calls "luck in one's circumstances—the kinds of problems and situations one faces" and "luck in the way one's actions and projects turn out." The other two deal with "luck in how we are determined by antecedent circumstances" and derive from the problem of determinism and free will. We would be wise to set them aside here for they can only lead us down a dark and digressive path.

First, luck in the way things turn out. Will the motorist be charged with reckless driving merely or with manslaughter? Will the bank robber with the murderous intentions be charged with murder or with attempted murder only? Imagine that a "little bit of negligence," through bad luck, leads to a child's death. In a luckier case, the same degree of negligence does not lead to anyone's death or injury. Is the luckier negligent party to be judged morally better than his unlucky counterpart? I had assumed that the moral judgments we make in such cases, as opposed to judgments of civil and criminal liability, would restrict themselves to what was within the actor's control and thus eliminate luck from the moral realm. But Nagel at this point surprises us by making the actor's moral status a function of the whole immediate outcome of his acts, including parts of that outcome that were quite beyond his control. "How things turn out," he says, "determine what [the actor] has done"[14]—whether, for example, he has endangered, threatened, or harmed another, where the verbs "threaten," "endanger," and "harm" are each the name of a different action. "Actual results," he says, "influence culpability or esteem in a large class of . . . cases ranging from negligence through political choice."[15]

I think that what Nagel says here is true of some legal judgments, but it seems highly paradoxical when said of moral ones. Perhaps the restriction of *moral* praise- or blameworthiness to what is under the control of the actor is part of the definition of the moral, or part of the point of the distinction between legal and moral judgments in the first place. Nagel's illustrative examples may seem to him to strengthen his position, but to me they seem closer to a *reductio*: "If one negligently leaves the bath running with the baby in it, one will realize, as one bounds up the stairs toward the bathroom, that if the baby has drowned, one has done something awful, whereas if it has not, one has merely been careless."[16] Luck does play a vital role in this example. It is, from the actor's standpoint, a matter of luck whether the baby lives or dies. But it does not follow that it is a matter of luck whether the actor is properly judged blameworthy or praiseworthy in his actions, right or wrong, good or bad, conscientious or indifferent. In both the fortunate and the tragic versions of Nagel's story, the actor's conduct is exactly the same. What is different is the unforeseeable contributions of outside factors to the outcome. It can hardly be true of the two actors in these parallel cases that their beliefs, desires, motives, and intentions were identically the same, but that the moral quality of their actions is radically different, one the work of an "awful" killer, the other the product of mere carelessness. Where Nagel is misled, I think, is in his assumption that the *actions* in the two stories are themselves different, contrary to what is actually given in the telling of the story. To be sure, "killing a baby" is a different action from merely "endangering a baby," but the actual conduct in the two stories is precisely the same. "Killing a baby" is causing a baby to die through one's faulty behavior; what distinguishes it from merely endangering a baby is the outcome (whether or not the baby dies) and that is at least partially beyond the control of the actor, and therefore a matter of luck. But it is not a matter of luck whether the actor's conduct is truly judged blameworthy.

Even the element of luck that is assuredly enshrined in the criminal law might in principle be subject to removal, or at least modification, without hindering the pursuit of any reasonable aim of that branch of the law. That could be done by eliminating the causal requirement from the definition of all crimes, for example, by eliminating the requirement in the law of homicide that the actor's victim *die* as a consequence of the actor's attempt to kill him.

If we took that step, then we would never have to decide whether the defendant was guilty in the sense of responsible *for* the harm or to blame *for* the death, but rather only if he were guilty *in* acting as he did, or guilty *of* breaking the law.[17] Perhaps the explanation of the persistence of the causal requirement in criminal law is that there is still a confusion between the aims of criminal and tort law. A terrible harm occurs to someone, and a cry goes up—"Someone must pay for this!" Then a search is undertaken to locate a wrongdoer whose criminal act *cum* criminal mind was "the cause" of the harm, and that party must "pay" for it. In tort law, there typically has to be a causal connection between a given harm and a faulty act that was its cause. The whole point of tort law is to *compensate* innocent parties for the harm they suffered as a consequence of the defective actions of others. If there is no harm to begin with, there is nothing more for tort law to do, since there is no loss for which to make compensation.

There may still be something, however, for the criminal law to do, for its function is to punish the parties who perform criminal acts, whether or not harmful consequences actually ensue. To be sure, legislators should enact prohibitory statutes only to prevent types of conduct that tend to cause harm to others. But it does not follow that such statutes should be enforced only when their violation actually causes harm. On the whole, the rationale of the criminal law is that it reduces the net amount of harm all around by discouraging conduct that is in fact dangerous. But it does that job more efficiently when it punishes disobedience and neglects its confused mission of making people "pay" an additional surcharge for actual harms. An alternative worth considering would be to say that tortfeasors are civilly responsible for the harmful *consequences* of their acts and omissions, whereas criminals, as such, are criminally responsible not for subsequent states of affairs, but for their own criminal actions in disobedience to law.

Another category of moral luck, according to Nagel, is "luck in one's circumstances." "It my be true of someone that in a dangerous situation he would behave in a cowardly or heroic fashion, but if the occasion never arises, he will never have the chance to distinguish or disgrace himself in this way, and his moral record will be different."[18] World War II ended before my infantry division was ever assigned to combat. I shall never know, therefore, how I would have behaved under fearsome combat conditions. If we assume, for the sake of understanding the philosophical point merely, that my unactualized disposition was to behave heroically under such conditions, then it would have become part of my moral record that in one important arena, at least, I behaved heroically. On the contrary assumption, that I was disposed to act cowardly, hysterically, or freeze in terror in such activating circumstances, then the judgment that I responded uncourageously to the call of duty would have become a permanent and irrevocable part of my moral record.

But in fact no reference to combat heroism or combat cowardice appears in my moral record because there was never an opportunity to put the matter to the test. It does not follow, of course, that I had no disposition at all in respect to combat duties, one way or the other. I think that probably the correct account of the matter is that I did (indeed, that I still do) have some kind of disposition to act in some way or other in extremely dangerous circumstances, but that since those circumstances are now unlikely ever to be actualized, neither I nor anyone else can know just exactly what that disposition is. It may be, as Michael Dummett says, that there simply is no disposition to be known since the only circumstances in which such a disposition could be formed have never become actual.[19] It seems much more plausible to say, however, that there is a disposition to be known if only its activating circumstances would come into existence. However I would have behaved in the invasion of Japan of which I was scheduled to be a part in November 1945, I would have revealed a disposition to respond in *some way or other* to combat danger, whether I charged an enemy machine gun, ran away, or lay down to sleep.

Nagel concludes that in respect to the circumstances that can activate my dispositions, "Here too one is morally at the mercy of fate."[20] By this he means, presumably, that what appears on one's moral record is subject to the occurrence or nonoccurrence of the circumstances that would activate one's disposition, themselves unknown and beyond one's control. What follows from this, of course, is that what ends up appearing on one's moral record is often a matter of luck, not because the existence of the pertinent disposition is a matter of luck, but rather because the occurrence or nonoccurrence of the activating circumstances is. One's moral record, in Nagel's sense, is part of the historical record. It lists the events, the actions, the omissions, the impelling thoughts and desires that happened in public time and space, not the mere potentialities that might have been actualized in different circumstances, but in fact were not. So when Nagel says that the moral record is partly a matter of luck, he does not mean that one's moral character, itself consisting of one's dispositions to act or feel in certain ways in certain situations, is a matter of luck (at least not in virtue of the argument from lucky circumstances that we are presently considering).

We can concede then that it is luck that determines in what situations we find ourselves, and even how our dispositions mesh with unusual or unprecedented circumstances to yield our concrete historical actions. But God, presumably, would see our character dispositions and make accurate moral judgments of them even when they are opaque to all finite vision and even to the person whose dispositions they are. In general, our actual moral character need have nothing to do with luck. Except for its severe oversimplification, a physical analogy might illustrate the point. In the period before the properties of sugar were well known, a given sugar cube may have been preserved in its solid state for many decades. Even if that sugar cube were never placed in water, it would surely have remained soluble, even though the liquid circumstances that foster its dissolving were not present, and none of the people who *were* present had any reason to suspect how it would behave in water.

Nagel says that "we judge people for what they actually do or fail to do, not just for what they would have done if circumstances had been different."[21] We do praise and blame people's actual behavior far more often than we assess their characters as a whole, but that should not be surprising given how many serious practical issues ride on our judgments of actual behavior. Moreover, the relative infrequency of character assessment is partly to be explained by our humility in the face of what is highly speculative and uncertain. It is only because we lack confidence in our knowledge of a stranger's disposition that we surmise that in the country churchyard of Thomas Gray's poem lies "some Cromwell, guiltless of his country's blood."[22] Very likely there were contemporaries of Cromwell whose lives (moral records) were far better than his, and who were innocent of murderous atrocities like those of Cromwell's troops only because they lacked the opportunities, in the circumstances that prevailed, to do the same. We cannot know of any given person that such a description fits, lacking as we do evidence of such potential in his behavior, but it is an intellectually titillating speculation that there were such disguised moral monsters, as there may be in our time unsuspected potential Hitlers (though surely not many). Indeed given the "banality of evil" that Hannah Arendt gleaned from the Adolf Eichmann story,[23] there may be thousands of moral Eichmanns in towns and villages all over the world—luckier people than the German organizer of death camps, but in the eyes of God of no better disposition.

Our modest conclusion thus far is that there is such a thing as circumstantial luck, but little reason to posit a corresponding dispositional luck. That is to say that it may sometimes be a matter of luck in what circumstances we find ourselves (what background conditions—physical, biochemical, social, political—as well as what conduct initiated by other persons in a manner requiring our response), but that rarely if ever are our dispositions to act in certain ways in certain circumstances equally based on luck. Moreover, the word "moral" is used misleadingly if it is made part of the label ("moral luck"), for unforeseeable variation in circumstances is a matter of luck and has nothing to do with morals or with character. It is the dispositions themselves that ground moral judgments about our character, and these are to a large degree subject to our own control. The presence or absence of activating circumstances does not in itself determine our moral merit or demerit, and a good thing too because they *are* largely a matter of luck. If I am right in this analysis, the word "moral" goes with our dispositions but not with our circumstances, while the word "luck" goes with our circumstances but not to the same degree with our dispositions. It seems to follow that there is little room amid these concepts for the hybrid idea of "moral luck."[24]

More about Dispositions

Dispositions are ascribed to people by sentences of the form, "Usually in circumstances C, actor A does x." Spelling out the circumstances and qualifications, the probabilities and exceptions can make such statements complicated indeed. Some conditional statements of this general form are too complex and specific to be definitions of single-word propensities like the names of virtues (honesty, benevolence, calmness under pressure, and so on) or flaws of character (dishonesty, self-centeredness, excitability). Moreover, we are reluctant to call such a singular disposition a "tendency" or an "inclination," not to say a "habit," because these words all suggest that the activating circumstances mentioned in the antecedent clause of the complex conditional sentence are frequently encountered, whereas some of them are only infrequently or even not at all encountered by the person who may truly be said to have the disposition in question. It may be true of such a person that whenever she is in complex circumstances C, or it may be true that if she were in such circumstances, she does or would do x, even though she has never been in C and is never likely to be in C. In that event we might have no way of learning whether the person really does have the disposition in question or even the general inclination associated with it, except perhaps by making shaky inferences from the dispositions we do know she has, and even those may give us little guidance. We can say that God, being omniscient, does know whether the statement attributing the disposition is true even though the activating circumstances mentioned in the antecedent clause have never existed and even though they may never exist in the future. In other words, there is a fact of the matter here even if it cannot be known by mere mortals. "If ever she were in C, Jane would do x" may be true or false though we may never know which.

A person can be said to suffer bad luck when his disposition to do something morally wrong is activated by circumstances that are extremely unusual, and which before they occurred were correctly judged extremely remote and unlikely. It may be true of me, for example, that when and only when huge volcanic eruptions fill the skies with darkening debris for at least twelve months do I become inclined to commit mayhem, counterfeiting, and embracery,[25] and that I will in fact commit that miscellany of crimes at the point when the skies lighten again. This is such a bizarre disposition that there would be no discovering it by inference from my analogous dispositions, so probably it could be known only to God. It certainly could not have been known, before its activation, to *me*. Now let us suppose that the skies darken to the requisite extent and for the requisite period and then begin to lighten again. Without showing any (other?) signs of madness, I commit mayhem on my neighbor; I make crude copies of $100 bills and distribute them as widely as I can; then I seek out a criminal trial, befriend a juror, and attempt wrongfully to influence him. I am, of course, captured, convicted, and sentenced to severe punishment. I was unlucky in that conditions that occur only once every four or five centuries, on the average, occurred in my time and led me to commit acts of undoubted wrongfulness.

I am not "unlucky," however, in having the wrongful disposition in the first place. That would be an instance of what Nagel and Williams called (bad) "moral luck." It would indeed be bad moral luck, for instance, to have a moral record containing instances of behavior deemed immoral because of factors beyond one's control and contrary to one's intention. Similarly it would be bad moral luck to have a disposition properly deemed blameworthy even in those of its aspects that are beyond one's control and contrary to one's predominant values.

But, putting aside all of that, what *is* unlucky is that one should stumble into the unlucky circumstances, rare as they may be, which unknown to the person in question, can actualize one of her wrongful potentialities, which in turn may also have been unknown to her. It is important to note, however, that the disposition remains a wrongful one, quite apart from the bad luck suffered by its possessor in its unlikely activation. A permanent bachelor's disposition to be unfaithful to his wife, if only he had one, is an immoral character trait even though it never can lead to an immoral action of the kind we call "adultery." What makes that disposition immoral is something quite other than that which makes it difficult or impossible to exercise. A similar judgment applies to a permanent civilian's tendency to be a cowardly soldier in combat. Both the civilian's cowardice and the bachelor's infidelity, however, may be particular instantiations of general failings of an analogous kind, so that the bachelor might be more inclined than most to betray people who trust him, and the civilian might be inclined to cowardice in a dozen other contexts, such cowardice leading those who know of it to expect that if he were a soldier he would be cowardly in that context too. The reason why the earlier example of the linkage between volcanic explosions and the counterfeiting of currency was so bizarre and incredible is that we cannot infer from it any more general kind of failing of which this strange one is only an instance.

Some Moral Judgments

One argument meant to minimize the guilt of a person who has been successfully manipulated by police agents into voluntary behavior that would seem out of character for her begins with a distinction between the *initiative* taken in an interpersonal transaction and the degree to which that action reflects the character of the actor. Typically, the strategy of an entrapment attempt as well as the decision to undertake it begins with another part. The behavior that eventually seals my doom, if I am the one induced into action, originates in the mind of the police agent. But for her initiative it would probably never have occurred to me at all to do the acts she was trying to get me to do. On my own, I am completely innocent. Of course, she did not use force or the kind of deception that would vitiate the voluntariness of my response to her. But she did bring into existence the condition mentioned in the antecedent clause of the conditional statement that defined my disposition, and that took a great deal of doing. The action she desired from me is linked to few dispositions of which anyone can know in advance, and in this case the triggering condition is very unusual, of a kind infrequently and improbably encountered by me. Since it was her initiative and not my disposition that is the critical element in the explanation of my criminal action, that action reflects more on her than on me. My doing, we might say, was primarily *her* doing, since the initiative in the first instance was entirely hers.

That argument, though on to something, does not quite succeed. It is not an automatic reducer of the guilt in someone's action to show that the original initiative for that action was taken by someone else, who undertook to persuade the acting party by noncoercive manipulation. Indeed, the greater part of our morally interesting conduct, and our challenging moral dilemmas, requires us to decide how to respond to the initiatives of others. You offer to sell; I decide whether to buy. I propose that we get married; it is now up to you to consent or not. You offer me a financial inducement at just the time when I need the money most; I wonder whether to accept your terms or not. You ask for my signature on a political manifesto; I must decide whether my agreements with it are more or less important than my disagreements. In none of these commonplace examples do I later have the excuse that in the beginning it was another person's idea, not mine, and that even though I responded as I did to her initiative of my own free will, the responsibility or guilt for what I did must be hers, since she started the whole thing. In short, locating the initiative in the other party does not automatically, with nothing more, provide the voluntary actor with an exculpatory excuse.

The point to emphasize is that while the other's initiative is not the whole story, it can be a crucial part of the story. Showing that your initiative was behind my voluntary act does not by itself reduce my guilt. What must be shown is that the disposition of mine that your initiative was meant to activate had certain characteristics. If I were known to be a skilled and experienced bank robber, you might propose that we do a job together and split the profits. Moreover, you may have a detailed proposal for my consideration in which you identify the bank, propose the date and time of day, provide the tools, and so on. If I agree and then get entrapped, because unknown to me, you are now a paid agent provocateur, I will certainly point out that your initiative was behind the criminal act, not originally mine. But that true observation will do me little good unless I can show that the predisposition to such acts, which I obviously had, was a very weak one. Indeed, the weaker the disposition, one might say, the less dangerous is the criminal, and the less guilty is he of any criminal act that another party induces him to perform. That rough rule of thumb is the best statement we have of the mitigating effect of another party's initiative.

We come finally to the problem of private entrapment. When a sexy person entices another person into the commission of a crime, the criminal actor cannot plead, either in a criminal court or in "the court of heaven," that the enticement excuses his otherwise criminal behavior *unless* the sexy person is an undercover police officer. Why should there be this exception? The entrapped victim, it would seem, is equally guilty, since the only difference between the two cases is one unknown to him. Two answers are often given. The first is the answer of "the objective theory of entrapment." According to this view, the person entrapped by police agents should not be convicted at all (in the most flagrant cases, not even tried) not because such a person is without moral blameworthiness or guilt, but simply because the police in a democracy must be kept honest and trustworthy. This rationale is essentially similar to that frequently proposed for the exclusionary rule, which renders inadmissible evidence seized in violation of the Fourth Amendment's stricture against unreasonable searches and seizures.

The other answer contains some elements in common with the first, but it is somewhat more interesting to the moral philosopher. When the state has license to test the virtue of any citizen, randomly selected, then for a substantial number of such citizens the circumstances that can trigger the criminal predisposition are artificially created and would not otherwise ever have arisen. This is quite another thing than randomly setting up police roadblocks to test drivers for drunkenness. People who are disposed to drive after immoderate drinking are punished not just for that disposition but for actually driving while drunk. So far as I know, no undercover police agent has ever been hired to offer them free drinks in the parking lot as they climb into their cars for the trip home from work, thus tipping the odds against the drivers they successfully persuade to accept the gift. That is the nub of the complaint against entrapment practices when they are objectionable. People who might otherwise never be in trouble with the law are convicted and punished anyway because and only because the police have intervened, without sufficient cause, in their lives. They have set out deliberately to alter the odds that are otherwise so unthreatening to law-abiding citizens.

If police have the power *randomly* to intervene in people's lives just to determine whether they have wrongful predispositions, then we are all subject to a great danger from those who are supposed to be our protectors. If they proceed in a genuinely random way, as their colleagues, for example, in the case of the drunkenness-testing roadblocks, then they can exercise their power to intervene in our lives without any evidence, even without any suspicions or hunches of wrongful doing on our part. That would appear to be a violation of our liberty, according to our traditional interpretation of the constitutional limits of police activity. But the increases in police power can be even worse if they are *not* random, as when, for example, they are put to political uses through the virtue testing of the leaders of dissident political factions. In that case, the police powers are being used to harass, and when a given dissident is not merely harassed but actually entrapped, he is treated even worse.

It may be more palatable, however, to put responsible government officials, federal judges, and members of Congress, for example, to a test of their honesty, since disposition-triggering circumstances (temptations) occur more frequently in their offices, and the chance of being put to the test of honesty is already high. Moreover, occupants of these positions have special responsibilities to be trustworthy, since they are the makers and appliers of law, and securing assurances of their reliability, even in the absence of any suspicion of their unreliability, is more pointedly in the public interest. It is plausible to tell them that being subject to a special scrutiny is a reasonable price to pay for their power. That argument is weaker when applied to a less powerful group (like college professors) and downright pernicious when directed only at political dissidents, religious heretics, and so on.

Most of these reasons against permitting police to test for virtue, and thus alter the odds that testees would ever become prisoners, apply more or less to the private seducer who, without using deception, force, or violence, lures another party, who might otherwise never have committed a crime, into being her partner, not for the purpose of betraying him to the police, but rather for her own private criminal purposes. So it seems that the ultimate difference between private seduction to crime and police enticement to crime is, after all, found mainly in our need to control police power in a democratic state. But this solution cannot be the whole of it. It really is more satisfactory knowing that the "natural odds" against my ever committing a crime and going to prison for it (now extremely high)—odds that include among their data the chance (now quite low) that I will be lured into a crime by a seducer for her own purposes—remain unaltered by the manipulations of the very state agency that is charged with my protection. I, for one, will be happy to take my chances with the natural odds, though unfortunately, in this imperfectly reliable world, even they give me no guarantee.

4

CRIMINAL ATTEMPTS

Equal Punishments for Failed Attempts

A Proposal for Reform

Every bona fide philosopher of law tries his hand at least once at the ancient problem of punishing failed attempts.[1] This may seem surprising, given that one's first impression of the problem is that it is an amusing riddle of no theoretical importance. Once one gets into the thick of it, however, and undertakes a critical examination of the arguments on both sides, one finds that many of the deepest issues of criminal law theory are implicated.

The puzzle I have in mind is ultimately a problem for the sentencing judge or the authors of sentencing guidelines. Should there be a "gap"[2] between the penalty for a completed crime and that for an unsuccessful attempt to produce the same forbidden result, other things being equal?[3] The standard way of illustrating the problem is to describe, through the method of hypothetical contrast, a matching pair of examples. In the first of these, we are introduced to an angry man with a gun. He bears the simple but appealing name of A_1. In the story, A_1, with the conscious objective of killing his enemy, B_1, gets B_1 in the sight of his rifle and carefully squeezes the trigger. Except for his later arrest and conviction for murder, everything works out as A_1 planned. The bullet emerges from the barrel of his rifle at high velocity and strikes B_1's body in a vital place that is the exact spot at which A_1 had aimed, and as A_1 intended, B_1 dies as a result.

Now consider another narrative with only a slight variation in the facts. This involves A_2, a man of similar disposition to A_1, but who despite his similar name, is unrelated to the killer in our first example. He too has an enemy, a person named B_2, and he has precisely the same hatred for him that A_1 had for B_1 in the first story. He too sets out to kill his enemy. He has precisely the same morally relevant past experiences with B_2 that A_1 had with B_1, the same motivating beliefs and emotions, the same fully formed intention to kill another human being. I mention all of these factors because I want it to seem plausible that A_1 and A_2 were equally blameworthy morally, and blameworthiness is normally compounded out of such factors as beliefs, emotions, motives, objectives, and intentions, in respect to all of which A_1 and A_2 are exactly equal.

But now we inject into the stories the first significant differences between them. A_2's enemy, B_2, escapes alive, while A_1's enemy, B_1, is killed according to plan. In different versions of this much-told tale, B_2 is wearing a bulletproof vest and B_1 is not, or at just the moment A_2 starts to pull the trigger, a mosquito lands on his nose, throwing him off target, or a speck of dust causes him to sneeze, or his target coincidentally moves at the last second. In all versions of the story, A_2 misses his shot, and therefore escapes guilt for murder, since there can be no murder without someone dying as its consequence. On these facts, A_2 will be guilty only of attempted murder and typically subject to a term of five years or less in prison.[4] His unfortunate counterpart, A_1, on the other hand, could be convicted of first-degree murder, and in most states he would be condemned to either life imprisonment or the death penalty.

The difference in the sentences inflicted on two persons whose criminal wrongdoing was the same and whose degree of moral blameworthiness was identical seems to indicate that the legal system which countenanced it is not committed to the principle of proportionality, which requires that the severity of the punishment be proportional to the moral blameworthiness of the offense. In these examples, the moral blameworthiness of the criminals is identical, yet the punishment is much more severe in one case than in the other. Unless there is some reasonable explanation for this discrepancy, the sentences seem to be more arbitrary than rational, the difference between the fates of A_1 and A_2 being determined not by their deserts but by luck, plain and simple.[5] The full explanation of how identical intentions produce importantly different results in these cases must appeal to factors that were beyond the control of one or another of the would-be assassins. Surely A_2 earns no credit for the antecedently unlikely survival of his enemy, B_2. He did not provide B_2 with his bulletproof vest, nor arrange for a mosquito to land on his own nose.

When such momentous matters as a choice between the death penalty and a minor term of imprisonment ride in the balance, we want the decision to be as free of arbitrariness as possible. Reliance on good or bad luck, or assigning weight to factors beyond the foresight or control of the central players, introduces an element of arbitrariness into court proceedings. Arbitrariness is the absence of rule, as in the bare will of an authority who can exert his power free of accountability, in a manner without rhyme or reason, which in turn makes predictability and security from abuse difficult, and fairness an inapplicable notion (except perhaps in reference to the honesty with which a randomizing procedure, like a roulette wheel, is used). Arbitrariness is to a legal system what corrosive rust is to machinery.[6] For this simple reason I line up with those theorists who would treat completed crimes and unsuccessful attempts as essentially the same, other things being equal. Since most legal practice throughout the world treats failed and successful attempts quite differently, the position I have taken here is a reformist position, and its logical denial can be called the traditionalist or retentionist position. I am a reformist on this issue because I believe that if the law is arbitrary in some respect, then provided we can improve it in that respect, at a reasonable cost in other values, we should improve it.

What I would propose, first of all, is that we eliminate the causal condition in the definition of all so-called completed crimes. Thus, in respect to the crime of killing, there would be no necessity that a death actually result from the criminal acts in order for the actor to be found criminally liable. Of course this change in practice would require a change in terminology. If a resultant death is no longer covered by the definition of "murder," for example, then participants in the criminal process would start saying some very odd things, such as "Jones murdered Smith although Smith is still alive."[7] I would prefer to have a more comprehensive crime with a new, technical-sounding name, like "wrongful homicidal behavior." Then we could say that Jones is guilty of wrongful homicidal behavior (WHB) toward Smith without saying something that sounds silly or even contradictory like "Jones murdered Smith but did not succeed in killing him." The definition of wrongful homicidal behavior would look much like our current definition of murder, except that the definition would have no component clause requiring that the victim actually die. The word "murder" then would become functionless and drop out of the law altogether. Moreover, no effort would be made to reinstate something like the old distinction between murder and attempted murder. Every act of endangering, threatening, or taking life that is judgable within the system would be either an instance of WHB or else legally innocent.

Perhaps legislative draftsmen would wish to distinguish WHB in the first degree from WHB in the second degree, because they believe, plausibly enough, that some accompanying motives are worse than others; or that some culpability conditions, like acting on purpose, are worse than others, like inadvertent negligence; or that premeditated crimes are *ceteris paribus* worse than impulsive ones; and so on. On first impression, at least, I see no reason why these judgments of comparative blameworthiness need be arbitrary,[8] and I would have no objection to them so long as they did not rely upon luck factors which, being beyond the criminal's foresight and control, are neither his fault nor to his credit. The important advantage of this change would be that luck factors would be purged from the sentencing guidelines. Some defendants convicted of WHB could receive more severe penalties than others, but only when their conduct seemed more blameworthy than the others, not simply more lucky.

The obvious defect in this proposal is that the drastic changes it requires in our terminology will cause confusion. Perhaps then we should seek a way to downplay the moral significance of the distinction between murder and attempted murder without such radical departures from ordinary as well as technical language. We could do that by continuing to use the terms "murder" and "attempted murder," while letting nothing substantive hinge on them. Our penal code, for example, could forbid WHB on pain of severe penalty, defining WHB as "any act of murder or attempted murder which . . ." and so on. The rest of the definition would specify *mens rea*, *actus reus*, and other definitional elements, except for the causal condition, which is left out because it has no relevant bearing on blameworthiness, and that being the case, the most blameworthy criminal actions may or may not satisfy it. In other words, when we look at the whole motley collection of lawbreaking actions and isolate those we want to call the most blameworthy (or morally culpable) ones, some of them will actually cause some victims' deaths, and some will not. In short, there are two distinctions here that can overlap: that between murder and attempted murder (expressions in ordinary language which could still be useful but which would have no legal importance), and the relatively high or low degree of blameworthiness manifested in one's criminal actions, whether they be killings or only attempted killings. The severity of punishment would depend on the latter distinction (high or low degree of blameworthiness), not on the former (attempted versus completed crime). Assessing blameworthiness, of course, is the hard part, but no harder than in any other penal code that is committed to proportionality.

These refinements should help disperse confusion, but they are not yet sufficient. The genus in which our definition places WHB must be made more inclusive. We could include in it, for example, in addition to failed and successful attempts and degrees and types of blameworthiness, conscious and unconscious risk creation, so as to capture all the types of WHB, all instances of endangering, threatening, attempting to take, taking, and risking another person's life. So the definition of the crime of WHB might be something like this: "Any act of killing or attempted killing or the faulty or blameworthy creating of an unreasonable risk of killing, whether or not the actor was aware of that risk, is an act of WHB." Then a further discussion of an *actus reus* condition, various *mens rea* conditions, circumstantial conditions, and so on would make the definition more precise and permit us to distinguish the various categories of WHB. (If the word "homicidal" is confusing in this usage, perhaps "survival-affecting" would be better.)

I will belabor no further the points that reliance on luck in the law is a kind of arbitrariness, that arbitrariness is a bad thing in a legal system, and that it is inconsistent with the principle of proportionality to which most of us give regular lip service. What puzzles me is the fact that among those who have considered this matter, and among penal codes here and abroad, now and in the past, almost all of them advocate treating attempts more leniently than their corresponding completed crimes, the few exceptions being almost all recent. Legal theorists and philosophers, however, are found on both sides in this controversy. Perhaps even a small majority line up with me on the reformist side. This reassures me that I am not abnormally insensitive to intuitions that others find irresistibly compelling, but beyond that, I am surprised at the number and high quality of my opponents. It is sobering to learn that among those who disagree with me on this question, including only recent writers, are Michael Davis, George Fletcher, the team of LaFave and Scott, Michael Moore, and Judith Thomson. Among the allies of these luminaries, there is often a perplexing tone in their prose, perplexing to me, which suggests that they feel they must defend the status quo on this question as though the survival of Western civilization itself depended on it.

Before considering some of these arguments, I should clarify one presupposition of the whole debate. We reformists are arguing primarily for a kind of equality. We insist that equal degrees of blameworthiness should be punished to an equal extent. But to what extent is that? When we begin with a sentencing code that decrees unequal punishments for crimes that we think ought to be treated equally, there are two ways that equality can be achieved. Either we can "level up" or we can "level down." If murderers are sentenced to forty years' imprisonment and attempted murderers to ten years, we can make the prison terms equal either by raising the penalty for attempted murder, say, from ten years to forty years, thus achieving equality in the sentences by "getting tough on criminals," or we can level down, and achieve equality by reducing the penalty for murder, say, from forty to ten years, or we can do both at once: raise the imprisonment term for attempted murder from ten to twenty-five years and reduce the term for successful murder from forty to twenty-five. Which option we should choose depends on a diversity of things that make it impossible to answer in a perfectly general way. We would have to look carefully at the conditions peculiar to given communities. Moreover, our decision would depend not only on our reaching agreement on the problem of failed attempts; it would also require a choice among the major theories of the justification of punishment generally. The position of this essay would put only one constraint on how those larger issues are settled. Unless impossible for practical reasons, punishments for what we now call attempts and corresponding completed crimes would have to be equal. One consequence of this point is that the reformist thesis is neither one of greater harshness nor one of greater leniency. What this position demands is greater consistency.

Bad Argument Number One: Misinterpretation of the Harm Principle

The argument I present in this part is simply the standard case for reform recognized even by retentionist writers as having some prima facie cogency. It is not complex, subtle, or ingenious. All it does is begin the debate by moving the burden, ever so gently, onto the retentionist's shoulders. The retentionist then offers his arguments ("proof" is much too strong a term) for maintaining the status quo. Only a small handful of these multifarious arguments are represented here. Those arguments are subtle, and often ingenious, probably because the assigned burden is so difficult. What puzzles me is how bad many of them are. It might be especially instructive, therefore, to examine the bad arguments of some good thinkers against it.

Bad Argument Number One is the work of Professors W. R. LaFave and A. W. Scott, authors of one of the best-regarded recent treatises on criminal law.[9] These genuinely distinguished authors appear to argue not only that unsuccessful attempts should be punished less than already accomplished crimes, but that mere attempts should not be crimes at all. Their case is put succinctly: "Since criminal law aims to prevent harm to the public, there can be no crime without harm."[10] This pithy statement the authors call a "basic premise of the criminal law."[11] I can only guess at their reasoning, but perhaps it could be reconstructed as follows. They may think that lawmakers should criminalize only behavior the predominant tendency of which is to cause harm to people other than the actor. This statement formulates the liberal theory of the proper limits of the criminal law, and is close to a principle that I have defended,[12] which has been called the "harm to others principle" or "the harm principle," for short. Anyone who approves of the harm principle will disapprove of penalizing so-called victimless crimes (criminalized activities of a kind that do not tend to do harm). Liberalism on this question, in effect, recommends to legislators that if an action is of a generally harmless kind, then it does not matter that they sincerely disapprove of acts of its sort; it is not their business to interfere with the liberty of those citizens who do not share their judgments of disapproval. So far, so good. But it does not follow that unsuccessful attempts to perform an act of a type that is very harmful (murder, for example) should not be criminalized! That is a well-intentioned but illogical conclusion drawn from a principle (the harm principle) that gives it no support.

Bad Argument Number Two: Confusion of Crimes and Torts

The second bad argument will tempt those who tend to confuse the functions of criminal and tort law. That would seem to be an easy kind of mistake to avoid, but language sets traps for the unwary at every turn. The advocate of this approach is likely to share with the other writers discussed in this section a fidelity to the principle of proportionality, together with a tenacious adherence to the retentionist position about attempts. She too effects a marriage between these unlikely partners by trying to show that the murderer is more blameworthy than the unsuccessful attempter even though they are, in all the respects usually thought to be relevant to blameworthiness, exactly alike. Why then does this person believe that blameworthiness is a function of actual harm caused? The answer might be that such a person has before her mind an inappropriate model for criminal law, inclining her to accept uncritically the following chain of inferences:

1. If Sadie is more blameworthy for her conduct than Sally is for hers, then Sadie is to blame for more than Sally is to blame.
2. That in turn implies that Sadie produced more harmful results than Sally did, perhaps killing two victims instead of one, or a married person instead of a solitary one. The point is this: If you are responsible for more harm, then you pay for more or, alternatively, the more harm you cause, the more harm for which you must pay. But this approaches self-evidence only in the law of torts, where we are adding up amounts so that we can present a bill to the harm causer, not trying to assess the exact character of her moral desert.

If our problem is to explain why so many people identify wrongdoing with harm causing, we should look at tort law as an example of the inextricable linkage of the two, and criminal law as an example of a much looser connection. Then we need only look at the different aims of these two branches of law for an explanation of why criminal law can get along without responding directly and exclusively to harm actually caused, whereas tort law's function does not permit it to respond to anything unless there has been actual harm caused. Here too we may find the explanation of why some people find it natural, even in a criminal law context, to assume that "more blameworthy" is entailed by "blamable for more."

The reformist on the problem of punishing attempts, as we have seen, proposes the removal of the causal requirement from the definitions of crimes, for example, by eliminating the requirement in the law of homicide that the actor's victim die as a consequence of the actor's attempt to kill him. If we took that step, then we would never have to decide whether the defendant was guilty in the sense of responsible for the death, but rather only if he were guilty of breaking the law.

Perhaps a part of the explanation of the persistence of the causal requirement in criminal law then is that there is still a confusion between the aims of criminal and tort law, and that a variety of English prepositions, such as "for," "in," and "of," exert their subtly different effects on meaning.[13] Another reason is the American penchant for commercial metaphors.[14] A terrible harm happens to someone, and an angry cry goes up: "Someone must be made to pay for this!" Then a search is undertaken to locate a wrongdoer whose criminal act cum criminal mind was "the cause" of the harm and who, once apprehended and convicted, must "pay" for it. The major, if not the entire, point of tort law is to compensate relatively innocent parties for the harm they suffered as a consequence of the defective actions of others. If there is no harm to begin with there is nothing more for tort law to do, since there is no loss for which to make compensation. Here then is a context, namely tort law, where LaFave and Scott's maxim that there can be no liability without harm is more at home. The maxim comes closer to the truth when the liability it refers to is tortious, not criminal.

Even where there is nothing for tort law to do, however, there may still be something for the criminal law to do, for its function is to punish the parties who perform criminal acts, whether or not harmful consequences in the individual cases actually ensue. To be sure, legislators should enact prohibitory statues only to prevent types of conduct that tend to cause harm to others. But it does not follow that such statutes should be enforced only when their violation actually harms someone. On the whole, the rationale of the criminal law is that it reduces the net amount of harm all around by discouraging all conduct that is in fact dangerous to others, even in particular instances when it does not issue in harm. But it does that job more efficiently when it punishes disobedience and neglects its confused mission of making people "pay" an additional surcharge for actual harms. A traditional usage worth reinstating would be to say that tortfeasors are civilly responsible for the harmful consequences of their acts and omissions, whereas criminals, as such, are criminally responsible not for subsequent states of affairs, but for their own criminal actions in disobedience to law—whatever the consequences.

Bad Argument Number Three: The Argument from Democratic Consensus

We come now to a more respectable argument for the traditionalist position on the punishment of unsuccessful attempts. In one of its versions, it is associated with the name of Oliver Wendell Holmes, Jr.,[15] and in more recent times with that of George Fletcher[16] and Judith Thomson.[17] The argument begins by surveying facts it deems relevant to its argumentative purposes, namely, that almost every developed legal system in the world distinguishes between attempted and completed crimes. Also, the overwhelming majority of sentencing codes and guidelines punishes completed crimes more severely than mere attempts that fail to cause harm. There is also evidence that a large majority of the adult population favors the status quo in this respect. These are significant facts in a democracy. If we do not respect the sensibilities of common people on a matter that they take seriously, we endorse by implication a government in which only an intellectual elite matters, and the genuine convictions of a majority consensus are dismissed as moral superstitions. In a democracy, Holmes insisted, those who make, enforce, and interpret the law cannot move too far out of harmony with the common people, else the law will seem tyrannical at worst, obscure at best.

George Fletcher, arguing for the traditionalist position on this question, gives his own voice to the consensus. In his book *A Crime of Self-Defense*, he concludes, "We cannot adequately explain why harm matters, but matter it does."[18] Some elitist professors may hold to the contrary,[19] but Fletcher is firm: Legal decisions should not go beyond the "sensibilities of common people."[20] Whether that is because of superior wisdom among the uneducated or political wisdom among those who rightly defer to their greater numbers, or both, Fletcher does not make clear, but I suspect that he would say both. That the bulk of the people believe that a particular proposition is true is a good reason, I agree, for tolerance and respect. But it is not a good reason, even in a democracy, for believing that proposition to be true.

There is a tendency, I believe, when discussing issues that have both a moral and a legal dimension, to conflate three independent questions:

1. Which rule, x or y, is the more rational (or otherwise superior)?
2. Which rule, x or y, is more widely accepted in this political community?
3. Which rule shall we adopt? Shall we retain x or reform the status quo by adopting y? (This is a question for a legislature or maybe a court, or any group with the de facto power to give shape to legal rules.)

There is, in addition to these questions, a principle that has been used by philosophers to generate answers to all three of the questions. We can call this, with all respect, the conservative principle, and formulate it as follows: People with the power to change legal rules ought not to do so unless some substantial percentage of ordinary people want them changed, or at least would approve the change were others to bring it about. At the least, it ought not to be imposed on a resentful, dissenting majority.

What is the status of the conservative principle? Clearly, it suggests an answer to question 3, not to question 1. It is, therefore, a fallacy to say that because "x is more rational (or more fair or more useful) than y, we should adopt x even in a community whose traditions and sentiments are strongly in favor of y." Many severe critics of the "fortuitous gap" between failed and successful attempts understand this well. Sanford Kadish, for example, concedes that "there are limits to how far the law can or should be bent by reformers [like me][21] to express a moral outlook different from those . . . common to our culture, irrational though they seem to me."[22] Kadish's combination of views goes well together, it seems to me. He is a conservative in the manner and timing of his public advocacy, but he holds on to liberalism and common sense in his private judgments. Professor Fletcher is powerfully impressed by the depth of our "cultural attachment" to the idea that actual harm makes a significant difference in the proper assessment of wrongdoing.

He is prepared to accept the probability of fire given all that smoke. Successful attempts, which actually harm people, he suggests, are more culpable morally, other things being equal, than equally genuine efforts that fail through lucky accident. If that is the case, then unequal punishment of the two crimes does not really violate the principle of proportionality after all. Fletcher, so interpreted, urges that we punish according to blameworthiness (ill deserts, moral culpability) alone, as the proportionality principle seems to mandate, but one of the chief determinants of blameworthiness, in turn, is actual harm caused. So Fletcher can have his cake and eat it too, only now instead of an odd theory of the grounds for criminal liability, he has an odd theory of the grounds of moral blameworthiness.

Bad Argument Number Four: The Argument from Defilement

One eminent philosopher who has argued audaciously for retentionism on the basis of the proportionality principle is Peter Winch. In Bad Argument Number Four, he does not attempt to win any advantage from a prior tinkering with the concept of actual harm. It is not the bungling attempter's lesser production of actual harm that makes him less blameworthy. Rather it is what seems to be an abrupt, moral sea change in his character. (I should point out that Winch is discussing the harm of death, which may be different in kind from any other harm.) "In doing something evil one becomes something evil," he writes, and when one has become something evil, like a murderer, one deserves blame and punishment if only for that reason. Those "defiled" persons who still have consciences will be "unable to live with themselves," and their networks of personal relations, Winch says, will be permanently altered, with further negative consequences for self-perception and self-esteem. As for the unsuccessful attempter, "if a person tries to do something and fails, then he does not become what his success would have made him, and thereby the possibilities of moral assessment of him are different."[23] In other words, he remains undefiled, and can still be a morally good person.

Yet the usual traps set by luck are waiting there for Professor Winch too. Winch's theory of moral change, unlike Aristotle's, does not build on habit formation, reinforcement, or gradual improvement or decline. It seems in contrast almost magical in both the abruptness of its onset and the inclusiveness of its sweep. If I were to shoot at my enemy now and injure him or bring him to the point of death only gradually, I would become a murderer (a morally worse person) only when he actually dies, and from that moment on, I would be invaded by floods of remorse. If my victim dies six months later in the hospital, then my supremely miserable moral status will not commence until that moment, and I may be miles away and uninformed. In the meantime, during that period in which I cheer the doctors on, how am I to be punished? As I interpret Winch, he implies that if my enemy finally dies six months after I shoot him, then I become a murderer and thus a morally worse person. During the waiting period, when my change of status is pending but very likely, I can be punished in anticipation of that change. The being I am about to become deserves that judgment, so I deserve it even beforehand. That is how clever philosophers avoid a direct linkage between actual harm caused and desert. The harm (death) changes the harm causer's essential moral status to that of murderer, and in anticipation of that change of moral status, we judge him highly blameworthy. His blameworthiness is not *directly* because of what he *did* back at the time before he became defiled, but rather because of the new person he has become, itself, of course, a product of what he did. Winch, in other words, has introduced a new intermediate stage between causing harm and being blameworthy, namely, becoming a morally worse person, a fate the luckier failed attempter may never suffer.

That and other consequences of this theory are little short of bizarre. If an attack victim will die one day later, his assailant has only twenty-four hours of moral respectability left before he (the assailant) is defiled, and then suddenly, at the moment of his victim's demise, he becomes Mr. Hyde or Dorian Gray. The victim could die six months after his assailant shot him, in which case the attacker suddenly becomes a murderer who will be unable to "live with himself" from that moment on, and who will be filled with self-loathing and hate, perhaps for the first time, at least in connection with that particular crime.

Bad Argument Number Five: The Argument from Moral Emotions

The remainder of Professor Fletcher's discussion of the problem of punishing failed attempts is taken up with an analysis of "moral emotions," like guilt feelings and feelings of remorse and shame. The attention he pays to these feelings has the effect, I think, of converting his reasoning into another kind of argument from public opinion, at least as public opinion is revealed in such emotions as guilt and shame. If the failed attempter feels no guilt, for example, and most others behave as if they do not expect him to feel guilt, then he and we are entitled to infer that this public, at least, believes that the harm caused by criminal acts is an independent determinant of moral blameworthiness. If we do not feel guilt, this suggests that we do not believe that unsuccessful attempts can be as morally culpable as successful ones. This kind of argument, common in ethics, is designed to convince the reader that he already holds the belief that "is to be proved," so that further demonstrative argument is hardly necessary.

To make his view more familiar and appealing, Fletcher has us consider what emotions are thought appropriate (in our culture) first to one's own near miss, say, in a murder attempt, and second to one's successful, intentional killing. His answer is that feelings of guilt and remorse are appropriate when the killing attempt was successful but not when it fails after a near miss; it is shame that we should expect the bungling assassin to feel, but not guilt. Moreover, if the would-be killer feels guilt at his near miss anyway, the guilt is probably morbid or perhaps neurotic.

Feelings of guilt and remorse are appropriate where harm is done, but if all is the same after as before the act, there would be nothing to be remorseful about, and the actor's feelings of guilt would make us wonder why he wanted to suffer inappropriate anguish.[24] Fletcher apparently treats "remorse" and "guilt feelings" as synonyms, which I think is a mistake. On the other hand, what he says about remorse, quite apart from its relation to guilt, seems right, though the advantages he gets from that insight are more than offset by the disadvantages he incurs through his mistaken account of guilt feelings. So I shall put aside, for the moment, the subject of remorse, and focus on Fletcher's theory of guilt.

One of the more common motives for murder attempts is passionate jealousy. If a modern-day Othello, while consumed with that jealousy, attempts to shoot Desdemona, but through lucky accident just barely misses her, he might well feel, appropriately, other emotions a couple of hours later—renewed tenderness and affection toward his wife, self-hatred and loathing, maybe remorse (I am not sure), but certainly guilt. That is to say that if Othello has the normal sort of conscience that internalizes the teachings of one's parents, teachers, and ministers of religion, imprinting on one's character the precepts that fraud, theft, cruelty, rape, torture, and murder are intolerable and inexcusable acts, and he nonetheless behaves against his own conscientious convictions, he will not feel very happy with himself. We might even expect, appropriately, that he will beg forgiveness, demand punishment, or release torrents of self-abuse.[25] Except for the "conscienceless killers," who are often up for hire, attempting murder is no frivolous or routine thing to the would-be killer.

Would it be some obvious moral category-mistake to add to this description of expectable or "appropriate" responses the word "guilt"? Is it some kind of conceptual solecism to suggest that a rational person in Othello's position, aware that only a lucky accident for which he should get no credit at all prevented his near miss from being a brutal obliteration of a fellow human being, might feel some guilt over what he intended to do? Professor Fletcher's account of guilt seems to me to be an accurate description only of the conscience of a simple sort of utilitarian. But surely people who are committed to moral codes that are at least partly nonutilitarian can feel guilty whenever they act, feel, or desire contrary to their own superegos. Adolescents express their guilt to priests for having enjoyed lascivious thoughts, with no obvious harm to others. Indeed self-blame for such fantasies is sometimes thought to be the very paradigm of a guilt feeling. And it is not only sexual taboos whose infractions can produce such feelings. The same is true, though usually to a lesser degree of intensity, of sabbatarian and dietary taboos. To be sure, these are examples of what Fletcher would call "nothing to feel guilty about." If he means by this remark that he rejects the substantive moral beliefs embodied in the prohibitions, then I have no disagreement with him. But there is no denying, it seems to me, that there is conceptual coherence in using the language of guilt even for acts and thoughts that are morally innocent in the judgment of others. The mistake is moral, in those cases, not linguistic or conceptual. But there is no comparable mistake in judging that a failed attempt to murder is morally guilty. Such language is both conceptually and morally appropriate. And if the unsuccessful killer has no guilt feelings, there is something wrong with *him*, not with the language. In other words, it is not a case of right feelings, wrong words.

This is not the place to analyze the concept of moral guilt, but let me suggest that the element in the concept whose absence is especially conspicuous in Fletcher's argument is the idea of disobedience. At any rate, to whatever extent moral guilt is a kind of legalistic notion transferred to an extra legal world, disobedience of authority is a quite essential feature. Consider the following weak effort at moral phenomenology, a picture of what one of my guilt feelings might be like. Actually, I think there are two distinct models of moral guilt. The following feelings would fit the first model. I succumb to temptation to do something that has been forbidden by some rule or person whose authority I unquestionably accept (mommy, daddy, God, or the municipal penal code). The authority is internalized. When I act, "he" is watching. He knows! I squirm with the inescapable awareness of the insolence in my rule infraction. My pain comes not primarily from the hurt or harm I may have caused incidentally and not from having embarrassed myself in public. (There may have been no witnesses.) I am upset simply because I have disobeyed, thereby alienating myself from the source of moral authority, and also perhaps for fear of the punishment I know I deserve.

The moral appropriateness of the quite different feelings that satisfy the second model of guilt is more controversial. But there is little controversy over the linguistic appropriateness of labeling them "guilt feelings." Consider some standard examples. Through a fluke, I survive the concentration camp while all the other prisoners perish, or I survive all of the battles, while my best friends among my fellow soldiers are all killed or maimed. Why me? I was not the most talented or virtuous nor the most deserving on balance. Now I feel unworthy of being alive. In another example, for some unknown reason, a teacher gave me an A in the course, whereas Tom, Dick, and Harry, who are plainly more talented than I, got Bs. I can hardly look them in the face. I am so burdened by my unworthiness that I slink away whenever I see them coming. The first description of guilt feelings follows the older established concept of guilt (disobedience of moral authority) and sin (disobedience of the sort that implies rejection of a rule maker's authority). The essence of the first conception is disobedience or rejection, whereas the essence of the second is unworthiness. Remorse characteristically (that is, when dissociated from moral guilt) involves intense regret, a painful wishing that the episode could be called back, that the hurt or harm to others or embarrassment to one's self had never happened. I suspect that remorse is more often worthy of respect than guilt is in either of its senses, and is more directly linked to contrition.

The first of Fletcher's contentions, then—that it is appropriate to have moral guilt feelings only for completed crimes—seems mistaken. The second—that shame rather than guilt is the appropriate feeling to have in reaction to a luckily failed attempt—does no better. Unlike guilt in Fletcher's account, shame at one's own conduct does not require that actual harm to anyone be caused. Thus, he writes: "If I contemplate killing the Pope and never do anything about it, I might feel ashamed of myself, but it would be out of place to feel guilty about my intentions. Feelings of shame are triggered by the realization that one is not the kind of person one thought one was; feelings of guilt by acts that rupture our relationships with other persons."[26]

I find much to quarrel with in this brief passage. First, however, we should look for common ground. All parties to the dispute should agree that it is possible to feel guilt and shame both, to some degree and in some fixed proportion, as a response to the same act or thought. I might feel shame in reaction to my bare consideration of the possibility of shooting the pope, though it is more likely that I would visit a psychiatrist for aid in dealing with such a downright crazy thought. So it is much more likely that I (for one) might experience a kind of moral alarm that I could even come as close to doing wrong as only to think about it. This, in my case, would be more like highly sensitive guilt than like shame. I feel guilty when I sin against moral authority (as I conceive it); I feel shame when I sin against my own ideals. Now part of my ego ideal, part of what I feel proud of when I feel good about myself, is my impeccably morally negative conduct (the part of morality that is relatively easy but also the most important). I never kill people, beat them, rape them, cheat them. I am honest and trustworthy. I even have some of the easier positive virtues, like friendliness, for example. All of that is of great importance, but it is also rather minimal. There is much more in my ego ideal than just not being a moral monster, and I imagine that is true of most people. Some people pack into their ideal self-aspirations some moral virtues that are more difficult to achieve than the bare minimal ones—heroism or saintliness, for example. When they fail to do something saintly, it is not necessarily because they do something immoral. So their consciences are left undisturbed, even though their self-image is tarnished in their own eyes and they feel shame.

Some shame has nothing to do with moral virtues of any kind. Part of my ego ideal may be to be a baseball star. I may then feel shame if I make several fielding errors in one game. Of course, what is called shame, in this sort of public arena, may in reality be little more than embarrassment. To have failed in front of all those people is what really hurts. Genuine shame is a kind of embarrassment in front of myself only. The aspiring side of my nature feels something akin to embarrassment when it is alone, face to face with that part of my nature that formulates and assigns ideals for me to live up to. When I do well in approximating one of my self-ideals, I feel proud; when I embarrass myself in my own eyes, I feel shame. When I make an ass of myself before others whose admiration is important to me, I feel embarrassed in the strict sense.

What do I feel when my deliberate effort to shoot another human being is foiled by a random sudden movement of my prey or a mosquito in my face? Surely not embarrassment; there may have been no one watching. Certainly not pride. Probably not a predominant shame, though there may be a trace of that element in the complex mix. (If I am proud of my ability as a marksman, I may feel shame at having missed an easy shot.) But unless I am a satanic immoralist or an amoral psychopath, what I feel, if I feel anything, will be guilt.

Bad Argument Number Six: The Argument from Natural Anger

This argument initially appears promising since it does not reject proportionality and formal justice so much as reinterpret them in a way that will seem plausible to some people and that also explains the traditional approach to the punishment of luckily failed attempts. The argument runs as follows:

1. One of the prime aims of legal punishment is to give vent to anger.
2. The more harm done, or believed to have been done, by a criminal act, the more anger, direct and vicarious, it is likely to produce.
3. The more anger produced by a criminal act, the more severe the punishment that is required to give it adequate expression.
4. Therefore (from 2 to 3), the more harm done by a criminal act, the more severe the punishment required to give anger adequate expression.
5. Therefore (from 1 to 4), the more harm done by a criminal act, the more severe the punishment that is an appropriate response to it, remembering (from 1) that a major purpose of punishment is to express anger.
6. Completed murders, as a group, do more harm than failed attempts to murder (especially when the latter fail to cause any physical injury).
7. Therefore (from 5 to 6), it is appropriate to punish murder more severely than attempted murder, which of course is the traditional practice.

There is no denying the central importance of anger and other retributive emotions to this whole discussion. One need only take a cursory glance at human behavior to realize that it is a natural response to pain inflicted on ourselves, or harm to our interests inflicted on us by others, to become angry. For most of us, anger is also a natural response to harm wrongfully inflicted on our friends and loved ones. Moreover, a kind of vicarious anger is a familiar and understandable response to wrongfully inflicted harms even on victims who are strangers to ourselves. We also naturally feel angry when we are able to avert threatened harm, but just barely escape actual harm, though that anger tends to be less intense and more like irritation mixed with relief. I do not deny that these feelings are natural and understandable, but I insist that they are *simply feelings*, like basic animal responses. If they turn out to be the main explanation of why ordinary folks want harm causers punished more than their equally blameworthy near missers, then it is those emotions rather than rational argument that are dictating the conclusion, and these are often somewhat unsavory emotions at that. Anger may be "natural" in the sense of common and universal, and it may be understandable in the sense of "easy to identify with," but for a couple of centuries now, critics have tried to point out how primitive it can be, and how independent of rational control. The nineteenth-century historian William Lecky, for example, wrote:

> If . . . the most civilized and rational of mankind will observe his own emotions, when by some accident he has struck his head violently against some door post, he will probably find that his first exclamation was not merely of pain but of anger, and of anger directed against the wood. In a moment reason checks the emotion; but if he observes carefully his own feelings, he may easily convince himself of the unconscious fetishism which is latent in his mind, and which in the case of a child or a savage, displays itself without reserve. Man instinctively ascribes volition to whatever powerfully affects him.[27]

At this point in the debate the retentionist could be expected to interrupt in protest. First of all, he will remind the reformist that he cannot take an opponent's anger, or any other merely personal trait, as evidence against his opinion. A belief that is produced by an emotion might still be true. To infer its falsity from the identity or the characteristics of the person who defends it is an *argumentum ad hominem*. To infer a proposition's falsity from the nature of its origin generally is a logical mistake to which C. D. Broad gave the name it most frequently bears now, "the genetic fallacy."[28] To be sure, the retentionist might continue, anger does tend to have the kind of unfortunate effect Lecky describes, but animistic superstition, which Lecky thought to be latent in all of us, just below the surface of consciousness, is nowhere as widespread now, at least, as he believed then, and there is surely no *necessity* that angry people become irrational either momentarily or permanently, as in the case of a person who acquires a permanent belief while in an angry state and still counts it among his convictions twenty years later. Furthermore, the retentionist might conclude, the role of emotion is far more complicated than our simplistic treatment of anger suggests. There is not one among us who would fail to experience a deep and profound emotion if one of her children were to die, and to die because of a deliberate act of killing by another person. Sooner or later extreme anger would have to be purged, but in the beginning anger would no doubt be swallowed up in a thick blend of anguish, despair, shock, disbelief, and frustration. "Wouldn't you too have such a feeling?" the retentionist will ask. Could there be anything "unsavory" about so universal an emotional reaction?

It is time to permit the reformist some rejoinders. (After all, he is *me*.) He begins by admitting that there is nothing clearly unsavory in the retentionist's examples of natural emotions. His description of the feeling of a parent whose child has been murdered is as accurate as it is eloquent. But there are examples and examples. People have lost their children to murderers in the past, and then have gone on murderous rampages themselves in search of revenge. Vengeance has fueled bloody vendettas that have decimated villages and lasted centuries, and those who kill in vengeance have a way of assuming self-righteousness when they sober up and justify their own killings. But the point I want to emphasize is not that one, but rather that angry human beings in vast numbers throughout the centuries have turned their vindictive emotions not only on those who have killed their loved ones intentionally but also, and perhaps more typically, on those who killed regretfully and reluctantly or unintentionally but knowingly, or unknowingly but recklessly, or not recklessly but negligently, or on people who faultlessly caused the death, or even on persons *not* believed to have caused the harm, but thought to be "universal objects" for other persons' vengeance, perhaps because of their known association with, or high opinion of, those suspected of being true killers, or perhaps simply because they are foreigners in the midst of alien tribes, and thus "naturally resented" outsiders. If we have outgrown that sort of tribalism, I have found little evidence of the change in our daily newspapers. Moreover, it is not only in the private affairs of single individuals, groups, and families that such responses occur, but also in established, respectable institutions, like courts of law and other government offices. It was in 1906, the twentieth century and in the highly "civilized" country of Switzerland, that there occurred the last recorded case of the trial of an animal in a human court of justice for a capital offense. In that trial in the village of Delemont, a dog was convicted of participating (with human accomplices) in a robbery and murder. In the Middle Ages, such trials and executions were frequent and commonplace.

Moreover, punishing animals for harms done to humans is not the only kind of example, in the sorry human record, of moral absurdities invoked in justification of acts and practices produced initially by uncontrolled emotions. Courts of law stopped treating animals as moral persons (that is, as eligible targets for the "satisfaction" of emotions "naturally" produced by other causes), but individuals continue to this day to destroy dogs and horses who have injured their children. There was a striking example of this in the film *Gone with the Wind*, and indeed an original example in the biblical directive to destroy morally tainted animals in Exodus. Transferred objects of danger are punished in all cultures, not just our own or that of our Jewish or Christian ancestors. According to Herodotus, the Persian emperor Darius, frustrated by stormy seas in his plan to invade Greece, equipped his troops with whips, and then commanded them to vent *his* anger by flaying the Hellespont. Similar rage-induced irrationality is illustrated by Shakespeare's Cleopatra, who upon learning of Mark Antony's infidelity, had her troops seize the messenger and punish him for bringing bad news, a practice that is not altogether extinct. The old English law of Deodand called for vindictive responses both against animals *and* inanimate objects. Subjects were required to forfeit the inanimate object or the animal which had in the most accidental way been the instrument of a man's death. Thus even the horse from which a fatal fall had taken place or the boat from which a man had drowned himself were made the subjects of this peculiar application of retributive justice, sometimes ceremonially beaten, dismembered, burned, and then "returned to God," no longer capable of its evildoing, more commonly repossessed by God's representative, the king, who knew how to put valuable property to use.

There are many other examples of astonishingly irrational moral practices generated by the disposition to respond, understandably perhaps, but nonetheless inappropriately, to particular harms without discriminating among the origins and sources of harm, some of these impersonal, as we should say, like disease, some the works of other persons, some the works of demons, spirits, and the ghosts of dead ancestors, some the works of human rulers and intermediate political authorities. Most striking of all was a near-uniform inability throughout the ancient world and persisting well into the modern history of Europe to distinguish between voluntary and involuntary homicide. The moral absurdities traced to this basic incapacity were not mere exceptional eccentricities or widely shared idiosyncracies. Rather, they were virtually unanimous reactions to harm, which seemed so natural that they became enshrined in most emerging legal systems without recorded criticism or complaint. This is what comes of paying disproportionately great attention to harm and too little attention to the multiform ways in which harm is produced.

Now it is time to hear rejoinders from the traditionalist. Having listened patiently but with a scowl on his face, he speaks earnestly in rebuttal: "I hope you won't suspect me of being willing to defend wild barbarisms, patent superstitions and fetishism, bizarre practices, and worse superstitions. Heaven forbid! I desire only to persuade you to have respect for quite unbizarre, ordinary, garden-variety emotions, and independently rational judgments of people like you when they suffer harm, and the contrast between those reactions and the experiences we have in the wake of near misses." When a near miss occurs, clearly produced by a human being's fault—his evil intentions his indifference, or his carelessness or clumsiness—we will respond with some alarm, some resentment, and even some anger. But these negative feelings typically remain under tight control if no actual harm were caused, and they usually cannot survive the inevitable positive reaction of happy relief. The emotional worlds of the near miss, and the far miss too, for that matter, are different worlds altogether from the world of experienced actual harm. We can try to give ourselves a sample of what real harm would taste like, but in normal persons it cannot reach the same intensity. Nor can it endure as long, partly because the good feelings are those that perceptions of reality bring, and partly from the clear awareness that we have to manipulate our feelings artificially to achieve even a pale semblance of the full emotional reaction to serious real harm. So there is not a parity between loss and near loss that can survive the awareness that one must use make-believe techniques to guide the near-miss reaction up to the intensity levels characteristic of our responses to actual harm. Retentionist philosophers may sometimes find it hard to find good abstract reasons for making moral desert or blameworthiness turn on chance as our opponents say we do. But here is the rub. Most of us make specific judgments of blame that fit this pattern exactly. We do not say that genuine moral blameworthiness could turn on chance, but we know that the degree and extent of actual harm caused by faulty conduct does often turn on chance, and our anger turns on it, which seems to us natural enough. Does not it seem natural for you to want to punish your child more for spilling her milk than for almost spilling it, more for running the family car into a wall than for almost doing so? The sight of the harm arouses a degree of anger and resentment that far exceeds that aroused by the nervous expectation about the harm. The reformist should be able to understand why near misses and actual harm production invariably elicit different judgments. That is because they invariably cause different amounts of anger, and the more anger, the more harsh and severe the reaction to it is likely to be. This approach naturalizes our position and makes it vastly superior to theories that, in order to defend themselves, must have recourse to such dubious entities as "rational intuitions."

Still, many retentionists want more than this, a more reassuring appearance of respectable rationality, not just the look of understandable anger. Adam Smith, in a much-quoted passage, describes the emotional incentives behind the traditional punishment differentials, but there is in his elegant language also the suggestion of a rational justification: "Our resentment against the person who only attempted to do a mischief, is seldom so strong as to bear us out in inflicting the same punishment upon him, which we should have thought due if he had actually done it. In the one case, the joy of our deliverance alleviates our sense of the atrocity of his conduct; in the other, the grief of our misfortune increases it."[29] Smith's summary at this point seems to bring the controversy full circle back to where it started. Both disputants now understand how and why people naturally respond both to near-miss attempts and to actual harm with anger, and why they respond with more intense and enduring anger to actual harm than to mere near misses. But that does nothing to establish the *correctness* of the traditionalist position. The missing link in the traditionalist argument is the one that would appraise the rationality of a sentencing policy by the test of how much anger produced it or is expressed in it.

My own view is that the emotional test for the truth of normative judgments is misguided. Experience shows that sometimes truth must overcome rather than reinforce emotion, even understandable emotion. This may be one of those occasions.

The key phrase in the quotation from Adam Smith is "our sense of the atrocity of his conduct." "Atrocity" is a term of moral condemnation, perhaps as strong as any morally condemning term we have. Smith joins the bulk of mankind in applying that term to certain harmful completed crimes. Why does he use the moral term "atrocity"?[30] Smith explains that in the case of actual serious harm or death, "the grief of our misfortune" and similarly, I suspect, our anger, increases the sense of atrocity or moral outrage. The linkage between completed harm and the truth of the moral judgment condemning it then goes as indicated in figure 1.

The connections between 1 and 2 are basic dispositions of human nature as they have presented themselves to trained and untrained observers for centuries. I take them to be noncontroversial. But the connection between 3 and 4 is not secure. It is an alleged linkage of a sort different from the others, not composed of empirically supported descriptions of mental states as they characteristically relate to one another. It is not, for example, an account of how certain feelings often give rise to certain judgments, but rather it purports to show a linkage between the mental states and the *truth* of those moral statements. Grief and anger are said not only to play a role in the explanation of the moral judgments, but they are actually part of the justification for those judgments, reasons for believing the judgments to be true. The traditionalist/retentionist uses the psychological story in rational support of the moral judgment that the person who caused serious harm was "atrocious," that his conduct was an "atrocity," and a much more wrongful atrocity, even, than a failed attempt to produce the same harm. That is precisely the point we have been debating all this time, and as far as I know, there has been no evidence offered in its support by anyone.

Those who use the elegant quotation from Adam Smith in an effort to support the traditionalist position on the failed attempts problem often fall into a fallacy of equivocation. (I have often thought that if one leaves an ambiguous word lying around long enough with little work to occupy it, like

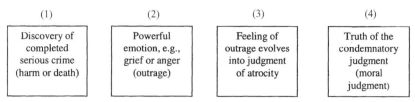

Figure 1.

a loaded gun, sooner or later someone will use it to commit a fallacy of equivocation.) A term like "atrociousness" can refer to certain negative emotions (so far, it is like "ugh" or "yuk"), or to judgments of moral condemnation of the actor or his acts. The fallacy that lies menacingly in the traditionalist's path consists in concluding that evidence supporting the empirical linkage of intense grief or anger with the making of certain moral judgments ipso facto shows a logical connection between that evidence and the *truth* of those moral judgments. That is a plain non sequitur. Supporting reasons for the moral conclusion, rather than empirical evidence for the psychological descriptions, is precisely the link that is missing in the retentionist case, at least when that case is based on the argument from anger. The retentionist claim all along has been that the unlucky harm causer is actually a morally worse person than the lucky failed attempter simply in virtue (not in spite of) of his bad moral luck. That claim remains unproved.

Let us be clear. Greater harms hurt more than lesser ones, and both of those more than no harm at all. Harm tends to cause grief and anger in proportion to the amount of harm caused and, in any case, is likely to cause those emotions to a greater degree than resented conduct that causes no harm at all. We all *prefer* no harm to harm, and even to like those who produce no harm more than we like those who produce little harm. Other things being equal, we *resent* the producer of great harm more than the producer of little harm, and both of those more than the producer of no harm. These are all highly probable truths that will surprise no one, but there is no logical or psychological necessity to them; they have exceptions. None of them is itself a moral judgment. None of them states or implies that harm causers are in fact morally worse persons than those whose equal faults do not materialize in as much harm.

So far, so good. But it does not follow that failed attempts to perform an act of a type that *is* harmful (like murder, for example) should not be criminalized! That is a well-intentioned but illogical conclusion hastily drawn from a noble principle that gives it no support (the harm principle). If the law prohibits *dangerous* behavior as well as actually harmful behavior, it will prevent more actual harm than it would otherwise. There is none likelier to cause actual harm than an armed and hate-filled person trying hard to harm someone.

Bad Argument Number Seven: The
Argument from the Value of
Immediate Gratification

Bad Argument Number Seven points out, as its first step, that a person who succeeds in her initial criminal purpose, a convicted murderer, let us say, has derived some gratification from her crime already, if only in getting what she wanted, namely, the death of her victim. She may not have exactly *wanted* that result, but insofar as she acted voluntarily, she must have been willing to bring about that consequence as a means to something else that she did want, so that for a moment at least her hopes of achieving her goal were excited and alive. Or perhaps she wanted the victim's death neither as an end nor as a means but as an expected by-product of her efforts toward her goal, a side effect that might have been a sign that her criminal project was proceeding smoothly toward its culmination, and *that* might have been a pleasant thought and thus, however momentary, a thing of value for her. Suppose, for example, that she packed a plastic bomb in her husband's suitcase in the hope of recovering the insurance compensation after his death. She knows that the explosion will also cause the deaths of the other passengers and the crew. She does not *want* that to happen, but on the other hand she *knows* that it will happen. Her regret about that is a cost she must pay, but one that is more than counterbalanced by her husband's death and the thrilling realization that the insurance money will make her rich. She watches from the ground as the plane explodes, and smiles inwardly at the thought that her plot is so far going well.

In contrast, the person who tries but does not succeed in his murderous attempt has no comparable moment of elation, no gratification at all, just an attempt and a failure. And now the seventh bad argument makes its big leap. If the failed attempter receives exactly the same punishment as his more successful counterpart, equal justice will not be done because the successful murderer will have had *some* benefit already from his crime, thus affecting his net balance of benefit and harm through the whole period of his subsequent incarceration.

One can only smile at the lighthearted, even childish attitude toward murder implicit in this argument. If we give the failed attempter steak dinners with champagne and ice cream each night for a week at the start of his term, will that even things up sufficiently so that equal punishments from that point on will meet the requirements of equal justice? Or perhaps we should sentence the murderer to forty years and the attempted murderer to 39½ years to make up for the early benefits enjoyed by one and not the other? I should think that from any reasonable conception of human rights and ideals these quibblings are *de minimus* and infantile. Furthermore the hypocrisy involved in the apparent acceptance of a claim by a would-be murderer to ice cream and wine as part of his "punishment package"—like change received for over-payment of a bill—seems to weaken the symbolic condemnation of the horrible act that was done (well, if not exactly done, than at least attempted).

Some of the more ingenious bad arguments on my list are efforts to secure for the retentionist the blessings of the principles of equal justice and proportionality and the exclusion of arbitrariness. He can then hold these moral principles constant and tinker instead with the facts and moral appraisals that he will subsume under them. The proportionality principle will tell him, for example, that in order for it to be right to punish the perpetrator of a completed crime more severely than an unsuccessful attempter, it must be true that he is more blameworthy than the attempter. "But that's just the point," the retentionist replies, "he *is* more blameworthy, even though his beliefs, desires, motives, and relevant traits are exactly similar to those of the mere attempter." How then could he be more blameworthy?

If our story were set in early, common-law England, then the death would have had to occur within a year and a day of the original assault. Otherwise, the late-arriving death could *never* be charged to the assailant. If especially creative medical care delayed the death for, say, thirteen months, the doctors would by that token have prevented the assailant forever from becoming defiled by assuming the moral status of a murderer, unless of course, he murders again. Even today, long after the demise of the year-and-a-day rule, there is enough arbitrariness in our understanding of legal causation to fill us with wonder at the powers of scientific medicine to produce or fail to produce momentous moral consequences.

Harm? From the point of view of maximum deterrence, I should think that we would be better off punishing *all* wrongful attempts. We want to discourage all attempts to kill, those done with resolute and wholehearted enthusiasm, those done reluctantly, those done self-confidently, those done by excellent marksmen, and those done by myopic haters who are dangerous and those whose general incompetence reduces their dangerousness. Why give an attempted assassin another chance after he has shot and missed? We can think of him as a person who *tried to commit a crime* but failed, say, because of poor marksmanship, and then just leave him alone, until he violates another law, or we can think of him as a person who *did* commit the crime of *attempted* murder, say, and who now must be apprehended, tried, convicted, and punished. I should think that the latter alternative would be the more stringent one, and the one more likely to "prevent harm to the public."

Suppose that we are starting a new country and designing a model penal code to "prevent harms to the public." We would first want a list of the generally harmful kinds of results of human actions and omissions that can be called "harms"—death, injury, material loss, psychological frustration. Then we can proceed to prohibit all attempts to produce any of these harms.

Then, applying appropriate procedural rules, we can punish *all* such attempts, or alternatively, we can punish only those attempts that succeed in causing harm. Which alternative would we select if our goal were the liberal one of "preventing harms to the public"? Should we ban all attempts to bring about results that are harmful? Or should we punish only those attempts that succeed in bringing about harm? From the point of view of maximum deterrence, I should think we would be better off punishing *all* wrongful attempts.

Summary and Conclusion

The reformist approach to the sentencing of unsuccessful criminal attempts seems highly plausible initially because it conforms to the principle of proportionality, which decrees that the just punishment for any convicted criminal is the one whose severity is proportionate to the degree of blameworthiness of that actor for doing what he did. The traditional approach, on the other hand, attaches more significance to the amount of actual harm caused than to the blameworthiness of the actor in contributing his share to the production of the harm, and does not exclude good and bad luck as major determinants of the severity of the penalty. To grant so large a role to luck is to invite arbitrariness to govern, and inevitably to corrupt the judiciary process. The principle of proportionality, after all, does not decree that the severity of the punishment be proportionate to the offender's good or bad luck, but rather to his good or bad deserts, or blameworthiness.

But when we looked at some arguments for retention, we discovered that none of them claim that the principle of proportionality is wrong in giving such an important role to moral blameworthiness. In fact, they all endorse the principle of proportionality but then go on to argue that the blameworthiness that punitive severity is to be proportionate to is determined by something else, namely, the amount of actual harm produced by the offender's contribution in combination with the contribution of parts of the natural world over which the offender had little normal control. Giving good reasons for that proposition—that moral blameworthiness is itself grounded in actual harm caused in the specific case—is such a heavy burden that it is no wonder the arguments we examined were so bad.

But to back up a bit, how is blameworthiness, as ordinarily understood, outside of the attempt problem? To begin with, the criminal's blameworthiness is not to be confused with the wrongness of what he did, for it is possible for a generally virtuous person to do the wrong thing in the circumstances and yet not be properly subject to much blame for doing it, or for a generally evil person to do what is right but not deserve any credit for it. But apart from the wrongness of his act, what determines the degree of praise- or blameworthiness of the actor?

A great number and variety of factors go into the determination, whether we are talking now of criminal sentencing guides or the moral judgments they partially incorporate. A sound if blurred insight is that the harm intended is much more important an indicator of an offender's desert than the harm actually caused. Far more useful, however, than the concept of intentionality, are the four "culpability conditions" first proclaimed in the Model Penal Code—acting purposely, knowingly, recklessly, or negligently in regard to some potentially harmful result. Then, of course, the concept of a motive, ruthlessly kept out of the original criminal trial, forces its way back at the sentencing stage and contributes its flavor to the emerging blameworthiness stew. Did the offender act cruelly? spitefully? from mercenary motives? out of greed? in an emotional explosion provoked by a sexual rejection? by sexual jealousy? through political conviction? out of mercy or compassion for another person's suffering? after forethought and deliberation? out of conscientious conviction or the determination to do at any cost to oneself what one sincerely believes to be one's moral duty? out of sudden violent impulse as mysterious to the actor as to anyone else? And, after all those questions have been answered and provocation considered, as well as other types of mitigation, diminished responsibility, and the questions they raise, now at last the more traditional justifications and excuses enter the arena with their talk of subtle coercion and mistakes, mistakes of fact and mistakes of law, defenses that undermine and defenses that affirm, defense of self and defense of others, with duress and necessity, involuntary and voluntary intoxication, insanity, and, short of insanity, a host of neuroses and psychoses, compulsions and obsessions, the great parade of syndromes, and on and on. There is surprisingly little disagreement about the factors that belong on this list, but much disagreement about the weight to be given different factors when they conflict.

Does the retentionist really wish to supplement all of that with a simple appeal to the harm actually caused? Is he willing to let the final judgment of moral blameworthiness be swayed by a luck factor reflecting nothing about the actor's character? If the incredibly complex test of blameworthiness now used pulls in the direction of extreme moral culpability, would he be willing to let the fortuitous absence of a serious harm pull it back in the direction of moral innocence? If so, how far back? I find no intuitive plausibility at all in first basing criminal liability on moral blameworthiness, but then basing moral blameworthiness in turn upon the actual harm or absence of harm caused. The ancient view, that liability should be based not upon blameworthiness at all but instead directly upon the amount of harm caused, seems to me more honest, though no more plausible. It seems almost as if the retentionist is so fixated on actual harm that he keeps searching for the question to which it is the right answer. Not the question: "What ought to be the basis of criminal liability?" Moral blameworthiness is a plausible answer to that question. Not the question. "What is the basis of moral blameworthiness?"

The traditional multiplicity of culpability conditions, motives, mitigations, aggravations, and so on, answers that question. How about the question: What is a necessary condition for tort liability? Now, that is more like it.

Why are good philosophers and legal theorists so determined to find a central place for actual harm caused (if any) that they are led into such bad arguments? I do not know, but I suspect that it may be partly because of a discomfort many persons have with moral concepts, which in order to be applied correctly, require our access to a human being's inner states, his emotions, passions, opinions, and distortions. Not only is the invasion of another's privacy unsettling; being required to make fine subtle appraisals of what we find there is even worse. How much less slippery is our task when we are asked only to take measurements, conduct tests, read laboratory reports, and the like. And it is much less daunting still to measure dollar losses, to subtract insurance coverage, and to apply the other, relatively objective, measures of harm and loss.

Finally, it is not as difficult for good thinkers to tumble into bad arguments as one might think. The subtle influence of compensation concepts on criminal punishment concepts has tricked many a complacent theorist. And it is an easy equivocation to think that one is praising the harm principle as a standard for the moral legitimacy of criminal legislation by urging the decriminalization of all unsuccessful attempts to inflict harms, even the harm of death. Professor Fletcher's mistaken analysis of guilt and shame, I realize, were animated by an unusually powerful (and commendable) motive to avoid elitism. Even though, on some scale of cognitive blameworthiness, these mistakes are not very blameworthy, they can nonetheless cause considerable mischief, intellectual and other, and in actual cases, can make the work appear the better cause.

5

"NOT WITH MY TAX MONEY"

*The Problem of Justifying
Government Subsidies for the Arts*

The Taxpayer's Challenge

Most of us think of art as a worthwhile but often profitless kind of activity, worthy of whatever financial support it can get. Unfortunately, in this historical period, few royal patrons or robber baron benefactors are available, and subsidies are more and more commonly expected from governments, which draw on their major source of income, tax revenues. Among those requesting government subsidies for art are, on the one hand, museum curators, repertory companies, and other groups that aim at preserving our cultural treasures and, on the other hand, creative artists hoping to add their own productions to the cultural treasury. Artists are not the only ones hoping for government aid. Scholars and humanists, like ourselves, are standing in line, too, hoping that the modesty of their requests will improve their chances. In addition, the applicants include mathematicians and theoretical scientists whose projects are so esoteric, or expensive, or both, that they have little hope of finding funding without government help.

A few decades ago, Congress established the National Endowment for the Arts, the National Endowment for the Humanities, and the National Science Foundation, partly to ensure that art, humanities, and scientific research be removed from the prevailing pork barrel system, by which lobbyists persuade their own representative or senator that there would be great political advantage for him if he could produce funds for some favorite local project, by inducing powerful committee chairs to attach funding for that project to an otherwise respectable appropriations bill moving toward passage.[1] Brian Kelly tells us that "some pork projects, like [a] North Dakota Senator's attempts to turn schlock entertainer Lawrence Welk's mud-walled birthplace into a museum, do not pass 'the laugh test.' "[2] Perhaps peer reviewers for the NEA are also capable of flunking the laugh test, but their procedures are somewhat more reliable, I should think, than the congressional pork delivery system.

The main challenge to the art and science subsidizers, however, is not how they spend tax money, but by what right they spend it at all. The problem raised by the indignant taxpayer is whether there is justification for using government funds derived from mandatory taxation of all citizens in order to promote the esoteric projects of a small number of people. Indeed there is a prima facie case for the proposition that such subsidies are unfair to those who are made to pay, not to protect their neighbors from harm, but to secure benefits for some of their neighbors that they (the complaining taxpayers) are not able to share. The principle invoked by the indignant taxpayer is that "Justice requires that persons pay for a facility in proportion to the degree they benefit from it." For convenience I shall call this proposed maxim of justice the "benefit principle." According to this principle, the appropriate model of fair taxation is users' fees, the price charged to visitors for their use of a zoo, or to drivers for their use of an expensive stretch of turnpike. Users' fees are paid voluntarily, and only by those who expect to receive benefits that are worth the price they pay.

Those defenders of public subsidies who accept the benefit principle must show that, initial appearance to the contrary, artistic endeavors supported by general tax revenues (instead of users' fees) are somehow universally and equally beneficial, whether some philistine taxpayers know it or not. If, as I suspect, that is too great an argumentative burden to sustain, then the determined advocate of subsidies for the arts may have to abandon the benefit principle.

An alternative is to abandon one's advocacy of subsidies for all but special cases. Opera lovers and zoo users, for example, might very well be able to collect their own funds from private sources. They can receive certification from the Internal Revenue Service as nonprofit foundations that are genuine "charities" (that is, worthy causes) and thus be immune from taxation themselves and also be eligible for gifts that are deductible from the taxable incomes of the donors. These measures, of course, are a considerable boost from the government. Moreover, they allow taxpayers to some degree to choose the direct beneficiaries of their own tax payments, and escape to some degree the requirement that they support causes from which they do not themselves benefit and of which they may even disapprove. The opera lovers and zoo visitors then could pay "voluntary taxes" in support of their favorite facilities and also users' fees on the many occasions they actually use those facilities, while other citizens, who are bored by opera and actually offended by zoos, could escape the compulsion that they support other people's pleasures.

I think that there is much to be said for this approach, but it cannot solve the whole problem by itself. There are exceptional cases in which the exclusive dependence on users' fees and voluntary taxes would clearly be insufficient. The more expensive the project, or the use of its finished goods, the harder it is to raise voluntary contributions for its support. Moreover, the more esoteric the project or its finished good, the fewer the persons who understand it, appreciate it, and are willing to support it. A number theorist may need an expensive high-powered computer to help him establish some truth about prime numbers. I, as a typical taxpayer, might admire him, but there is no way I could "use" his results. The whole idea of a users' fee collapses in this example.

The homely case of the zoo provides a less outré example of how the costs of operation, for practical reasons, could exceed the capacity of patrons to pay for them by means of users' fees alone. Suppose that the entrance fee to the zoo is $5 a person, so that a family of four must pay $20. This leads to a shortfall, so the fee is raised to $10 a head. For a large percentage of regular patrons, the new fee has crossed the line of what they can afford, so they stop coming, and that in turn creates another deficit, requiring another price hike, leading to further customer alienation, and so on. We can imagine at least some circumstances in which dipping into the tax revenues is the only alternative to giving up the valuable facility altogether.

These are some of the reasons we might have, in admittedly exceptional cases, for supporting facilities and projects at least in part with tax revenues. But to acknowledge cases of this sort is not to solve our original problem so much as to transform its character. It is now less a pressing policy question than a philosophical one. In respect to those expensive or esoteric goods that we feel impelled to support out of tax funds, we still have a problem, though it may now seem only a theoretical one, like justifying induction, justifying democracy, or the like. What can we say to the indignant taxpayer whose money we take to support things like zoos, which for the sake of the example, we can assume he never attends and does not like, and from which he secures no benefit and of which he morally disapproves?

The Search for Universal Indirect Benefits

The legitimacy of some tax-funded governmental activities, of course, is beyond all cavil. We all benefit from the protection of the police and the national defense, from public health agencies, from reliable treatment of drinking water, unpolluted air, sewer systems, highways, and so on. But only some of us benefit directly from school systems, museums, public parks, ballet troupes, opera companies, astronomical observatories, chess tournaments, mathematical treatises on number theory, and so on. Some of those who would not benefit directly from some of these activities can nevertheless be said to benefit indirectly from them. Single adults who have been educated elsewhere, childless couples, and couples whose children have grown up and finished their schooling do not themselves profit directly from the further maintenance of a public school system. Neither they nor their children will ever need further schooling at that level. But it is at least plausible to claim that everyone, even members of these groups, profits from living in a well-educated society, and the better educated our fellow citizens are, the better off we are likely to be. Nondrivers, similarly, benefit indirectly from a network of good roads. It is clearly in your interest, even though you may be permanently confined to bed, that the transportation of responsible persons and essential goods be efficient, and that is true whether you know it or not.

It is less plausible, however, to claim that opera companies are indirectly to the benefit of everyone, even those who are bored and uninterested, and that that is so whether the uninterested party knows it or not. At this point in the dialectic, the more thoroughgoing philosopher would have to decide whether a search for subtle indirect benefits will yield a justification for subsidizing the arts out of general tax revenues. She would have to survey the various dogmatic theories—aesthetic and moral perfectionism, aesthetic environmentalism, and so on—in her quest for the universal subtle benefit.[3] I am quite convinced that none of these theories is satisfactory, so I shall turn instead to the much more interesting arguments that proceed without the benefit of the benefit principle.

Imperfect Schemes of
Rotational Justice

First, let us consider a highly indirect way of appealing to benefits and harms exclusively. Some of those in the great majority whose interests would not be harmed by the reduction of government support, say, for the Library of Congress, would be harmed by the withdrawal of some other government subsidy—the weakening of support for the visual arts or highly theoretical sciences, or the loss of a tax exemption for churches (an indirect subsidy). This suggests that there may be a justification for the whole system of which these particular enactments are component projects. When this system works with approximate fairness, it may make it seem tolerable to the citizens it represents that sometimes, because they pay the bill, they should be net losers, provided they have a fair opportunity to be net winners on other occasions. Almost everyone may have reason to prefer such a system of fluctuating benefits to its more cumbersome alternatives in which unanimity, for example, is always required for tax-supported appropriations.

When it comes to political institutions, there is much to be said for the view that the primary subject of justification is the full institutional complex of rules and practices, not each small component or by-product of it considered in isolation from the rest. In our country, part of that complex consists of a democratically elected legislature, using majority rule to govern its procedures, making laws of which some confer powers, others prohibit or enjoin actions directly, others raise revenue, and still others set up programs to be paid for out of the revenues that were raised by virtue of the techniques and powers created by other rules. The system is meant to represent the interests and wishes of ordinary citizens and groups. Thus, if a given citizen is in the minority on one issue of how to spend money from a pool to which he has been forced to contribute, he will have a fair chance to be in the majority on another such issue. Different programs will create different patterns of protectees, beneficiaries, and indifferents, and each represented citizen will (it is hoped) win some and lose some, never feeling as a consequence that he is completely overlooked and impotent. Individual tax-supported programs win their moral legitimacy by virtue of being the end product of a legitimate procedure, a complex institutional practice without which, in turn, everybody would be a net loser. That is the sort of justification for legally compelling people to pay for particular programs, like the Library of Congress or the National Endowment for the Arts, that they may not want and from which they may not benefit. Citizens pay their money and take their chances, knowing that they will not win all the time, but also knowing that they may be protected from harm to some of their own valuable ulterior interests, which may not be widely shared.

The argument from rotational justice is admittedly imperfect. It does not guarantee that everyone will win and lose equally, and in fact even the best working of democracies will sometimes generate serious inequalities in the way tax funds are allocated. In our own Congress, projects that are genuinely worthy of government support on grounds recognized by this argument may in fact get caught up in the unfortunate pork barrel system of dispensations, which for so long has been the scandal of our government's operations. Moreover, in many or even most instances, the argument may prove to be unnecessary because the grievance of the nonbenefiting taxpayer can be obviated by the exercise of ingenuity in collecting users' fees and stimulating voluntary private contributions. Still, for the diminished number of cases that could not be supported privately because the project, though worthy, is too esoteric and too expensive to survive without government help, the argument from rotational justice often seems persuasive. It may well be the best we can hope to do if we restrict ourselves to the concepts of benefit and harm in our attempts to justify subsidies. On that level, it provides the best answer to the challenge of the taxpayer who disapproves in a particular case the uses for which his money is employed, who does not want his money used in that way, and who is unbenefited himself by that use of it. Perhaps we can do better still, however, if we cease restricting our justificatory efforts to such values as harm prevention and benefit promotion, and appeal instead to values of a quite different kind.[4]

Benefitless Values

In my book *Harmless Wrongdoing*, I argue that it is at least coherent to claim that some behavior is morally wrong even though it harms or threatens no one.[5] Some might claim, for example, that homosexual relations between consenting adults in private, simply because some interpretations claim they are condemned in the Bible, are morally wrong, even when they harm or wrong neither participant and offend no third-party witnesses. Even if there are such instances of harmless wrongdoing, I argued, they are none of the state's business, since the coercive arm of the law can legitimately intervene in human affairs only to protect unwilling victims from harm, not to enforce morality whether harmful behavior is involved or not. Similarly, I argued that there are, or at least could be, so-called free-floating evils, that is, intrinsically regrettable states of affairs that are evil for some reason other than that they harm or offend anyone. I cited as examples reputation-shattering false beliefs about the long dead (say, about Emperor Nero), voluntary contraceptively protected adult incest, hateful but repressed thoughts, and such single capricious acts as that of squashing an endangered beetle in the wild. If there are such free-floating evils, I argued, they too are beyond the legitimate concern of the state.

But now, as we consider problems of government subsidy policies, we come to the mirror image of the problems about the proper scope of criminal prohibitions, and we discover some initially disturbing asymmetries. When we discuss the subsidy problem, we must inquire whether there are free-floating values or benefitless good things, which means we must ask whether a thing can be truly valuable for some reason other than that it benefits someone. Further, we must consider, if there are some nonbeneficial values, whether it can be the proper business of the state, using tax funds extracted in part from the unbenefited, to subsidize them. Liberal impulses on the question of the propriety of subsidizing nonbeneficial goods seem at odds with those on the question of criminal prohibitions of harmless evils, for characteristically the liberal approves of the subsidies for nonbeneficial goods though he opposes the criminal prohibition of nonharmful evils. I see no contradiction, however, in this asymmetry. Sometimes the truth comes in displeasingly untidy forms, and at any rate, we might expect some stark and asymmetric contrasts when comparing concepts as opposed as good and evil.

I am happy to have as an ally in this inquiry so talented a philosopher as Tom Nagel, who attacks the assumption that "everything good is good only because it is for the good of some person or persons, and that its value is simply the sum of its value for the people it benefits."[6] Rather, Nagel reminds us, "Some things are wonderful in a measure quite beyond the value of the experiences or other benefits of those who encounter them."[7] I suspect Nagel has in mind here not only such sublime works of art as the great medieval cathedrals, the Beethoven symphonies, and Shakespeare's tragedies, but also such natural wonders as the Grand Canyon and the 125 surviving Siberian tigers, and such relatively nonutilitarian projects and achievements as the ingeniously proved theorems of abstruse number theory and the search for interstellar signals from possible intelligent beings in the Milky Way galaxy by means of an enormous radio telescope.

One needs little imagination to reconstruct the views of the fiscal philistines whom Nagel is attacking. "What do I care whether the Notre Dame cathedral falls into decay?" a provincial French citizen might ask. "Restore it if you wish but don't charge me with part of the bill. I don't profit, and most of the taxpayers I know don't benefit in any way from some pretty church in a distant place, so it is wrong that we should be compelled to pay in support of its restoration." Even more so, such a person would protest against measures to use his tax money to help save the tigers, since the tigers directly benefit neither him nor the bulk of the human race sufficiently to balance the harm of the taxation required to save them. And certainly our hypothetical taxpayer would balk at the use of government funds to allocate time on enormous computers so that number theorists can list the first two billion digits in the value of pi (the ratio of the circumference to the diameter of a circle) as part of a purely philosophical study of the concept of randomness. As for radio transmissions of signals to outer space, our hypothetical taxpayer would be better off not knowing that "since 1974 a signal sent from the giant radio dish in Arecibo, Puerto Rico, describing our solar system, our DNA, our species, and our culture, has been speeding toward the constellation Hercules, dispatched in the hope that an 'alien being' there might apprehend it. But since Hercules is 25,000 light-years away, an answer would take at least 50,000 years to reach Earth." Because these time intervals are so great, the urgency of the project is decreased and the most recent version of the undertaking has been funded for only $1 million over the next ten years.[8]

Not all or even most taxpayers are narrow-minded philistines. Many people would agree that there are precious objects and noble pursuits that are worth paying for even if their direct benefit to other citizens is an insignificant component of their value. But Nagel reminds us that even if these people "pay what the experience is worth to them personally, it may not add up to the value of the things themselves,"[9] and thus the remaining costs require some subsidy from other sources.

The Concept of Intrinsic Value:
A Quick Sketch

If "value" is not simply a synonym for "benefit," what then can a value be? To be valuable, I suggest, is to be worthy of being valued, just as to be praiseworthy is to be worthy of being praised and to be execrable is to be worthy of being execrated. The word "worthy" is the key term in the analysis, but we should expect that it will raise philosophical difficulties that must here be avoided. So I will not linger long with it except to point out two of its features. Judgments of worthiness, whatever response their subject is said to be worthy of, are often the occasion of controversy, but especially on those occasions we tend to think of them as objectively true or false, that is, correct or incorrect in virtue of something other than the opinions people may hold about them. Second, worthiness in the present sense is a relatively weak normative term. When I say that Jones is praiseworthy for what he did, I do not intend anything so strong as a command that he be praised ("He is to be praised"), or that he must be praised, or even that he ought to be praised. More likely, I imply that if there is a reason for withholding praise, it cannot be that he does not qualify for it. To praise him for what he did would not be inappropriate even if on this occasion it would be inadvisable. Considered on its own terms, praise would be an entirely fitting response to what he did, the response he deserves, even when there is an overriding reason in the circumstances for withholding it.

If to have value (or to be valuable) is to be worthy of being valued, to what then does this response called valuing come? To value a thing, I should think, is to have a relatively constant disposition to hold that thing in high regard, to appreciate, esteem, or admire it, and in the extreme case to revere, to cherish, or to treasure it. None of these words are precise synonyms of valuing, but each stands for its own type or degree of valuing. We judge that a thing has a great value when we think of it as worthy of cherishing or treasuring. According to some theories, this schematic definition is incomplete and will remain so until it specifies by whom the object is worthy of being treasured. Perhaps its character is such that it is worthy of being cherished by me (it is a photograph, say, of my grandmother) but not by you.

At this point we should add to our definition that the valuable object is worthy of being valued either for itself (that is, for its own characteristics and properties) or for what can be done with it (that is, for its causal or instrumental properties), or for both itself and its uses. The distinction between intrinsic and instrumental value, of course, goes all the way back to Plato's *Republic* and was no doubt a commonplace earlier still. Nevertheless, many philosophers purport to find difficulties with it. Their main problem is understanding how anything could be valued entirely for properties that are noncausal or noninstrumental. To their understanding, even the paradigm examples of intrinsic value are objects worthy of being valued for their causal capacity to produce effects of a desired kind on those who value them. Some people, for example, value the experience of eating broccoli because broccoli promotes good health; it is beneficial or good for them, as we say. Others value the experience of eating broccoli because broccoli tastes good; they like it for itself, as they say, for what it is, rather than for what it does. Similarly, sexual intercourse can be valued as a virtually indispensable means to the creation of children. Producing offspring may be valued by some people as the sole answer to the question, "Admitting that sex is good, what is it good for?" Others, most others, I should say, will value sex, at least in part, for its own sake, quite apart from its conducibility to some further end, like reproduction. But the skeptic about intrinsic value will point out that the broccoli appreciation, whether he values eating broccoli for its nutrition or for its flavor, values broccoli for what it produces: pleasant gustatory sensations in one case, good health in the other. Similarly, the sex appreciation, whichever camp he falls in, will value sex for what it does: producing children in one case or erotic pleasure in the other. Why then, he might ask, is one ground for valuing sex any more "intrinsic" than the other?

The questioner has a point. Most valuable things are valuable for what they do. But the distinction between intrinsic and instrumental value may nevertheless be usefully made. I suggest, in many cases, that we think of it as a matter of degree, a distinction of more and less. A pilgrim or an aesthete may value the Notre Dame cathedral for the infinite complexity and richness of its design, its stained glass, the texture of its stone, its soaring, vaulted interior. All of this causes him aesthetic pleasure or religious awe. A Parisian city official from the bureau of tourism might equally value the cathedral, but primarily for the money it attracts from foreign visitors into the Parisian economy. The old-fashioned way of making the distinction was to say that the pilgrim values the cathedral "for itself" and the official "for what it does," its causal capacity to bring in revenue. The pilgrim assigns intrinsic value to it; the official assigns instrumental value. The skeptic, however, points out that even the pilgrim values the cathedral instrumentally. He finds it thrilling and awesome and treasures its capacity to cause these richly emotional responses. But there still is a point, I would say, in distinguishing his valuing from that of the city official. The end to which the cathedral is a valuable instrument for the official (namely, municipal revenue) is relatively remote, and many intervening causes and conditions contribute toward its realization, whereas the effect for which the cathedral is valued by the religious aesthete is relatively near and certain, intimately linked to the perception of the valued object, and relatively independent of intervening causes and conditions. Most of the traditional examples of intrinsic value are like the cathedral in these respects. There may be some values that are in between the immediate causal effect and the remote consequence, and thus hard to classify as intrinsic or instrumental, just as there are moments at twilight that are hard to classify as day or night, but in neither case is the utility of the distinction seriously undermined.

There is another kind of reply that might be made to the skeptic who insists that all things worth valuing are so in virtue of their causal capacity to produce desired effects on users or observers. The second response is to insist on at least one class of exceptions to the skeptic's claim, namely, those values for which the words "ultimate" or "final" are often used. Aristotle thought of ultimacy, along with self-sufficiency, as the marks of what he called "the good for man." That good is the ultimate one, in that it is never sought as a means to anything beyond itself. It is where the value theory buck stops. An ultimate value, then, is not merely chosen for its own sake, like other intrinsically valuable things. It is chosen only for its own sake, there being nothing else that it could be a means to, or that it could be good for, that would increase its total goodness one bit. Final values are just one class of intrinsic values, namely, those that stand on their own feet and are not made better still by any further end to which they reliably lead. Not all intrinsic goods are ultimate in this sense, but all ultimate value must also be intrinsic.

The problem about intrinsic values that has traditionally divided philosophers is not whether there are such things but how many irreducibly distinct kinds of intrinsic values there might be. Pleasure, of course, is commonly counted as intrinsically valuable, an honor it shares with its near relatives, happiness and fulfillment, and also with virtue, even when virtue is its own and only reward. Knowledge too has its supporters, even though most knowledge is also valuable instrumentally, and therefore is ineligible as a candidate for ultimate value in Aristotle's sense. Knowledge of a difficult proof in number theory, for example, may have a value "in itself" way beyond any merely instrumental utility. Love has also been said to have an intrinsic value well beyond its incidental contribution to pleasure, happiness, knowledge, and such specific objectives as creating families with their own distinctive values. Some philosophers, departing from Aristotle's usage, are pluralistic. They are willing to attribute what they call ultimate value to all of the above candidates or to some subset of them. But if any of the other views are right, then there are some valuable things that are worthy of valuing for some reasons other than their causal capacities to produce relatively immediate valuable effects, since those effects add nothing to their total value. If there are ultimate values, then there are things that are valuable in themselves, as we say, and not totally for, or not at all for, effects of any kind that they characteristically produce. And that is precisely what it means to be intrinsically valuable.

We come now to a fundamental question about our understanding of the concept of intrinsic value. In those cases in which an object's intrinsic value can be correlated with the value to a beholder of states of mind reliably produced in himself by that object, do we explain the object's value by reference to the states of mind it produces or do we explain the states of mind by reference to the independently grounded value? For example, suppose that we find the sight of Notre Dame predictably thrilling or its soaring interior awesome and inspirational. Do we thrill because of the value we apprehend (that value in turn derived from some features independent of our thrilled state) or do we value the cathedral, at least in part, because it reliably produces a thrilled state of mind in us? Could the value of the cathedral itself simply consist in the state of mind it characteristically produces in a large number of people or do those people experience their aesthetic/religious emotion in response to the appreciated architectural value of the cathedral? If the value either consists in or is derived from the thrilled state of mind of "consumers," then it is logically on the same footing, say, as a bottle of good wine, whose value for some consists in its causal capacity to make people "high," relaxed, or euphoric. In the example of the wine, others may value it on other grounds, for example, its flavor, body, aroma, and so on, but these too are effects produced in the drinker by the wine. In either case, therefore, the wine is valued by a large number of drinkers because of the effects it has on them.

But must all intrinsic values be that way? I think not. Consider examples of another type. Suppose one of our giant radio telescopes picks up signals of a patterned kind suggesting an attempt to communicate on the part of some distant intelligent beings. Cryptologists, after working for years on the project, finally succeed in deciphering it, and sure enough it is a kind of message. We send back immediately a response in the alien language, and then sit back to await a reply in 50,000 more years. Almost anyone would be excited by this sequence of events, but the excitement would be a consequence of our appreciation of the importance of the discovery that we are not alone in the universe. It would not be the case that the appreciation of this point was simply a response to its capacity to cause us excitement. In short, we value the message because of its cosmic implications; we do not value it simply as another reliable means of "getting high," that is, of producing exciting mental states. Indeed, it is only because of those implications, as we understand them, that we can be excited.

Now, even though I have completed only the lightest sketch of the concept of value, we are in a better position to return to the main question. Are there valuable things that are valuable for some reason other than, or in addition to, the fact that they are beneficial? In particular, are some of these valuable objects and pursuits extremely valuable in the judgments of at least some persons, that is, are they deemed worthy of that kind of valuing we call cherishing, treasuring, or venerating? The only way of proceeding at this point is to search for examples in our common judgments of objects or undertakings deemed worthy of cherishing for reasons other than their production of benefits. We have already considered some likely candidates. A cosmic message whose sequel can be expected in 50,000 years can hardly be of any direct benefit to anyone now, despite its instructive and understandably exciting character. Yet surely such a message would be a wonderfully good thing in its own right even in the absence of direct benefit. The discovery of some tenth-century Arabic treatises on logic might be another example, a collection of overriding value, fit to be treasured by a small and narrowly specialized group of scholars. Those scholars can no doubt themselves be said to benefit, but their gain can hardly be the full explanation of why the ancient documents are objectively worthy of being cherished. A great amount of value remains to be accounted for even after we subtract the part that consists of benefits to specialized scholars.

Nor are all nonbeneficially valuable things treasured because they are surviving antiquities. Some are so new and so innovative that they neither interest, inspire, nor benefit anyone but their creators and a small circle of collaborators. Benefit then comes with time as belated understanding grows, until finally a later generation contains many who benefit by the existence of the formerly esoteric materials. But the original creators hardly have their remote descendants primarily in mind when they first cherish their own creations. Each historian of art will cite her favorite example of this process, the most striking examples perhaps being from the history of music.

Philosophers who reject examples of the sort I have just provided usually do so, not because they deny that the objects in the examples are worth valuing, much less worth cherishing. Rather, their denials are based on their judgment that these valuable objects and undertakings are really beneficial. They are able to hold their ground in this way, however, only because they employ an inflated sense of "benefiting." Typically, the objects and events we think of as beneficial are those that advance the interests of a beneficiary. But discovery of an intragalactic message with the promise of a once-in-50,000-years turnaround time does not obviously advance the interests of anyone we can now name.

Financial interests are the conceptual paradigm, I believe, for all talk of gain and loss, benefit and harm, though of course people manifestly have interests other than their financial ones. The problem with talk of nonfinancial interest is that it gets fuzzy about the edges, since it sometimes tries to apply the exactitude of the accountant's ledger to subject matter that is too fluid to fit it. Suppose a number theorist discovers a monumental proof of a complicated theorem about prime numbers that wins the admiration of most specialists in that abstract and narrow branch of mathematics. The theorist himself might be an indirect beneficiary of his own work, if by boosting his reputation it leads to a higher salary or a better job. But we would hardly describe his work as benefiting humanity, benefiting his countrymen, or even as benefiting his publishers, if any, since it is too esoteric to promise profit.

Why then would anyone want to say that the theorem proof, or the cosmic message, or the endangered species (say, Siberian tigers), or the atonal sonata, though clearly things of great value, are also beneficial things, objects that advance the interests of specific beneficiaries? (We must remember, of course, that a valuable object can have some benefit for someone or other, but have an overall value that cannot be accounted for by those benefits alone.) The reason people insist that value must be a function of benefit, and that the counterexamples proffered above are themselves subtly beneficial projects, is that they count among the benefits of a valuable object or undertaking the derivatively valuable states of mind they directly produce, particularly want satisfaction, gratification, and excitement. The cosmic message is exciting, gratifying, stimulating to the imagination, and therein lies its benefit. So the argument goes. Preserving the few remaining Siberian tigers has little direct benefit for people, since we believe that the loss of so few animals would not have an appreciable impact on the environment as a whole, and thus little consequence for human interests, but it would make most of us happy to think of these noble beasts remaining in existence, and the zoologists and environmentalists who work hard for this result will be especially gratified by the success of their labors. The argument concludes that these effects—mental states such as want satisfaction, self-satisfaction, and pride—are beneficial to those who experience them, and thus there is a necessary link between value and benefit, after all.

These arguments, I submit, will not withstand careful scrutiny. What is it in these examples that makes the original desire or ambition a reasonable one? What makes self-satisfaction, for example, natural, fitting, and proper? Why is the successful result in these examples best described as an achievement? The answers to these questions about the grounds of the resultant mental states must refer to something beyond the mental states themselves to something the mental states are about. We must already sense that the object or pursuit is beneficial (or valuable in some other way) if we are to experience any satisfaction at its production or occurrence. So the reason it produces satisfaction is that it is deemed beneficial or otherwise valuable.

I propose therefore that we distinguish beneficial achievements from other achievements in the following way. A benefit to someone is something that advances her interests in such areas as wealth, security, power, or health. It is, as we say, something "good for her," whatever her conscious beliefs about it and emotional responses to it may be. To a person who has lost confidence in herself, for example, her production of a valuable thing of a kind not normally thought of as beneficial may nonetheless be beneficial in her case by helping to restore her confidence. Her pride and self-satisfaction may be good therapy for her and therefore beneficial, even though production of the same kind of thing by a self-confident person may produce a self-satisfaction for which he has no therapeutic need. In that case, his achievement will have a value in itself equal to the value of the self-doubting person's creation, though his benefits no one, and hers benefits herself.

Consumers and creators of the arts, of all people, should need no argument to convince them that aesthetic value, at least, is not reducible to its beneficial properties. A painting might have a market value of $1 million, and therefore be very beneficial to its owner, who stands to gain enormously from its resale. But that beneficial capacity can hardly be the whole of its value, else it would be impossible to explain how it could have any monetary value at all. Surely, it is because some people judge it to be good as art that it can also be a good investment, that is, beneficial to its owner. A plain flat surface constructed from unfinished pine wood resting on a pile of bricks at each of its four corners can be a benefit to its owner in that it is a sturdy support for dishes or papers and functions well as a kitchen table or desk. An eighteenth-century delicately carved and decorated classic of craftsmanship may serve equally beneficially as a kitchen table, but that does not explain how its total value, all things considered, is so much greater. Obviously, it is valuable for some reason other than (or additional to) its beneficial utility. It is a cheat, I think, to identify that additional value as the pleasure in the minds of those who admire it, and then treat that pleasure as a benefit of the same order as its capacity to support papers and dishes.

Intrinsic versus Inherent Value

It may be useful at this point to complete our rough sketch of a theory of value by discussing briefly what might be called inherent (as opposed to intrinsic) value. While I think there are many things that are intrinsically valuable, although perhaps only a few kinds of such things, I do not think there are any inherently valuable things, in the sense I shall give that term, at all. What I mean by inherently valuable is similar to what G. E. Moore meant by intrinsically valuable, when he wrote that an intrinsically valuable thing is one that would be good even if it existed quite alone. His model here seems to be the theory of primary and secondary qualities of physical objects, as expounded by Locke and earlier by Galileo. Primary qualities are inherently part of the object itself—solidity, extension in space, figure, motion or rest, and number. An object's mass, in the sense of Newtonian physics, was thought to be a primary quality, that is, a quality an object would continue to possess even if there were no perceiving beings in the world. Secondary qualities, on the other hand, such as color, taste, smell, sound, and temperature, exist only when actually sensed, and then "only in the mind" of the one who senses them. What we identify as the smell of an object, for example, is the effect its vibrating molecules have on our olfactory nerves. A being without an olfactory nerve could not be affected in the appropriate way, and thus could never sense an odor, an aroma, or a stench. A world without properly equipped sniffers, then, would contain no smells. Would garbage then lose its stench if all perceiving animals disappeared? No, the garbage would continue to smell as it does, but only in a hypothetical sense. The statement that decaying meat has a rancid smell, for example, can only mean that, if any perceivers—animals equipped with olfactory nerves—are in the vicinity, they will have a rancid smell experience, and that hypothetical statement would remain true even if all perceiving animals were to cease to exist.

Inherent value is not like that, according to Moore. When Moore ascribes to an object what I call "inherent value," he will not settle for the hypothetical rendering of what he means. He explicitly denies that the inherent value of a thing is its worthiness to be valued by people in a position to value it, if there are such persons. The object's value inheres in it whether or not there are persons to value it, and it inheres in the object in a sense stronger than that of a causal capacity to produce effects on valuers, because those effects are already thought to be present in the valuable object itself. That is like saying that the vibrating molecules that can produce odors in the experience of observers with olfactory nerves are themselves inherently smelly, quite apart from their capacity to produce smelly sensations in perceiving beings.

Sidgwick found such talk about values incoherent, an opinion I am happy, one hundred years later, to join. But G. E. Moore expresses his own theory in the form of a response to Sidgwick in a once-famous passage. Moore begins by quoting Sidgwick:

> "No one," says Professor Sidgwick, "would consider it rational to aim at the production of beauty in external nature, apart from any possible contemplation of it by human beings." Well, I may say at once, that I for one, do consider this rational; and let us see if I cannot get any one to agree with me. . . . Let us imagine one world exceedingly beautiful. Imagine it as beautiful as you can; put into it whatever on this earth you most admire—mountains, rivers, the sea, trees and sunsets, stars and moon. Imagine these all combined in the most exquisite proportions, so that no one jars against another, but each contributes to increase the beauty of the whole. Then imagine the ugliest world you can possibly conceive. Imagine it simply one heap of filth, containing everything that is most disgusting to us, for whatever reason, and the whole, as far as may be, without one redeeming feature. Such a pair of worlds we are entitled to compare: they fall within Professor Sidgwick's meaning, and the comparison is highly relevant to it. The only thing we are not entitled to imagine is that any human being ever has [lived], or ever by any possibility can live in either, can ever see and enjoy the beauty of the one or hate the foulness of the other. Well even so, imagining them quite apart from any possible contemplation by human beings; still is it irrational to hold that it is better that the beautiful world should exist, than the one which is ugly? Would it not be well in any case to do what we could to produce it rather than the other? Certainly I cannot help thinking that it would.[10]

Moore cannot help holding his opinion, as he says, perhaps because he cannot help putting himself into the picture he imagines. He invites us to picture his two worlds not as they are in themselves unwitnessed by any human beings, not even ourselves. What we then succeed in imagining, of course, is a world observed by our own human, all too human, selves, quite contrary to the terms of the experiment.

Beauty and ugliness, I would prefer to say, are both in the eye of the beholder in roughly the same way that a smell must always be in the nostrils of the one who senses it. If there are no beholders, there may still be beautiful and ugly things, in the sense that if there were qualified observers of the proper (that is, human) sort, in a position to behold the objects being judged, then those beholders would be affected in a certain way, and their responses to that predictable effect on their experience might be objectively appropriate. That hypothetical proposition, of course, can be true even if there are no such beholders. But Moore wishes it to be true of his unobserved worlds that they are beautiful and ugly in some categorical sense, just as if he were to maintain that unsniffed garbage is categorically smelly in itself—a claim I find impossible to understand.

My use of the phrase "eye of the beholder" may bring to mind the traditional formulation of a kind of value subjectivism, that "beauty is altogether in the eye of the beholder."[11] This saying has often expressed the view that one person's judgment that x is beautiful can be neither more nor less rational than another person's judgment that x is not beautiful. I do not hold that subjectivist theory, nor do I think it follows from a denial that beauty is a kind of primary quality of objects, like physical mass. To say that an object has any of the types of intrinsic value (including, presumably, beauty), on my view, is to say that in virtue of its own characteristics, it is worthy of being valued by some class of persons (possessors, beholders, creators, and so on). The key term, I repeat, is "worthy." That is the notion about which some of us are absolutists, some relativists, some objectivists, some subjectivists, some rationalists, some sentimentalists. I hold that the value of a thing is not a property of that thing independent of its effect on persons, but that claim does not commit me to the subjectivist view that disagreements over worthiness cannot be settled rationally, or that there can be no reasons supporting the claim that one of two opposed judgments of worthiness is correct, the other incorrect. But my present point is not that value subjectivism is itself false, but rather that it does not follow from a rejection of the concept of inherent value.

The error in the "primary quality" theory can be expressed as follows: There are many examples of states of mind produced by a causal mechanism consisting of two necessary elements, one acting on the other. Intoxication, for example, may be produced by an intoxicating beverage acting on the brain (to which it has been transmitted by the circulating blood) of a human being or other biologically suitable animal. Without the intoxicating beverage, there could be no intoxication. Without the appropriately receptive sort of nervous system, there could be no intoxication. Both are necessary. Similarly, without molecular agitations of a certain kind and an appropriate receptive olfactory nerve, there could be no rancid smell, and without some kind of capacity to affect human beings as well as some human beings to be affected, there could be no value. Sometimes one part of such mechanisms (the human receptor) is missing, but it remains true that the other part (with the causal capacity to affect the receptor) can still be said meaningfully to have value, but only in the sense that were the human receptor present, then she would be affected in a certain way. The mistake occurs when one infers from the presence of the affecting mechanisms that the usual effect (intoxication, aroma, value) is actually there anyway even in the absence of an intoxicated (or intoxicatable) animal. As Santayana put it in discussing a closely related point, it would be to insist that "whiskey is . . . intoxicating in itself without reference to any animal; that it is pervaded, as it were, by an inherent intoxication, and stands dead drunk in its bottle!"[12]

For our present purposes, it is not so important to argue that what I call inherent value is a conceptual muddle as it is to show that the thesis that there are inherently valuable things, which I reject, does not follow from the thesis that there are intrinsically valuable things, which I accept. Most writers use the words "intrinsic" and "inherent" interchangeably so that confusing the two distinct concepts is a mistake as natural as it is frequent. What I have been calling "intrinsic value" is simply a thing's being worthy of being valued in virtue of its own qualities, as distinct from the qualities of other things to which it can serve as an effective means or instrumentality. I have conceded that this distinction is imprecise, but there are ways of dealing with its vagueness that preserve its utility. People do value some things primarily for what they are, as opposed to, or in addition to, what they do or what can be done with them. At least some of the time, the things that are valued intrinsically are worthy of being so valued, even worthy of being highly valued in some cases, or cherished. These objects then are said, and sometimes correctly said, to have intrinsic value. But it in no way follows from these commonsense observations that intrinsically valuable things are ipso facto inherently valuable. One can rightly judge a thing worthy of appreciating or cherishing for its own qualities without interpreting those qualities as properties it would continue to possess in a categorical sense if it were all alone in the universe. Commonsense observations about how and why things are worthy of being valued do not generate this brand of metaphysical oddness.

The incoherence of inherent value has relevance for the problem of justifying subsidies for the arts out of tax funds exacted from those who are not likely beneficiaries. If the justification for this otherwise unfair practice invokes the idea of objects and pursuits that are extremely valuable at least partly for reasons other than their benefits, we can be tempted to fall into metaphysical obscurantism when we describe these precious objects. The confusion between intrinsic and inherent value once again can be the source of the trouble. Professor Nagel, after arguing that certain "treasures of human culture" have a value independent of, and superior to, the extent to which they are beneficial or actually appreciated, rushes to reassure us that he will not walk into the inherent value trap. "I am not suggesting," he writes, "that the existence of these things would be valuable even if there were no one to appreciate them. We don't have to conclude, for example, that if there were a nuclear war and human life were wiped out on earth, but New York hadn't been hit directly, it would still be a good thing that the paintings were hanging in the Metropolitan."[13] I agree with Nagel about this, though I should add that a hypothetical value judgment about the paintings would remain true even in the absence of human beings, namely, that the paintings in the permanently deserted museum are still things of great value in the sense that if, contrary to fact, there were human beings about, then the paintings would be worthy of being valued (appreciated, cherished) by those beings, and that is true for reasons not restricted to the actual benefits the paintings would produce. If it is exclusively benefits we want in the aftermath of a nuclear holocaust, we should probably be better off eating the wax paintings than appreciating or cherishing them.

Appraising Nonbeneficial Value

A final point remains to be made about nonbeneficial values. How are we to tell when an object or a project has such a value, especially when we are dealing with esoterica like research into number theory or electronic music? I have heard mathematicians praise proofs of theorems in terms that musicians would reserve for Bach or Mozart. I have no doubt, on their authority, that some of the highest flights of the human intellect have been made by mathematical theorists in areas that yield no particular benefits for humanity as a whole. I am sure that the more talented members of this group deserve support for projects that cannot be funded otherwise. But do I think that the project of using expensive giant computers to calculate the digits of pi up to the ten-billionth, say, so that number theorists might search for patterns of digit distribution in this endless number, is deserving of government support? Well, I am not a mathematician, so how should I know? If we are impressed enough by the nonbenefical values produced generally by this kind of research to reserve some tax funds for their support, let the mathematicians themselves judge the worthiness of their colleagues' proposals. ("Peer review," I believe, is the appropriate phrase.)

There are risks in this procedure. An occasional selection committee, reserving a small proportion of a small budget for experimental innovation,[14] a sensible practice in all fields, might budget tiny sums to underwrite an art museum exhibit of experimental works like that initially approved in 1992 by the NEA for $10,000 at the MIT Museum and then vetoed by the director of the NEA. According to a newspaper report, "The M.I.T. exhibit included works by four artists that portray body parts, including sexual organs, in various ways. The works include wallpaper imprinted with female and male genitalia, a glass sculpture of sperm and sculptures of disembodied breasts and buttocks."[15] This sounds to me interesting, and I would be happy to go out of my way, to some degree, to see it. (You know, if I happened to be in Boston anyway.) The "risks" to which I referred are that such playful innovation will always be vetoed by overseers protecting the public morals, who are fearful of doing otherwise on the good chance that politicians will retaliate by canceling all programs of support for the arts.[16] For all of that, however, once we have determined that an area of human activity, like art (at its best), has a value beyond its benefits, then the projects in that area most deserving of support had best be determined by committees of leaders in the field in question. That will predictably lead, occasionally, to bizarre awards in the area reserved for experimentation, but the discovery of just one authentic genius otherwise certain to have been overlooked is worth the cost of many dozens of bizarre failures.[17]

Future Business: Dealing Anew with the Resentful Taxpayer

With the consent of my commentators, I have added this brief addendum to the essay they have seen and reviewed. I find it striking, not to say a little embarrassing, that both of them, but especially Dr. Richard Manning, point out that I overlook altogether a crucial strategic question my article raises, namely (partly in Manning's words), "Why is the resentful taxpayer who objects to the state spending his tax money on benefits for others that he does not share, any more likely to accept the spending of his tax money for the production of intrinsically valuable objects that he is unable to appreciate?" (Or, one might add, if he does appreciate them, he does not appreciate them enough to be willing to pay a share of their costs.) For Manning, the question appears to be about motivation, rather than, or in addition to, justification. His question challenges us to motivate the person who does not give a damn about what we call intrinsic value.[18]

My more limited aim was to distinguish benefits, direct and indirect, from benefitless intrinsically valuable things, to defend the latter conception by showing at least that it is coherent, and to sketch a possible analysis of it. But what makes me think that benefitless values will be any more effective than appeals to invisible benefits in motivating the philistine taxpayer, or justifying to him our use of his tax money? Could he not simply reply that he agrees that opera companies, for example, at their best produce intrinsically valuable experiences, yet deny that that is a good reason to tax unwilling citizens to support them?

If I had space to pursue this matter here, I would probably begin by developing in more detail my account of what intrinsic value is. It is important to emphasize that judgments of value are judgments of the worthiness or appropriateness of certain attitudes toward the object in question, characteristically expressed in language seeming to claim objective truth. If that is correct, then it would seem odd to admit that something is objectively worthy of being valued (esteemed, treasured, cherished) and then deny that the possession of such property is any kind of reason—or a reason of significant weight—for requiring people to protect or support it. Even the egoistic philistine taxpayer, I should think, would have to admit that the possession in high degree of intrinsic value is not a gross irrelevancy, neither here nor there. Its relevance and cogency as a reason worthy even of the philistine's respect derives from the fact that the judgment of value is an appeal ultimately not to the taxpayer's actual attitudes and wants, sometimes called his "values," but rather to the worthiness and propriety of attitudes that he might not in fact share.

It would be exceedingly odd, for example, to protest taxation meant to enable purchase of a Civil War battlefield for perpetual preservation as a national monument, while eagerly conceding that the once fiercely contested fields are worthy of cherishing, treasuring, and revering. Suppose for example that one speaks as follows:

> I too cherish the battleground at Manassas. Not only that, I think that there are reasons tending to show that it is worthy of being cherished in its present condition, at least by an American. Here is a burial ground full of dead soldiers of both armies, who bled equally over it. Here are unchanged rolling hills and woods, peaceful and quiet, an unblemished vista which may always make a suitable symbol of a healed nation, yet is evocative too of human suffering, folly, and tragedy. Surely such a place is worth cherishing and more than that, preserving, in the face of the relentless march of highways and shopping malls that tend to distort our history by burying irretrievably the record of our past. I for one treasure that holy place, but even if I did not, I could agree with the judgment that this inspiring locale, for the above reasons, is worthy of being cherished (by others) in the highest degree.

The speaker concludes: "But of course that is no reason at all for actually preserving and protecting the land, and using tax funds, if necessary, for its purchase and maintenance."

On the contrary, that is a genuine reason, though certainly not a demonstrative one, and perhaps not a sufficient one. Surely, it would be to misunderstand something essential to the concept of value to deny that value has any weight at all when it is considered in the abstract, that is, when stripped of its benefits.

A fuller account of the problem of government subsidies would distinguish at least the following three classes of reasons that can be offered in support of the expenditures of government funds:

1. to benefit recipients (all people indirectly? some people directly?).
2. to create, maintain, or preserve things of high intrinsic value even when they do not create benefits.
3. to prevent harms, that is, to rescue or protect persons from such harmful or dangerous conditions as malnutrition, disease, unemployment, and criminal violence.

This chapter has been primarily concerned with limitations on the first class of reasons listed above. I have been discussing the challenge of the egoistic taxpayer who insists that fairness forbids taxing him to support a result that produces no benefits for him. I have done this by rejecting the ancient position that all worthwhile things produce benefits and produce them directly or indirectly for everyone. So I have shown the liberal advocate of subsidies how to avoid a trap and to do it without reliance on any obscurantist notions, such as intrinsic value is often thought to be and inherent value really is.

But suppose that the quarrel is not between the egoistic philistine taxpayer, on the one hand, and the liberal art lover, on the other, but rather between that taxpayer and people threatened with serious harm, that is, with the deprivation or loss of what they need (not just "want" or "benefit from") in order to lead a good, or even minimally decent, life. It would be quite unconvincing for the taxpayer to protest that it is unfair to tax him in order to enable others to avoid starvation, criminal violence, disease, and so on. Other things being equal then, harm prevention trumps benefit production. (Actually, "trump" may be too strong a word here, because after all, elimination of a small harm might not have priority over the production of a great benefit.) The problem for liberal art lovers, however, is that given the immense costs of fighting harm, this priority ranking of types of reasons would lead to no subsidies whatever, either for intrinsically valuable things or for benefits. The tax money would always run out before we could spend anything on such luxuries as art and mathematical number theory. This transforms our problem. In the light of the above, how can we justify subsidizing any benefitless intrinsically valuable activities at all? or, for that matter, any activities that are merely beneficial while not preventing or curing harms? Even in the world of private funding, where private donors and charitable foundations must sometimes choose between, say, donating a million-dollar painting to a worthy museum or donating the money instead to cancer research, parallel problems of choice arise. But the use of tax funds in the governmental example adds a further level of moral complication. Our political leaders struggle not only over what causes should be supported and in what order of priority. They must also choose whom to coerce into paying the costs.[19]

6

EVIL

Language Families

It is commonplace that confusion over responsibility in criminal law stems from the mutually unintelligible vocabularies we reserve for talking about these things. It is as if one group were speaking one language, that of the psychiatrists, the other were speaking the language of the moralists, and further that no one has ever bothered to translate the terms of one into the terms of the other. (Perhaps there is work here for unemployed philosophers?) Actually, the problem is even worse than I have suggested. The crucial but untranslated words seem to fall into natural groupings. In this essay, I call them "language families" and point out that there are more relevant families than we might have supposed.

In the first place, we have more than just one moral or moralistic family. At least three of these should be mentioned, although one of those is completely archaic, being a functionless survival of terms used by upper-class persons to condemn the manners and morals of the "common" people. These terms are still in our language but they are no longer reliable ways of expressing forceful denunciation. Social democracy has overtaken them, and they are now strangely pallid and toothless. My list includes the words scoundrel, rascal, knave, rogue, scamp, blackguard, ruffian, bounder, cad, base, vulgar, and vile.

A second family of moralistic terms is also uninteresting but for an opposite reason. These are words for the typical kinds of moral blameworthiness in garden-variety crimes. They are terms for the ordinary criminal, but we are also familiar with them from our everyday experience in nonlegal contexts. These are the names of the commonest ways of going wrong or being morally blameworthy. They are the terms that most moral philosophers have in mind when they think of specifically moral judgments. I have no complaint against moral philosophers for dealing with standard cases of immorality. I fault them only for failing to include in the scope of their inquiries rather more peculiar specimens too. The following is my list of the leading garden-variety moral faults: deceitful, dishonest, dishonorable, untrustworthy, evasive, mendacious, cheating, prevaricating, aggressive, quarrelsome, choleric, hotheaded, cruel, selfish, indifferent to the sufferings of others, insensitive to the interests of others, insensitive to the feelings of others, ruthless, and unscrupulous.

At this point I would add a third moralistic family, which I call the "wickedness family," despite my misgivings about the word "wickedness," which, though far from being archaic, is historically associated with the archaic class of words already discussed. At any rate, the wickedness family is especially interesting in that its characteristic terms are closely related to terms in the "triple-sick" category discussed below, so closely related, in fact, that we must be especially careful not to get them mixed up. The wickedness family contains among others the following relatively infrequently used terms: flagitious, nefarious, plain evil, sheer wickedness, depraved, a malignant and abandoned heart, mere wanton barbarity, baleful, turpitudinous, heinous, diabolical, satanic, fiendish, weird, monstrous, inhuman, ghoulish, ogre-like, and bestial. The persons to whom these extravagant words are applied may seem simply bad. They are at least that. Along the line from the "ordinary criminal" to, at the opposite end, the insane and therefore totally nonresponsible person, the wicked person in days past was closer to the ordinary criminal, fully responsible for his evil deeds and subject to moral condemnation for them. Jeffrey Dahmer, to whom most of these words apply, seems not only wicked but as sick! sick! sick! as a criminal can be. Indeed, we can cognize his behavior only by thinking of it as essentially inhuman, either superhuman—diabolical, demonic or fiendish—or else subhuman, that is, beastly or monstrous. Devils and wild animals are not sick human beings; they are healthy inhuman beings. Psychiatrists are not best described as trying to "cure" them. Rather, the attempt with these criminals is to restore them to their essential humanity, to rehumanize them. In short, both the sick and the wicked in their most extreme forms are likely to appear inhuman and almost unrecognizably so.

We leave the moralistic language families as we turn to the fourth family, which is the last refuge of the medical model: the triple-sick or severe mental illness family. This is a troublesome clan if only because many of its words seem to straddle a line connecting this family with one of its neighbors. Its relatively unambiguous members include crazy, screwy, nutty, incomprehensible (as to motives), demented, deluded, emotionally twisted, conscienceless, retarded, deranged, hallucinatory, disoriented, and psychotic.

Sick! sick! sick!ness, I suspect, is determined not by what a criminal perpetrator did to his victim but rather by what the perpetrator himself got out of it. Dahmer's most prominent crimes were first-degree murder, for which he qualified by deliberately killing a number of human beings; sexual abuse, for which he qualified by imposing sexual behavior by force on his victims; and aggravated battery, for which he qualified by imposing physical beatings on his unwilling victims. If he had murdered in order to silence a blackmailer, to inherit life insurance money, or to remove a barrier to his planned burglary at a convenience store, his motives would have seemed to almost everyone as at least minimally rational. No one would judge him, on these facts alone, to be sick! sick! sick! His goals would seem both rational and intelligible.

Which would be the more grave or serious crime, that of the real Jeffrey Dahmer, who was both evil and sick! sick! sick! or that of a hypothetical Dahmer who, let us imagine, is cold-blooded, deliberate, and rational but commits the same crimes (first-degree murder, sexual abuse, battery)? Given the recent devaluation of mental illness, and its apparent decline as a moral mitigation, I am not sure how people would vote on this question and what the moral judgment of the majority would be. Our chances for a just and coherent system of criminal penalties would be improved, I think, if we pondered the question.

Before leaving the triple-sick language family, let me register one more suspicion about its interfamiliar relations. My suspicion is that it is not perceived triple sickness that has undergone a reevaluation and loss of mitigating power. Neither is it perceived wickedness that has lost that status. Rather it is perceived *oddness* that has become more important. Mental illness often makes crazy people seem strange. The craziness is one thing, and the strangeness is another, though in many cases it is the former that produces the latter. The connection between oddness and nuttiness is so close that it is easy to mislocate them and place them in the same language family. In fact, triple sickness and oddness are in different families. And there is some reason to think that many people find oddness (or even unusualness or differences per se) harder to forgive than the mental illness that sometimes underlies it.[1]

We need a new category therefore in which to put extreme oddness. I suggest for this important word family a French family name, the bizarrerie (bizarreness) family. Some of these word-family members are bizarre, odd, oddball, queer (in its original meaning), strange, (extremely) unusual, out of the ordinary, foreign, alien, (extremely) eccentric, way out, weird, deviant, abnormal, (too) different, and unusual. Some of these words may belong on the sick! sick! sick! list too, but by and large the families are distinct.

One final family will complete the survey of vocabulary groups that might be relevant to our purposes. I refer here to the repugnance and offensiveness family. The following words are a small sample of those in the repugnance family: repugnant, offensive, sickening, nauseating, revolting, disgusting, repellent, and gruesome. Some of these terms are virtual synonyms; others are otherwise equivalent terms taken to an extreme. The extreme of bizarre, for example, is grotesque.

The Occasional Indistinguishability of
Triple Sickness and Sheer Wickedness

I will consider now some consequences of the closeness of sick! sick! sick!ness to sheer wickedness. First, what do we add, if anything, to wickedness when we qualify it as "sheer"? What, if anything, do we add to the word "evil" when we add the adjective "pure" or "plain"? Sheer wickedness, as I understand the term, is pure, unalloyed, neither more nor less than, that and nothing else, unmitigated, unqualified, absolute. Apparently, wickedness gets so mixed up with the things that produce it or follow from it, or are difficult to distinguish from it, that moralists find the sheerness vocabulary an invaluable means of sorting things out. And when we deal with wickedness, it is often sick! sick! sick!ness that needs to be disassociated from the target of our investigation, for its symptoms can be difficult to classify, resembling, as they often do, the illness symptoms that look so much like the real thing.

Plain evil is unmixed, pure, something familiar, even "old-fashioned." Samples include beatings inflicted for no reason, wanton barbarity, utter gratuitousness, and cruelty for no purpose or reward beyond itself.[2] Purely evil killers, when questioned about the conscious objectives of their wantonness, are likely to reply that it is great fun to cause another person pain, to see his last twitchings and death agonies, or similar horrifying statements. This tells us that his cruel actions were not means to any other end. They were in that sense "plain" and "pure." On the other hand, he might answer our questions by saying that he does not think about things like that; rather, he just felt like killing his victim and he did. Insofar as we disconnect the crime from any clear goal that might contribute to our understanding of his motivation, his evil act is "pure" or "sheer," the characteristic of evil that troubles us most. Pure evil troubles us so much, I suspect, first because it is the most puzzling kind of human wrongdoing, and second because it comes out of the blue without apparent rhyme or reason and thus is more threatening to us. I doubt, however, that the *purity* of pure evil reflects on the evil person himself, that he is more blameworthy than the unscrupulous or ruthless killer who takes another's life as a means to one of his own goals, or even the cold-blooded, businesslike criminal who kills on contract. All three of these types are wicked, but only the first is *sheerly* wicked. Moreover, one wicked act can be more sheer than another without being more wicked.

Pure wickedness often resembles triple sickness in that they both defy reason and puzzle the investigating intellect as much as they offend moral judgment. Since triple sickness and sheer evil are often nearly indistinguishable, we are not surprised to find that some theorists reduce sick! sick! sick!ness to sheer wickedness, and others travel in the opposite direction, reducing sheer wickedness to triple sickness. Until recently, it has been triple sickness replacing sheer wickedness more often than the other way around. One example of this is the thermostat analogy. The idea of mental illness came into promi-

nence at first in large part because of the difficulty both professionals and
laypeople had in coping with "sheer evil." Criminal hearings in particular
seemed to require that various states of mind be put in a ranking order of
moral blameworthiness so that one evil act could be more purely evil than
another without being more evil, on balance. There came a time when the
whole upper part of certain scales of moral evil threatened to disappear, so
that what used to be the "wicked" part of the scale was called "mental illness," and what used to be middling blameworthiness or medium immorality
is now as close as one could come to perfect wickedness before a kind of
"conceptual thermostat" turned evil off and something else (triple sickness)
on. Those criminals who are likely to be thought of as sheerly wicked, then,
may actually be hard to distinguish from psychotic or legally insane people.
The scales of wickedness and mental illness may seem, even in the absence
of a conceptual thermostat, to circle back and culminate at the same place,
and although the moral and the medical diagnoses are supposed to be dia-
metrically opposed—the more wicked, the *more* responsible and blameworthy,
and the more sick the less responsible and the *less* blameworthy—we find that
extremely wicked persons tend to resemble the most bizarre and crazy ones.
The more bizarre, unrewarding, and incomprehensible the crime, the more
sick it seems to ordinary people on its face.

While people are understandably disturbed by the concept of pure evil,
they make a mistake in replacing it with concepts of sickness and cure. As
we have seen, the historical model for understanding the wickedness family
of terms is not the sick human being, but rather the smoothly and rationally
functioning nonhuman being, the subhuman animal (ghoul, ogre, beast,
monster) or the superhuman (demon, devil, fiend). The sheerly wicked are
understood to be entirely different from merely human beings, even from
gravely ill, depraved human beings. They have little choice but to be wicked.
It is "in their natures to be evil," they often say. And there is little reluctance
in the way they pursue what is "in their nature." However else the Devil
(Satan) is represented in Western art and literature, he is essentially a being
who enjoys his work. When the Devil's tortures cause the expected pain in
his victims, the Devil is immensely pleased and roars out his diabolical laugh-
ter at full volume. When the Devil's lies seduce another sinner, he may voice
a diabolical chuckle. He is not only dutiful and industrious, he is basically
happy and fulfilled. His relation to God, against whose authority he leads a
rebellion, equally establishes his bonds to humans, all of whom are a mixture
of godly and beastly elements. Part of the Devil's image, according to the
artists who have tried to give visible shape to literary descriptions of Satan
(the Evil One, the Deceiver, the Prince of Darkness), is a humanlike visage,
alternatingly ugly and beguiling by human standards, with menacing expressions, like sneers and scowls. But traditional graphic artists have had
trouble keeping subhuman, animal parts out of their portraits of the superhuman fallen angel. Frequently his animal characteristics are unhidden:

fangs, horns, claws, tail, hoofs. In literature, the Devil is described as howling, snickering, and growling. Perhaps, apart from that, we can imagine that the Devil's evil work is much like that of Jeffrey Dahmer, who, while "bloody in tooth and claw" from defective table manners, punctuates his remarks with growls and grunts. Even lesser demons enjoy their work. Their victims' sufferings amuse them. They too have a hearty laugh with a touch of the monstrous in it.

The Identity of Extreme Opposites: A Paradox?

Generally speaking, there are two ways in which triple sickness and pure wickedness can be assimilated. We can follow the scale of triple sickness until it runs out and turns into wickedness or, just the opposite, we can follow the scale of wickedness until, at its extreme point or near it, it turns into triple sickness. Either sickness absorbs wickedness or wickedness absorbs sickness, and in either case the tendency is for the two concepts to fuse, to our great puzzlement. We discussed earlier the significance of downplaying triple sickness. In the previous section, we emphasized the opposite tendency, that of turning wickedness into triple sickness as the conceptual thermostat kicks in.

In the nineteenth century, it was common for psychiatric and criminal law theorists to attempt to merge their disciplines by speaking of moral flaws as themselves forms of psychological impairment and to do this by blending parts of the moral and therapeutic vocabularies. The moral realm was then still respected, and something like old-fashioned moral judgments could still be made, but the moral realm was treated as a species of the mental. So we find word combinations like "moral insanity," "moral imbecility," "morally diseased," and the like. Such hybrid phrases designated forms of "mental illness," as it came to be called. I do not know whether motives for adopting that invented terminology were clear to anyone, but a century and a half later it surely seems as if these ways of talking were early attempts to have one's cake and eat it too, that they were used to treat "moral imbeciles" as mentally ill and morally blameworthy at the same time.

Similarly, criminals suffering *defects* (as opposed to diseases) of the mind were thought to be incapable of knowing the difference between right and wrong and incapable of understanding and fully appreciating the truth of some quite obviously true moral judgments. In a word, they were thought to be *stupid* when it comes to moral judgment. That is what a "morally diseased" person or a "moral imbecile" is.

I do not mean to suggest that it is impossible for some of one's behavioral or emotional dispositions to be blamable morally and at the same time symptomatic of mental illness. It may even be the case that the criteria for some particular "syndrome" and some complex moral failing coincide exactly, so that the same litmus test applies to both. Indeed, the leading checklist for psychopathy, now called "antisocial personality disorder," proposes to be a set of criteria for identifying people who have that psychiatric personality disorder. But the criteria that specify moral flaws read in some ways like an annotated Ten Commandments. A psychopath, one might almost conclude, is simply a person who habitually, from whatever original motive, violates basic moral requirements and is nothing more complex than that. But even if we want to leave this simple possibility open, we should not want to arrive in this fashion at definitions with moral and psychiatric criteria all intertwined.

Some ways of fusing the concepts of mental illness (particularly triple sickness) and wickedness (especially sheer wickedness) do breed paradox. Suppose that we rank character traits, including those that are virtuous and those that are vicious, on a progressive scale. As persons line up to be assigned their places in the rankings, they are judged steadily worse as they are linked to steadily more blameworthy traits. So, for example, a murderer is ranked worse than a rapist, a rapist worse than a batterer, a batterer worse than a minor con man, a cold-blooded harmer of others worse than a passionate harmer, a deliberate harmer worse than an impulsive harmer, a knowing harm causer worse than a reckless one, a reckless killer worse than a negligent one, and so on until every degree of blameworthiness is represented at its proper place in the rankings. As a person descends the scale to each ranking position, he gets worse and worse, that is, he qualifies as more and more blameworthy until he reaches some maximum point at which he is as evil as he can be, and yet from that point, if he should get one degree worse still, he will not be evil at all, but rather something in stark contrast to evil, namely, sick.

A Word of Caution

In the sense that I give the term, "moral" is a word used primarily to classify subject matters. Consider the following: There are terms for concepts and terms for judgments. Some concepts are *moral* concepts; some are *nonmoral* concepts. The concept of a home run is a baseball concept, not a moral concept. Some nonmoral concepts (e.g., gravity) are scientific; others (e.g., melody) are aesthetic; others (e.g., existence) are philosophical. Some judgments ("She is schizophrenic") are psychiatric; some are musical; some biological. In this essay, for the most part, when I use the word "moral," I intend to contrast it with any or all nonmoral judgments. I do not intend to contrast it with "immoral." If I meant by "moral" simply "not immoral," then I would be asserting something to be to someone's credit. After all, it is good to be moral and bad to be immoral. But in this essay most of my uses of "moral" are entirely neutral, such as "When I say that Jones is brave and generous, I am making a moral judgment about him." *That* use of "moral" (as opposed to "musical," "biological," "psychiatric," and so on) judgment gives neither credit nor blame to anyone. What I am doing when I speak in that neutral way is to classify types of judgment and give a particular judgment a place of its own in the classification.

Words Defined in Terms of the Attitudes
Appropriately Held toward Their Referents

Many highly derogatory judgments, including various moral ones, fall into this class. These definitions do not merely permit reference to attitudes. They actually require such references. To say of a person that she is sheerly evil is to say that she is, in virtue of her conduct or character, a proper object of certain distinctive, unfavorable attitudes to an extreme degree. These attitudes include, in one combination or another, elements of righteous anger and vehement ill will; elements of dread, horror, and awe; and elements of un-qualified abhorrence, unreserved loathing, utter detestation, the soil of re-vulsion that leads one to shrink from its object with uncontrolled shuddering. This is purple prose, I admit. But how else can we react to Jeffrey Dahmer?

Wickedness or Sickness?

This section is about serial killers, people who kill more than one person, but only one at a time. Some of these criminals are prepared to kill whenever doing so will help promote their own interest, such as the cover-up of an earlier crime by eliminating a possible witness. Others kill only for the sake of killing. For them, murder is a way of life, and they kill frequently simply because they enjoy it.

In recent years, there have been a number of well-publicized serial killers. The name that first comes to mind is that of Jeffrey Dahmer, whose atrocities, I presume, are well known to you and need not be dwelled upon, except perhaps to mention that they included multiple dismemberment, torture, rape, cannibalism, and even necrophilic mistreatment of corpses. Almost everyone would acknowledge that these amusements of this polite, pleasant-looking young man from Milwaukee were "sick! sick! sick!" (At least three reiterations are needed to adequately convey the speaker's disgust.)

It is easy to make a mistake at this point. We must not assume, without evidence, that the more bizarre desires are necessarily the more powerful ones, that a sick! sick! sick! (or triple-sick) appetite must be at least near compulsive strength, that a pedophile's sex drive must be stronger than that of a person who prefers adult partners, that Dahmer's crimes were the prod-uct of an immensely powerful, intensely lustful appetite, whereas a murderer who kills for a more standard motive (money, other gain, revenge, lust, jeal-ousy, or ideological zeal) must act from a lesser, and hence more resistible, passion.

The pattern of events from this point on is familiar. A suspected serial murderer is arrested, and further investigation reveals that he is a killer of sensational barbarity and wildly bizarre living habits. Soon after the story breaks, the great debate about him begins. One side refers to the killer as "mentally sick" and in need of therapy. The other side refers to him as "sheerly wicked" or "plain evil" and demands that severe punishment be inflicted on him as soon as he is proven guilty. These are not mere quibbles. How we come to categorize him determines in large degree how we come to treat him and others like him, and putting him in the right category, essentially a philosophical task, is no easy matter.

A number of preliminary points should be made. First, we should distinguish between medical and nonmedical conceptions of sickness. It is one thing to use the word "sick" to give vent to one's disgust and quite another thing to use that word to make a medical diagnosis. Indeed, in the sense that I am describing, there is nothing "medical" in its use at all. In that respect, the current sense of the word sick differs from older, more established senses. Imagine a hospital nurse cautioning a noisy child visitor to be quiet on the ground that an elderly patient needs her rest. "She is a sick woman," the nurse might say, using the word sick in the older, customary way. Surely, that is not to say that the patient, her wants, or her actions are sick! sick! sick!

Triple Sickness

Every decade seems to produce its own candidates for the century's most revolting crime. In the 1920s, the most shocking felony was committed by Albert Fish, "a mild-mannered man approaching sixty and father of six children," who in 1928 "kidnapped, choked to death, and for nine days ate parts of Grace Budd, a girl of ten."[3] He had molested, over the years, at least a hundred children and murdered in similar ways at least fifteen of them. Attempting to atone for his sins and free himself of obsessive guilt feelings, he had eaten his own excrement; he had inserted cotton soaked with alcohol up his rectum, and then set fire to it; and he inserted needles beneath his fingernails, causing intense pain.

In the 1980s and 1990s, this country produced a number of murderers whose crimes were as bizarre as those of Albert Fish—and as sickening. Most serial killers were thought at the times of their best-known atrocities to be triple sick. Since this section is about mental illness and some of its implications, I should say a preliminary word also about "madness," a word of the poets, and "insanity," a word of the lawyers, both of which denote only a special form of mental illness, a kind of going berserk.

Madness and Insanity

A madman is a person whose behavior is often, but not always, downright crazy, and that introduces another distinction of some importance into our discussion, that between mental sickness, or triple sickness, and the more cognitively based "craziness," which may or may not go with it. Dahmer and the notorious rapist-murderer of the 1980s, Ted Bundy, were certainly sick— triple sick—but it is unlikely that many people would describe the criminal activities of Ted Kaczynski (the Unabomber) or John Hinkley as triple sick. That would be a bit extravagant. Kaczynski and Hinkley were crazy in the sense of acting irrationally by employing means obviously ill-adapted to their ends. It is prototypically crazy to court a movie star with letters sent from a distance and then to try to impress that Hollywood actress (Jodie Foster) with one's historical importance and the genuineness of one's love for her, as John Hinkley did in 1980, by shooting the president of the United States. That strategy has not generally been effective as a means of winning a lady's hand in the District of Columbia. And Kaczynski's plan to set back technology worldwide by a series of individually addressed mail bombs to various scientists was no less irrational.

If the facts are as alleged, then Ted Kaczynski and John Hinkley acted irrationally in concocting their bizarre crimes, but apart from reference to these gross mistakes in reasoning, I would be disinclined to call their behavior "sick." Behavior can be crazy without being particularly sick. They acted irrationally in making their murder attempts. An ordinary person, I suspect, would not call their actions sick! sick! sick! Rather, they might say that it was a plain crazy thing to do, wild and nutty, demented and psychotic, but not sick! sick! sick!

The Trilateral Functions of Triple Sickness

The best way to interpret the triple-sick language is to point out its simple although trilateral ambiguity. When a person makes a triple-sickness judgment, she will be doing at least one of the following three things. First, she may be describing her own subjective feelings and propensities. The use of the reiterated idiom claims objectivity for her initial remark. The first meaning can be rendered as follows: "When I look at or think about these things, they make me sick." So the primary focus of the expression may be on the speaker herself. She may mean by saying "sick! sick! sick!" the following: "When I look at or think about these things, they make me sick, and in fact they are likely to make any reasonable person of normal sensitivity, at the very least, squeamish." The speaker's reference to a "reasonable person" is a second use of the reiterated idiom, namely, to claim objectivity for her initial remark by appealing to any reasonable person, actual or hypothetical. So, clearly, she is not merely describing her own subjective impressions.

The second meaning, then, adds to the first: "Moreover, they are likely to make any reasonable person of normal sensitivity, at the very least, squeamish." In the first use, the speaker might be simply voicing her own repugnance or disgust at another person's behavior and its visible consequences.

But she could almost do that much by uttering "ugh!" or "yuk!" The second use makes the much stronger claim, that her reactions would be those of any reasonable person, which is just another way of saying that disgust is among the emotions that can be meaningfully called "reasonable" or "unreasonable"; and of course, in this case, that (negative) emotion, disgust, is said to be reasonable. In this example, that would also be the intended message of the speaker. Even though feelings are often contrasted with reason, it makes perfectly good sense to say (even to say falsely) that a given feeling in a given context is quite reasonable. It is reasonable in appropriate circumstances to feel gratitude, depression, resentment, affection, and, yes, disgust.

The assessable disgust in some contexts is a reasonable reaction to conduct such as that of the more notorious serial killers. In the first use of the triple-sick language, the focus is all on the speaker and her own states of mind. In the second use, the focus is on the "reasonable person of ordinary sensitivity," a hypothetical construct long familiar to students of the common law. The third emphasis is on the person being talked about. Imagine that A is a conspicuous sufferer from mental illness. B witnesses A's behavior and responds by addressing a triple-sick judgment about A to C, a third party. B's remark also focuses on the "reasonable person," a kind of hypothetical judge. The third emphasis or focus of the triple-sick judgment is simply the person that the judgment is about, in this case, the person named A, but in general it refers to the actions of still other people. The disgusted person who makes the judgment in most cases would find her message distorted if it were merely taken to be an introspective account of her own sensations without even minimal cognitive content. If we take away belief, truth or error, and objectivity from a judgment of disgust, we are left with something close to simple nausea, like that produced by indigestion.

Finally, there is the most obvious and straightforward of the uses of triple-sick judgments. In this use, the judgment is about the person addressed or identified by the speaker. It is not an introspective description of the speaker's own state of mind, and neither is it an application of a standard of rationality to which all reasonable persons aspire. The speaker, B, is talking about A, the person she may actually accuse of being triple-sick, and what she may be saying is that A frequently exhibits the characteristics that lead to impairment and malfunction and are commonly listed as symptoms of one or another mental disorder, such as excessive or deficient emotion, craziness, depression, paranoia, and so on. After A calms down, B might find it appropriate to say to him something like this: "Man, you are sick."

Mental Illness as Moral Mitigation

The typical outbursts of genuine madmen (persons who are both crazy and unstable) would have led the psychiatrists of an earlier generation to classify them as psychotic, and a trial lawyer would have had little difficulty in persuading juries that the mad defendants on trial were legally insane. In the Anglo-American criminal law, insanity has always been a complete exculpation. Insane people can be stored forcibly in a hospital, but they are incapable of the legal guilt required for incarceration in a prison. I shall not be saying much about insane people in this essay. Instead, I shall focus on convicted criminals, mostly murderers, who have some degree of mental illness, enough for us to call them "disturbed" but not enough to render them totally nonresponsible "because of insanity." Dahmer also fell into this category, but his mental illness makes it extremely difficult for him to be constantly in conformity with the law in question. It seems no more than what is required by good sense and fairness to assign *degrees* of responsibility in proportion to the degrees of difficulty a given sort of person in a given kind of circumstances would have avoiding infractions of law. Why indeed does it matter that law abidingness is not impossible if, for persons of the defendant's type, it is extremely difficult, just short of an impossibility?

The extreme difficulty need not lead to the defendant's total exculpation, but only to less severe punishment. Anyway, in recent times it has become increasingly difficult to convince impartial observers (for example, jurors) that a person (for example, a criminal defendant) has violently attacked another person despite his own efforts to restrain himself, as if his choice had no effect on his action.

The "diminished capacity" system at least avoids the unrealistic assumption that all mentally disturbed persons are either wholly unaffected by their mental illness or else they are "insane," that is, impaired to such a degree that they are unable to do what is required, and obedience is simply impossible. It is more realistic, it seems to me, to think of the capacity to obey as a matter of degree. People find some things easy to do or to omit doing. Other things are harder for some persons than for others.

One reason why the diminished capacity test has not caught on in the United States is that Americans have looked in a variety of places for sources of difficulty and have not restricted their attention to internal barriers to law abidingness, such as mental illness, but have also considered "difficulty factors," such as parental abuse, severe poverty, and slum environments. This expansion of the difficulty test threatened, for a time, to inundate us with acquittals and to release some of the most dangerous criminals from imprisonment.

I have given no compelling empirical evidence for the changes that will be predicted and described herein. In fact, I do not possess such evidence for or against the changes I expect to occur. I have only unorganized impressions and word of mouth, and these do not constitute strong evidence. Even if it should turn out that the changes I have expected do not materialize, however, a philosopher can contribute insight by considering what such changes would be like if they were to happen. These musings will increase our understanding of the concepts with which we must work and, more substantively, provide guidance and a warning in case we are truly drifting in an unpromising direction.

If a disturbed person who has just shot someone must either be held wholly responsible or not responsible at all for killing that person, and thus for committing murder, then perhaps it is preferable that he be held responsible "100 percent." But if blame and responsibility are properly interpreted as a matter of degree, as on the British model, a whole range of intermediate treatments are still open, insofar as we have full sentencing discretion or its moral equivalent. In recent times there have been rhetorical revivals of enthusiasm for individual responsibility, and to many people who have thought about judgments of blame, it has seemed clear that criminal defendants, even under a deeply conservative regime, are free to take the legally required path and are indeed free, in an appropriate sense of the word, to take that path at any point if they prefer to do so. Self-restraint is possible even in situations where it is difficult. Even Jeffrey Dahmer's actions were probably under his control in the sense required by the law if they were to qualify as voluntary. So, we have the case of a sick! sick! sick! crime committed voluntarily by a sick! sick! sick! person, who will be held responsible for it, and rightly so.

That is not to say that the concept of mental illness over the years has had no softening effect on our moral judgments. This point can be appreciated in the case of the criminal who is genuinely ill but whose illness was causally independent of his crime.

Anglo-American criminal law assigns the role of moral mitigation of an act of homicide only to instances of that crime in which the defendant pleads provocation as his defense. It is assumed that there are cases in which we would not want to exonerate the defendant altogether, and yet we feel a certain bond of sympathy with him anyway. We may even concede that had we been in his shoes we might have acted as he did. When this happens, the penalty is reduced to match the reassessment of guilt, and the murder charge is reduced to manslaughter.

In the past, when interested parties tried to decide whether a given defendant was sick! sick! sick! on the one hand, or immoral, say, on the other, it was understood that, practically speaking, what was at issue was whether the person was an appropriate object of pity or, instead, a fitting object of moral condemnation. These were considered mutually exclusive alternatives, so that to whatever degree a person was judged sick, to that degree he could not be morally condemned; and sickness, as we have seen, had the tendency to weaken the moral case against the sick person, to change our opinion of the appropriateness of certain negative attitudes toward him, and to at least partially excuse him for what he did. Since, *ex hypothesi*, he was not insane, we assume that he knew what he was doing when he committed his crime and that he could have taken the honest path if he had chosen. Therefore, it is only proper to consider him a responsible moral agent, answerable for his conduct.

Traditionally, moralists and jurists believed that evidence of mental illness in a criminal defendant had a clear and precise sort of significance. It weakened the moral outrage naturally felt toward the wrongdoer even in the normal case in which he was not forced to act nor deceived into acting as he did. Mental illness, as such, does not normally exculpate; that is, it is not an excuse, but neither is it altogether irrelevant to the degree of blame placed on the criminal. We tell the mentally ill actor that his conduct was inexcusable; nevertheless, we can find it understandable, and that is precisely the aspect that mitigates.

Sick Desires and Immoral Actions

Human desire in any given community can meaningfully be labeled "sick" (or, for that matter, "healthy" depending on what the facts should turn out to be). It is at least not gibberish to say that a set of actual desires are, as we say, "sick." Dahmer's desire at some point to have a solitary banquet of human flesh and his desire to have sex with a dead human body are sick! sick! sick! But simply to have desires like those is not sufficient for deserving condemnation so long as one does not act on them. I suppose that one would actually get greater moral credit for not acting on a sick desire than for "resisting" a comparatively weak one, so that in general the stronger the sick desire not acted upon, the more favorable the moral judgment deserved by the omitter.

When is a sick desire culpable in itself? The subtle answer to this difficult question uses conditionals frequently, as philosophers are prone to do. A desire is itself blameworthy when it is such that if its possessor were to act on it, then the action would be immoral. According to Dr. Robert Schopp,[4] as I understand him, evil is something potentially present in a desire, which becomes actual when the person with the desire acts on it and thereby brings about harm to an innocent party—which was part of his intention all along. In this example, it is the act itself that is directly blameworthy; the desires that led up to it, by overcoming a person's defenses, are culpable only in a derivative and counterfactual way. If one were to act out the desires in reality, then that dreamlike intrusion, scattering harm among all those in its path, would deserve condemnation.

The concept of mental illness, which has had a softening effect on our moral judgments, has been interpreted in a fairly standard and undeviating way for more than a century. Its mitigating function can be appreciated in the case of the criminal who suffers from a serious *physical* illness. That is a reason for punishing him more leniently. (The argument for this unpopular position [mine] is that the reduction of his life expectancy, the deterioration of his creative capacities, or an increase in intense pain can all be assimilated, in our understanding, to his punishment.) If we do not punish him less, we shall be punishing him more.

The Sheerness in "Sheer Wickedness"

The British classify mentally disturbed prisoners in a distinct category of relatively moderate criminals whose capacity to conform their conduct to the requirements of law has been diminished and whose responsibility after the fact for their failure to conform is therefore "diminished" too. I have some sympathy with the British system, although it is uniformly rejected in the United States as cumbersome, impractical, and expensive. The alternative, however, can seem to be morally unpalatable. In theory, we Americans can punish severely a person whose "disease of the mind" is so extreme that it puts him right at the margin of insanity, and we can exempt from serious punishment a person whose mental illness creates only a minor handicap. The British system would punish the severely ill criminal slightly because his mental illness is so severe that he is, after all, nearly insane. But it would reserve its more extreme punishment for the person whose mental illness is mild and whose responsibility, therefore, remains strong enough for a severe punishment. Thus, proportionality, a requirement of justice, is more likely to be observed in a system in which diminished capacity is accepted.

Our ordinary thinking (if we can call it that) about the relation between moral blameworthiness and mental illness is muddled. Many more views of the connection than those considered here are possible. We have heard judgments both in the law and in the views of the ordinary person in the street that suggest a variety of different kinds of relationships between sickness and wickedness. Sometimes it is suggested that sickness and wickedness bear an inverse relation to each other (the more sick you are, the less wicked, and the more wicked, the less sick). At other times, sickness and wickedness are said to vary directly; the sickest crimes are judged the most wicked and inspire the strongest moral outrage. Some writers, we have seen, even judge that sickness aggravates character flaws, that is, makes them more flawed than ever.

There are difficulties in this interpretation of responsibility that stem from efforts to keep the concepts of sickness and wickedness separate. The crimes that appear most sick are often also considered most wicked. When a man rapes and murders his own mother, surely every licensed psychiatrist will interpret this as the clearest example of an act that is sick. But with equal unanimity, moralists from Sophocles and Euripides to the Christian fathers and beyond have claimed that the incestuous matricide is the most wicked sinner imaginable, and the history of sermons and sentences would seem to bear them out as well. Thus, the most typical and extreme moral sins seem to correspond to the most extreme and disabling (mental) illness. It is but one small step to the claim that, at least at the extremes between sickness and sin, there is no difference.

My own guess is that "sickos" are sometimes persecuted not because they are perceived to be wicked or sick, but rather because they are perceived to be odd or bizarre in the manner of ethnic, racial, religious, or sexual minorities, who are mistreated for no better reason ultimately than that they are different, and thus unacceptable.

It may be that there are few bigots lying in wait among crazy people for the opportunity to mistreat them. The real enemy in the eyes of the bigot is what seems to him the strangeness of those he mistreats, and nothing more effectively makes a person seem strange than an underlying craziness. There is some reason to think that many people find that sort of oddness, or even mere unusualness or difference per se, harder to forgive than the mental illness that sometimes underlies it and sometimes does not.

Cultivated Fantasies

Fantasies are fictitious stories about oneself, composed by oneself for oneself, though rarely put in written form. As a person becomes more preoccupied with the stories he keeps in his imagination, he is really shifting from hopes and goals, celebrating successes, and slowly becoming a different person. No mental element plays a more vital role in self-creation than fantasies, and not only sexual ones. Obese people often knowingly aggravate the diabetes they have had since childhood. Hence, we perversely injure our bodies in a way analogous to our mistreatment of our characters when we indulge in counterproductively poor dietary habits. Or character flaws can take root because of what we do to cultivate and promote them. Indeed, "cultivation" is an especially good word for what we do to make over our characters when we make them worse.

When we cultivate a character disposition in a responsible and effective way, we convert the disposition inevitably into something as new to us as to anyone else. In time, if one can, one will exert a central control over a dominant aspect of one's character. In short, it is not just a matter of luck what kinds of elements make up one's character.

The Crucial Concept of the Strength of a Desire

There are different dimensions along which desires can vary: how good or evil they are and how strong or weak they are. The more evil they are, the more blame there is for acting to satisfy them. Suppose, however, that the only statistical data we have bearing upon these variables in a concrete case justify us in claiming that this specific person was unable or unwilling to suppress this particular desire. Was the desire a weak one? Well, it must have had some strength. After all, this person failed to control it. Perhaps that argues for the strength of the desire, but it could also argue for the person's weakness. If A wins a boxing match against B, that may be because A is strong, or it may mean that B is weak. The only way to tell is to match A and B against other contenders. And when State U. wins its game by preventing the team from Siwash Tech from scoring, it may be because of State U.'s powerful defense, or it may be because of Siwash Tech's inept offense. It will be difficult to tell which is the case until there are more data comparing these two teams with many others.

Much the same point applies to assessments of the strength of a desire. If Mr. Triple Sick desires to make love to a corpse, that may be because of the overwhelming attraction of necrophilia to him, or it may be because of his inept defense against a desire of routine strength. We can then compare data on the percentages of those who have the admitted desire to make love to a corpse and clear opportunities to do so. If few of these other persons ever act on their desire, that would increase the probability that the necrophilic desire in his case too was a good deal less than compulsive.

A Sea Change in the Attitudes toward "Sickos"

An indication of how the term "sick" has changed its tone and associations is found in the remark of a survivor of the only death caused by the unknown bomber at Centennial Park in Atlanta during the 1996 summer Olympic Games. He had only this one angry word for the terrorist who set off the explosion: "He must be sick!" Why must he be sick? Has "sick" come to mean what "wicked" used to mean?

Schopp reports that when people speak of convicted triple-sick killers like Dahmer, they sometimes say that ordinary execution is "too good" for him, that "for him they ought to turn down the current and let it take a while." Many would say that such people are sick and also are deserving of increased blame, condemnation, and suffering, presumably for being sick in the particular way that they are sick.

Note the new terminology for ill people and the sea change of basic attitudes it seems to express. A sicko, like a weirdo and a wacko, by definition is sick in such a manner that his illness actually aggravates his moral guilt and deservingness of punishment. Instead of being a kind of softening excuse, mental illness has become in some quarters a kind of hardening aggravation. Instead of saying, "He is mentally disordered, poor fellow, go easy on him," some now say, "He is a damned sicko, so draw and quarter him."

Professor Schopp suggests two explanations of how these changes have come about. The first is not meant to be the fundamental one, but it is certainly part of the story. People who describe repugnant conduct as both sick and deserving of severe punishment do so because the sick culprits they describe are among the criminals we most fear. No wonder we are hard with them; they "elicit the most undifferentiated loathing and anger."

Some of those who said such things to Dr. Schopp were no doubt expressing their wishes for a kind of vicarious vengeance. They would like the "satisfaction" of seeing the criminal suffer as much as, or more than, his victim did. If the speaker proceeds to help himself to a portion of such satisfaction, then his action, especially if it harms a third party, is immoral. So we have a conceptual scheme in which mental sickness can logically coexist with moral condemnation of the sick person provided that the sickness is predicated on desires only, the immorality applies to actions only, and neither applies directly to the person in abstraction from her traits and dispositions.

Pure Wickedness: Plain and Simple

Definitions and Examples

What leads people to speak of "evil, plain and simple," "pure evil," or "sheer wickedness"? Usually these phrases introduce a moralistic account of criminal wrongdoing, with emphasis on blame, guilt, and sin. People lose patience with the medical model, with unconvincing tests for exculpation, with expressions of sympathy for perpetrators, and with attempted elucidations of motives.

Primarily, however, the concern behind these terms is just what one would expect from the language used. "Evil" is not exactly a new word in English, but it is having an increased use these days in scholarly books, essays, lectures, and symposiums. The increased interest in the subject is also easily explained. The twentieth century, may it rest in peace, was the period of the Holocaust and the Stalinist mass murders, and there are still alive many thousands of people who have lived through all of that, just as we have lived through similar atrocities on a smaller scale.

Our strong tendency, I think, is to reserve the word "evil" for wrongdoing and harm causing that we cannot understand. The realm of evil is not that of the petty criminal, the nasty cheat, nor even the raving madman. It is where the sane and responsible wrongdoer produces huge amounts of harm with no gain in it for himself or anyone else. The apparent evil person is one whose conduct not only shocks and angers us but also puzzles us. "How could such a thing have happened?" is often our first question in response to evil, and before we begin to search for an answer, we fear that no explanation is possible, a kind of pessimism that did not exist when the Devil was always available for us to pin the rap on. Without the Devil, some writers fear,[5] a strange moral complacency will take over the world, and the full horror of fiendish evil will not be properly appreciated. This nonchalant indifference to evil, some think, is itself a serious evil.

"Pure" evil requires exclusion. It is evil undiluted, two hundred proof, served in an old-fashioned shot glass and taken neat, without a chaser. It is all evil and nothing but evil, and its impact is unweakened as it ages.

When we examine the characters in history and in fiction who are the leading candidates for the status of sheer wickedness, we discover first a strange sort of serial criminal who seems to have no plausible motivation of sufficient strength to account for his peculiar habits. He performs his actions for no apparent reason. They are to the rest of us, therefore, incapable of being understood.

Sometimes sheerly wicked actions are done calmly, but often those cases are no less perplexing than those done from a peculiar, powerful passion. The passionate evil killer who murders without explicable motive elicits this query: "What on earth is he so excited about?" The motiveless but calm killer, on the other hand, if only because of his superficial resemblance to the rest of us, may strike us as an irreducible mystery, but his very calm in other cases may contribute to his sinister eeriness.

In a different context, the Victorian criminal court judge James Fitzjames Stephen described a "purely evil murder" in which "a man passing along a road sees a boy sitting on a bridge over a deep river, and out of mere wanton barbarity," calmly pushes him into it and so drowns him.[6] Imagine that the boy is a stranger to the man who assails him. He sits on the side of the bridge, his legs dangling toward the deep water below him, and his back turned toward the other pedestrians on the bridge. The wanton man walks purposely up to his victim and without pausing, calmly activates his "impulse." (Of course, I elaborate Stephen's example.) The victim never even gets to know who his executioner is, or in what worthy cause that person acts.

It might not be quite true to say that all killers of this bewildering sort appear to have "no reason" for doing what they do. When asked later by the police why he did it, such a killer might have replied, truthfully: "I don't know. I never thought about the matter. I just felt like doing it, so I did." We can tell him, of course, that *that* is no reason, but by then he might have shifted his ground just a bit. Now he might reply in a somewhat different way. "I don't know," he might say. "It must have seemed to me at the time that it would be fun to do." This alternative response has the form of a "reason," but not much of a reason. It suggests that the killer acted on hedonistic principles, and that his "reason" for killing the boy was that it seemed likely to give him pleasure ("fun"). But this is not exactly a comprehensible explanation. How could killing a child (of all things!) give the killer pleasure? Until we know that, his conduct is no more intelligible than that of the other confessed killer, who had no reason at all.

Most of those who read about serial killers in their newspapers will say that they cannot understand how the profitless killing of a stranger/child could appeal to anyone at all or move anyone to action. And they remain puzzled about this even after all the facts are in.

The puzzlement that is part of the natural response to evil is of the same kind, though more intense and disturbing, as that of a jealous lover, who says, "I cannot understand what she sees in him." In both cases the speaker puts himself imaginatively in the other person's shoes and finds that his experiences in those shoes are quite different from those of others. Killing children has no more appeal to our imagination than it has influence on our motives, and one cannot easily conceive of any people being otherwise. If there are such people (and, alas, it appears that there are), then most of us cannot identify with them.

It is one thing to identify evils and quite another to understand or explain what we are saying when we pronounce a thing "evil." Few of us have any hesitation in judging things evil, but most of us find it surpassingly difficult to explain what we are doing when we make and support such judgments. This is the dark corner where I hope to cast some light.

To begin with, "evil" is a term of negative appraisal. We all understand that we are not saying something nice about a person or her works when we call her "evil." But evil is not the only such term. The English language is particularly bountiful in its provision of terms of negative appraisal. How does evil differ then from such terms as bad, wrong, ought not, and all the others?

I have suggested that at least one of the features that distinguish evil from other bad things is its capacity to generate puzzlement. When we examine the most atrocious crimes, we will often discover that the actor had no apparent motive or that he appeared to act in a way that we would call sick! sick! sick! (triple sick) and to do so for no apparent reason.

Moral atrocities are also sometimes called "pure evils" or "sheerly wicked" actions. Perhaps it is because evil typically causes puzzlement that pure evil, undiluted and disconnected from the actor's goals and purposes, has an air of mystery about it. At any rate, pure evil might be distinguished from other evils by the puzzlement it produces by its motive or reason, or by the fact that it seems to have had no reason at all. A preliminary working definition, therefore, is that an evil act is wrongful behavior done for no intelligible reason.

Not all pure evils are actions, but when a state of affairs is deemed purely evil it is normally because of the character of the actions from which it follows or the actions to which it leads. So there is something basic about the idea of behavior or conduct. (One exception to this will be discussed in the section below on unsavory emotions.) A human action properly appraised as purely evil will be an instance of

1. wrongdoing,
2. moral blameworthiness for that wrongdoing,
3. considerable harm to a victim, and
4. the unintelligibility of the actor's reasons or motives for her wrongdoing and for the elements that ground her moral blameworthiness.

Category 4 contains reference to the puzzlement and unintelligibility discussed above. If we consider unintelligibility to be not merely a typical element of evil, but an invariant element, then the following definition of "pure evil" is plausible:

Pure evil is wrongful behavior or its upshot, for which the actor is blame-worthy, done for no intelligible reason, and which people understandably find extremely perplexing.

Abject Wickedness (Impulse
Control Disorder)

The psychiatric writer Carl Goldberg has a perfectly typical example of pure evil.[7] I quote:

> After seventeen years of trying to reform Wesly Allen Dodd by conven-tional methods used to treat sex offenders, the state of Washington executed him. When he was arrested for the last time, in the fall of 1989, he con-fessed to stabbing to death an eleven-year-old boy and his ten-year-old brother and to killing a four-year-old after repeatedly raping him.
>
> "I knew what I was doing," Dodd said, adding that he killed the children because he enjoyed doing so and because he thought he could get away with it. "I knew I would get the death penalty if caught. I killed them anyway."[8]

Dodd's case is different in some important ways from that of a philosophy professor I know, who teaches at a large midwestern university, but the pro-fessor's story is also strikingly similar to Dodd's in other ways. Here is that story in the professor's own words:

> In 1949 when I was twenty-two years old, a fellow student and I spent the summer studying Spanish in Mexico City. We rented rooms in a private home in a moderately prosperous middle-class neighborhood. The family with whom we stayed contained a father and mother, both of whom worked for the Mexican federal government, two teenage children, and an Indian maid and her out-of-wedlock three-year-old daughter, Luisa.
>
> My American friend and I were very fond of Luisa, who was an ex-tremely cute, lovable little thing. Because of her fondness for European-type sweet rolls (on sale next door at a neighborhood bakery), we called her "Pan Dulce."
>
> On most days before leaving for the university, either my friend or I or both found a few minutes to play with Luisa Pan Dulce. She especially enjoyed the game I played with her, in which I would grip her under the arms, throw her vertically up in the air and catch her as she came down.
>
> The frightening episode occurred on a day when my friend had left early for his class. Luisa Pan Dulce and I were on a kind of mezzanine balcony that extended out over a tiled entrance parlor. I threw her up a few times as usual and then I "found myself" (it seemed as passive as that) holding her firmly by her wrists as she dangled over the tiled parlor one floor below. If I had dropped her, obviously she might have been seriously injured. She seemed to have perfect trust in me at first, but then I felt her body become

tense. She returned to silence from her squealing and giggling, and an un-accustomed look of alarm was on her face. Then it happened. My arms went weak and felt like jelly. My fingers were cold and sweaty. I began to tremble uncontrollably. I wondered if I was going to open up my hands and let her drop. I felt my fingers twitch. My arms felt weak and shaky from the wrists to the shoulders, and I was terrified. Then I pulled her up and gently set her down. I was so weary in the aftermath of an adrenaline surge that I lay on the floor for ten minutes.

For many years, I told this story to no one. There was, of course, nothing for me to be proud of in the story. But I had "wondered" about myself ever after, and I was, at the very least, puzzled and curious. One of the things that puzzled me, but also reassured me, was the singularity of the experience. Nothing like it had ever happened to me before, nothing like it was ever to happen again. It was absolutely unique.

About a dozen years later, when I was forty years old, I won a fellowship at the Center for Advanced Standing in the Behavioral Sciences in Palo Alto, California. There I met social scientists of every sort. One of the fellows I befriended was a psychoanalyst. One day I told him about the episode with Luisa Pan Dulce, and asked whether he had any quick and easy explanation for it. He did.

First, he asked me if I had any siblings. "Yes," I said, "I have a younger sister."

"How old is she?"

"Twenty-two months younger than I am," I replied.

"Was she a very attractive little girl?"

"Yes, she was always attractive, both as a little girl and as a bigger girl and an adult. My male playmates, and later, my high school friends, could not keep their eyes off her."

"Did you have a very intense sibling rivalry with her?"

"Fierce."

The psychoanalyst had other things to do, so that is where we left the story of Luisa Pan Dulce. A little bit of insight made my evil disposition, if there had been anything left of it to begin with, utterly disappear. I was able to talk about the matter in a relaxed way. I was no threat to anyone. There was just that one time in a lifetime of seventy years.

The philosopher in me, however, could not be so easily handled. What about that one time when I *was* a danger? No one will ever be able to convince me that I did not come *close* to inflicting serious injury on a three-year-old child, for no reason at all. My adrenaline surge, my fatigue, my rubber legs, my itchy fingers seemed inconsistent with any other story. My *mind* was not a conspirator, but my body (arms and fingers) almost failed me and injured her. And then I must wonder: how many persons who are very much like me in relevant psychological and moral respects, have found themselves murderers to their great surprise and confusion? "Why did you do it?" the authorities (I imagine) would ask. The only honest answer would be "I don't know."

An uneducated and inarticulate killer would probably not do even that well in answering this question.

The criminal who does not understand his own motives, who seems both to others and to himself to act for no reason, whose criminal actions are surprising even to himself and out of character in apparent defiance of his own principles, who acts neither to benefit himself nor to harm others, and in fact acts without profit to himself or to any others, is properly called "wicked," but only if we invent a kind of wickedness to fit him. If he seriously regrets his episodes of wrongdoing, tries as hard as he can to prevent them (if only he knew how), and still fails to do so, he is abjectly miserable and helpless, as indeed the professor in the Pan Dulce case *is* abject and helpless. The professor feels as he would feel if he believed he was at the mercy of an unknown internal enemy, who can strike at any time. Above all, he does not wish to do what is wrong, and feels terrible if he learns that he has killed or injured someone. The professor in the story is wretched not because he pointlessly killed someone, but rather from the realization that he might have, indeed that he *could* have, done so.

The shock to his psyche may persist even in the case where his luck is good and no harm is done to the child, and even though he conquers his tendency, if he has one, to damage little girls, and never repeats. Imagining that his fingers did lose their hold, and Luisa did lose her life, we could say that he *killed* her, and that would become a memory he would have to live with forever in abject self-hatred. This is an extreme and unlikely case but a possible one.

Atrocious criminals like Jeffrey Dahmer often seem to be beyond any possibility of our understanding them. It is the fourth element in our definition of evil (the agent's reason or motive) that is the source of our difficulty. We do not know his motive, so we cannot understand his action. Further, the motive appears either nonexistent or beyond the possibility of comprehension either by observers or by the agent himself. In the latter case, we can say that the agent is both wicked and abject.

Predilection for the adjectival modifiers "pure" and "sheer" is the mark of those writers who put forth evil as a rival to sickness or illness as their recommended rational response to atrocious crimes. They are likely to say such things as "Atrocity committers are not necessarily sick. To so classify them lets them off the hook too easily." We must insist that such people are pure evil, old-fashioned evil, "plain and simple." A definition of "perfectly pure evil" could then expand it as follows: Perfectly pure evil is morally wrong and extremely harmful behavior, done without excuse or mitigation (hence blameworthy), and mysteriously without intelligible motive.

The Devil and Inverse Utilitarianism

The Devil is still useful as an analytic model, even though he is irrelevant for other constructive moral purposes. If we want to understand what pure evil is, let us ask ourselves what a perfectly evil being would be like, a being who, but for his unlimited nature, is more or less human in his psychological make-up. Perhaps such a being would be a kind of maximizer in ethics. Just as God, the perfectly good being, would, in his infinite benevolence, create as much happiness as possible in those affected by his actions, so the Devil, the purely evil being, would in his infinite malevolence create as much misery as possible in those affected by his actions. This might give us a start at understanding what we could mean by perfect evil and, through contrast, by perfect good. If Satan had the same power that his master has, and knew that he had such power, he might well aspire to do for misery what God has done (allegedly) for pleasure, namely, spread it far and wide. The satanic legends give us every reason to suppose that Satan would embrace his self-assigned duty to maximize pain.

One gets the impression that Jeremy Bentham did not have any personal experience with the diabolic sort of person among the philosophers and lawyers he knew in eighteenth-century Great Britain. Nevertheless, when he comes to "prove" his own "first principle" of ethics by eliminating all of the alternatives to it, one of the alternatives that he takes seriously enough to eliminate is one that would probably please a genuinely evil person. His own favorite theory, propounded in his *Introduction to the Principles of Morals and Legislation* (1789), he calls the "principle of utility" or the "happiness principle." That principle imposes a moral duty on us to produce through our own voluntary actions and omissions as much happiness as possible. The position of the lover of evil that must be refuted ("eliminated") if the happiness principle is to be "proved," Bentham calls the "principle of asceticism" or the "unhappiness principle." He defines it, in effect, as utilitarianism turned upside down, which requires us always to act in such a way as to create the largest balance of pain over pleasure in those affected by our actions.

Perhaps Satan himself, if he ever read philosophy, would endorse this kind of inverted theory, which justifies creation of as much misery all around as possible. I think, however, that we tend to reserve the term "ascetic" for actions deliberately performed for the purpose of creating pain for the actor. A truly diabolical inversion of the happiness principle would require that we promote the greatest possible balance of pain over pleasure in ourselves as well as in other people. But I do not think Satan is particularly eager to cause *himself* pain. *He* is no ascetic.[9]

What sort of human being might it be who is utterly devoted to producing maximum pain all around? Some possible motives are familiar and intelligible. Perhaps he is a bitter, unforgiving person who wallows in his own frustrations, always blames them on others, and then moves toward a full misanthropy, through vengeance and spite. Perhaps he is not only paranoid but, even worse, poor at logic. The agents who have caused him harm in the past have included all kinds of human beings, white and black, male and female, and so on. Underlying their diversity, however, is one feature they all share in common: They are all human beings. Therefore our upside-down utilitarian will have us hate them one and all, and hate them equally. In that way one slides spitefully from egalitarianism to the impartial promotion of unhappiness in all those one encounters, which is what the inversion of Bentham's happiness principle would require from us as our duty.

Does Satan himself acknowledge duties? Is he merely doing his duty to God when he produces harm to others? Or is he simply paranoid and spiteful? "If I cannot find happiness in myself," he might say, "I will make damned sure [in the literal sense of "damned"] that no one else can find happiness either." Satan as described by John Milton in *Paradise Lost* is not only a superhuman being (a fallen angel), he is also basically human by nature, if only because Milton meant to write a moral and psychological study of Satan based on the poet's knowledge of human beings, the only species whose psychological nature is accessible to us.

Objectivity is actually one of the advantages of the utilitarian moral philosophy of Jeremy Bentham and John Stuart Mill. Everyone is to be treated equally with no partisanship and no arbitrary exceptions to basic commitments. Insofar as he has the time to deliberate in the face of a moral quandary, the utilitarian is required by his teachings to create the greatest possible balance of happiness over unhappiness or, if all of the acts open to him will have bad consequences for others, the smallest possible balance of unhappiness over happiness in all of those people who will be affected by his conduct. Satan, a thoughtful fellow of pure evil disposition, will be tempted in his own case to embrace (perhaps secretly) an "inverse utilitarianism," utilitarianism turned upside down, a view that requires everyone to act so as to maximize unhappiness and minimize happiness all around. In the ensuing calculations, no one would be favored over anyone else. "Everyone is to count as one and no one as more than one."[10] The abundant pain and suffering throughout the world that would result if the Devil could persuade people conscientiously to inflict maximum pain, each on most of the others, would no doubt have a certain appeal to Satan, but in the end, I think he would choose a system that permits his own self-preference. Everyone else should count as one, and only Satan should count as more than one. That would be a more diabolic moral principle, a description of it that seems to Satan to be high praise as he understands it.

In any event, I think that Satan is happier with a personal moral code that requires us to maximize pain for others while exempting ourselves from the requirements that we contribute to our own pain. Diabolic pain then is more than Benthamite utilitarianism turned upside down. The traditional utilitarian, a benevolent sort of person, is perfectly impartial in the way he seeks to distribute benefits to others. Employing the same assumptions, Satan would be absolutely egalitarian in his distribution of pains to others. Nobody is to count as more (and nobody less) than one. But whoever occupies the office of Devil must be treated with partisan favor.

I have been proposing here that what is most distinctive about evil is its unintelligibility to observers, which in turn is a consequence of its apparent motivational inadequacy. What is there about the behavior in question, we might ask, that moves the actor to undertake it? If the actor himself cannot answer in a way we can understand, and the motive would seem to be incapable of inducing behavior in a normal person, then if it satisfies the other criteria of negative assessment, it is the kind of bad thing we call "evil."

The purely evil wrongdoer may be taken by surprise by his own voluntary action. His conduct will seem mysterious to other people and likely will remain mysterious even after extensive study. If his conduct, like that of the abject professor, remains a mystery, it may remain a mystery *to him* as well as to everybody else. His harmful action, having no motive intelligible to him or to anyone else, was done for no apparent reason and seems even to him to be incomprehensible. That must be what pure evil feels like from the inside. At its best, it is an astonishingly opaque phenomenon. At its worst it is, well, plain evil, nothing more, nothing less.

Not even a philosophy professor will know whether it is rational for him to feel remorse or guilt, when all he can understand of his conduct is that it was an unpredictable eruption. Worse even than being a surprise to the point of amazement, it may be behavior that is totally out of character. Fate seems to offer the professor, in such a case, only two interpretive options: to cultivate irrational (morbid) guilt feelings or to be taken into diabolic "possession." These are not very appealing alternatives. Irrational guilt feelings and remorse without actual guilt are purely destructive, and when the Devil is in possession of one's self (the other alternative), then one's wrongful actions are the Devil's, not one's own, a paradoxical result destructive of our common sense of responsibility.

Because there is nothing in the professor's experience of himself in relations with other people in the past that provides him with a credible motive, we find him unconvincing. That would be a serious defect in a work of fiction. It is worse in an allegedly realistic portrait of a human being. Inhuman beings do not make believable human beings. They make at best permanent mysteries. Some of the evildoers, like the professor in the case of Luisa Pan Dulce, resemble the hypothetical person who, while walking hastily and inattentively, finds himself suddenly staggering on the brink of an unknown chasm, off guard and shocked by his imminent jeopardy.

If the philosophy professor's injury to the three-year-old, had he allowed it to come about, would not have fit in with his character at all, then even though it would have been voluntary, it is not clear in what way he would be responsible for it. If friends were to read about the literal "dropping" of

Luisa Pan Dulce, most of them would respond as follows: "The person we read about who injured the child was not the John Doe we have known and admired all these years. This terrible accident must be something that *happened to* that Professor Doe, not something that he did" (as Mr. Hyde was something that happened to Dr. Jekyll).

In any case, that action not only fails to fit in with the various components of his character, it positively *conflicts* with them. It is against everything he believes in. So the killer (if that is what he would have become) would forever more have no alternative but to wallow in his not-understood guilt, or else feel that his true self had been preempted by an alien resident within him who simply used his host's true self as a place to hide.

It is difficult to avoid speaking in this context of distinctions between mixed and unmixed bad things, between intrinsic and extrinsic badness, or the Platonic formulas—"for its own sake" or "in itself." The evil person will glory in what is in fact something bad. Such a person's perversity gives us an element for another model of pure evil, to be examined in the next section. A person like that is evil if she values things that are bad in themselves, and values them because they are bad.

Other persons may also like to produce bad things but they are not evil persons unless they value those things for no other reasons than that they are bad. A bad person of another type might produce or promote the same bad thing, but not because it is bad, but rather because it is a useful means to further ends, which may or may not be bad in themselves. Terrorist bombings, cruelty, ruthlessness, and the unscrupulous pursuit of worthwhile ends by the use of cruel means, in the absence of some extraordinary complication, are all examples of immensely harmful wrongdoings. The actions themselves are wrong, and the perverse and voluntary doing of those wrong acts precisely because they are seen to be wrong reflects blame on the character of the actor, and insofar as the actor is disposed generally to act in similar ways from similar motives, he is an evil person, though not necessarily a purely evil person. A purely evil person is interested in evil only as an end in itself.

The criminal who kills for no reason then should be distinguished from the unscrupulous or ruthless killer who takes another's life as a means to one of his own goals and from the cold-blooded, businesslike criminal who kills on contract. All three of these types are wicked but only the first is *sheerly* wicked (*purely* evil).

Not everything that is "sheer" is some kind of evil. Some acts are sheerly wicked, to be sure, but some give sheer pleasure. Others are sheer joy; some are moved by pure malice or sheer hatred. The chemistry of evil admixture is indeed odd. Any kind of thing that *can* mix with evil can only dilute it. But it is not obvious that diluted evil is less evil, only that it is less purely evil. At any rate, the Devil as usually interpreted before Milton prefers his poison straight. Anything else would be unsatanic.

Perverse Wickedness as Analyzed by Ronald Milo

The optimism and self-confidence that came with the modern scientific out-look on the world has weakened where people have come to regard nature as an enemy. Frustrated and inarticulate, the victims of calamities begin to listen respectfully to those who would abandon attempts at naturalistic explanation and speak of evil as itself a basic principle or ultimate kind of explanation. Evil is just *there*, waiting to be done, as accidents are often said to be "waiting to happen." Pure unqualified evil, then, is thought to be part of the basic structure of the universe, and there is simply no explaining how it got there or how it can be removed. Of all the many confusions that have impaired our efforts to understand the fusion of moral and medical judgments, this one is, in my opinion, by far the worst.

"Pure evil," as I use the term, corresponds closely to what Ronald Milo in his penetrating study, *Immorality*, calls "perverse wickedness."[11] This comes close to "desiring to do what is wrong as an end in itself," which (Milo adds) "might be thought of as the most evil desire of all."[12] The perversely wicked person decides to do an act which he believes wrong in itself, whether or not it is also wrong for some other reason. He voluntarily chooses to do this act because moral wrongness appeals to him. But how, we might ask, can a person get such a positive thrill out of doing something of which he presumably disapproves (else he would not judge it to be "wrong")? Perhaps he understands the meaning of words like "wrong" differently from the way we do.

To ordinary, nonwicked people, this description of the perversely wicked person makes very little sense. It implies that a person might choose to do x in circumstances C even though, indeed precisely because, she strongly believes that doing x in C would be morally wrong. To see how difficult this kind of perversity is to understand, contrast it with various other choices that a person can make. She can choose *not* to do x in C because that would cause some other party, S, to suffer severe pain, and she believes that causing suffering in circumstances like C is wrong. But in her motivation she does not refrain from x because it is wrong, but rather because it causes pain to other people, and she values pain avoidance more than wrong avoidance. Even if she thought that doing x in C would not be wrong, she would choose not to do it, because it causes pain, and she regards not causing pain as even more important than not doing wrong. Even though wrongness and pain causing rarely, if ever, diverge, she would be prepared to opt for pain avoidance in preference to wrong avoidance, just in case they should ever diverge. And there may be no other ground of wrongness than the wrongness of unnecessary pain causing, to which she would give automatic priority over wrongness itself.

Because of these difficulties, the picture that emerges of the perversely wicked person is likely to seem incoherent. "It is tempting," Milo adds, "to

think that these [perverse desires] . . . are always symptomatic of some path-
ological condition,"[13] which is a fancier way of saying that the perversely
wicked person, for all her "plain evil," is mentally ill, therefore not fully responsible for her conduct, therefore not unqualifiedly wicked at all. Once
more, medical and moral judgments blend and merge.

The atrocious act to which the professor is tempted in the Pan Dulce story
would be cruel, harmful, and blameworthy. It would also be morally wrong.
Suppose that he does this act not because it has these negative features, but
rather only because it is morally wrong. It may have the other negative features too, but it is only wrongfulness that appeals to him. He is tempted to
drop the child only because he believes it would be morally wrong to do so.

There are possible paths out of this paradox. We could deny that people
are necessarily expressing their disapproval or rejection of something when
they pronounce it morally wrong. Or we could deny that when a person
appears to do something that she believes to be wrong in itself, she is really
exhibiting a desire to do the wrongful act for the sake of the attendant properties that make the act wrong, not from a desire to do something wrong for
the sake of wrongness. For example, hurting another person might make an
act wrong (*any* act insofar as it has this characteristic could plausibly be said
to be of a kind that *tends* to be wrong). Nonetheless, one might inflict pain
on another person because one likes causing others pain, not because one
wants to do what is wrong.

A wicked person who is somewhat less perverse than the one who has
enlivened our examples thus far may be a nasty fellow, cruel and sadistic, and
his actions may often, incidentally, be morally wrong. In his position we might
do the act because of some weakness in our moral make-up, not because we
believe it to be morally wrong and we like wrongness. Most of us would either
omit the action or do it *despite* our belief that it is morally wrong. The perversely wicked person will do it precisely *because* of its wrongness. In other
examples he might do it despite its cruelty, its harmfulness, and its sadism,
but *because* of its wrongness. How is it psychologically possible for a person
to be so much in love with moral wrongness?

In a way, that question paraphrases John Milton's similar effort to explain
the legend of Satan in Milton's monumental poetic work, *Paradise Lost* (1667).
In the seventeenth century, the period of Shakespeare and the King James
translations of the Bible, writers were greatly impressed by the poetic resources of the English language. The capacity of the language to promote the
expression of difficult ideas was inspirational primarily to those storytellers
who could illuminate the shadowy corners of human nature and reconstruct
essentially human motives for the inner life and actions of humanlike beings.
Traditional Christian theology slipped through the dramatic and poetic nets.
Its subject matter was a being who lives outside of space and time, who is in
every relevant respect unlimited and unchangeable. Unlike poetic drama,
which tells stories about finite beings who change and grow, who act and are

acted upon, and who struggle and quarrel, traditional theology has no room for its central figure to move or grow. Ordinary human beings, as they exist in our experience, must be the models for the understanding of angels and demons as well as for comprehension of the infinite God, whose actions must be made plausible, like any other actions, to those with the soundest understanding of human psychology (the only psychology to which we have extended access). But the poet's task is impossible if in addition to expressing his psychological insights, he must also garb in humanlike personality an infinite and unchangeable abstract entity. Yet that is what Milton tried to do.

In *Paradise Lost*, Milton retells the Christian story, dealing with God as if he were only first among equals, one humanoid character among the others in the drama. He tells of the fancied grievances of one of the angels (Satan), who becomes so disgruntled that he leads a rebellion in heaven against the ultimate and infinite authority himself.

Applying an essentially human psychology to a fallen angel, the poet portrays a being in as dramatic and frightening a situation as anyone has ever imagined. Satan must truly be crazy to take on such a formidable foe as God. But if he is crazy, he must have a mental defect that prevents him from functioning properly, and in our world, at least, such defects of reason are typically produced by what we call "mental illness." Indeed the connection between irrationality and mental illness is so close that we take the former to be a reliable symptom of the latter. We also take mental illness to be an excuse for otherwise blameworthy actions. And now we are back, full circle, to our starting place. Even a rebellion against the ultimate source of all morality, arguably the gravest of all conceivable moral crimes, a treasonable betrayal of an infinitely good maker of moral commands, does not prevent us from sympathizing a bit with this archdemon. He has a human side! He struggles and suffers with his emotions, including some partially disreputable humanlike emotions, such as vanity and greed. However unwholesome such emotions may be, he has to struggle to remain loyal to them, and he also surprises us in places by experiencing tender sentiments of love and mercy as, for example, when he looks down from a celestial vantage point upon Eve, who is to be seduced in time by him in the garden of Eden. The archdemon's character flaws do not long vanish from view; his selfishness and boastful pride remain dominant. But his nonprurient tenderness toward Eve and his occasional self-doubts give him a mixed character. As a leading Miltonian critic put it more than a half century ago, "Surely it is exactly because he is capable of such a lapse from evil that Satan is so deeply tragic."[14]

Confused as Satan is by his assigned and voluntary roles, and by conflicting sentiments and principles, he never loses his courage, and only rarely his dignity. Who can escape feeling at least a little sorry for him? C. S. Lewis can, that's who.[15] And so can his fellow critic, Charles Williams.[16] Lewis finds Satan, as Milton depicts him, much too absurd to be a hero. After all, virtually the only things we can find to admire in his conduct, something resembling courage and integrity, are based on misconceptions which have the tinge of madness to them. He is determined to go down fighting against superior forces, and that sort of virtue he shares with some of the heroes of Shakespearean tragedy. But one cannot very well be a hero in a struggle against a being that one acknowledges to be infinitely powerful (that's crazy!) and (even worse) a being that one acknowledges to be unerringly good. That is a declaration to one's moral command giver that, although the commander is absolutely right in his side of their quarrel (and about everything else as well) and furthermore, he is so powerful that he is certain to put down any insurrection of lesser persons, nevertheless, Satan will struggle to do what he knows to be impossible (like Albert Camus's Sisyphus, "a blind man eager to see, who knows that the night has no end, but does not abandon his struggle against the darkness").[17] Satan fights back. That of course is crazy. But insofar as we can find anything nice to say about Satan at all, it is that his errors, tactical and moral, are very human, familiar to us, who share with both the poet and his subject a human nature. Even a poet of Milton's brilliance cannot succeed in making Satan both appealing and inhuman, a fiend or a ghoul.

If one can make any positive sort of mitigating statement at all about Satan, for example, that some of his character flaws render him human, all too human, in our eyes, then we can feel a little sorry for him, at least, and find that even his weaknesses are in some ways appealing. It is only because we recognize his humanity and share it with him as if he were a brother that this is possible. One cannot be a "brother" to a subhuman beast or a superhuman fiend.

Satan's "lapse" into virtue raises many more problems for our understanding of plain evil. When Satan does good, and admittedly that is very rare, he is acting, one might say, "out of character," and similarly, when he has certain feelings of tenderness, sorrow, and even on occasion something like remorse, he is "feeling out of character." Aristotle said that to be a good person on balance is to have deeply rooted dispositions (sometimes his word is "habits") to act or feel in certain ways in certain circumstances. In this sense, Milton's Satan is not a predominantly good person. His habitual responses are weak and unreliable. He is not rocklike in his virtue. But there are the germs of good habits in him, potentially capable of becoming stronger.

Even though a consensus among literary critics about Milton's Satan may still be lacking, his case raises an important question for ethical theory. When a predominantly good person (a person much more reliably good than Milton's Satan) acts out of character, does that deviation from his habitual path make his conduct better or worse? Does it mitigate or aggravate? If his usual way has been taken often, he can cite in his defense his own better behavior in similar circumstances. He can show that he *did* act out of character, which might show that he is basically a good person who on rare occasions goes astray, not some common hoodlum who is thoroughly reprehensible in his character, hence more deserving of blame and punishment. The prosecutor might scold him by saying to him, "You have had every advantage and no excuse. You knew better, and yet you persisted in this foolish crime. You are a member of the respectable classes, not some helpless ignoramus. Shame on you!" To show that the wrongdoer departed from his usual praiseworthy ways then can be taken as aggravation. He knew better but acted worse anyway. Paradoxically, it can also be taken as mitigation. A good man uncharacteristically gone wrong should have his virtues as well as his flaws counted in the final appraisal of his desert.

I do not think there is any easy way to get a question like this answered. The language of morals unavoidably generates absurdities and incommensurabilities that sometimes can be resolved only by a kind of existential flip of a coin, as reason flees to a perch of impartiality. Neither is there any easy way to preserve pleasing symmetries in our explications of moral concepts. It would be a mistake, I think, to expect tragic virtues to work the same way as tragic flaws, or all-good divinities to have emergent properties perfectly parallel to those of all-evil demons, or a mixture of various moral properties in a person to affect our judgment of that person in a way no different from judgments of him as wholly unmixed. Again we must ask: Why is pure evil worse than impure or mixed evil? Is mixing always diluting? The Devil does evil just "for the hell of it," that is, just because he, being evil, loves the thought of evil being done for its own sake. His nature is all wound up to do evil, and he enjoys discharging his native spring. As we declared in our governing metaphor, the Devil would like his evil neat or straight, drunk without dilution in an old-fashioned shot glass. But that may just be a matter of taste. There may be in existence not just one but a diverse plurality of devils. Some may practice inverse utilitarianism, being rational calculators out to maximize human suffering; some might be perversely wicked in Milo's sense; some might be wholly arbitrary devils who can give no reason at all for promoting what they themselves think of as evil, except perhaps the fact of its being evil, but that would be to take the position of the perversely wicked person. It comes close to being also the position of Milton's Satan, when in a spirit partly grim and partly resigned, he makes his famous avowal: "Evil be thou my Good." Here Satan must suppress every last semblance of goodness in himself, squelch his tender feelings and his sense of honor, and then, motivated by anger, resentment, and vengeance, create suffering in other people and do other noncontroversial evils, just as if he really thought them to be goods. All of this in order to upset God's morally ordered universe and achieve a soupçon of revenge. At once, Satan really believes as a matter of genuine conviction that certain occurrences that are almost universally loathed and condemned as evil really are evil, and also that the best thing for him to do about it is to create and preserve as many of these genuine evils as possible. This, I submit, is close to being contradictory but not clearly and explicitly so. It is without question as morally complex a state of mind as it is possible to sustain. That it can be sustained at all is a tribute to the psychological strength of resentment and envy as motivators.

Let us reintroduce Milton's Satan. He is of course the very epitome of evil. And insofar as his evil ways seem self-serving, ideologically derived, or passionately and self-righteously motivated, there is no doubting their evil status. But Satan takes the production of evil to be his job; that is "what he is for." He likes his work and labors hard at it. Apparently he understands that his employment is the consequence of some special agreement made with God, and he expects God to live up to *his* end of it. What foolhardy arrogance! He is also somewhat offensively proud, vain, and boastful, likable only in those rare moments scattered thinly throughout *Paradise Lost* in which Satan is overcome by the great natural beauty of the world and the beauty of innocence in Adam and Eve before the Fall. These moments lead a sensitive reader to a new appreciation of the good in Satan, mixed though it be with his dutiful perfidies. We can add to G. R. Hamilton's point that it is in virtue of Satan's capability to relapse from evil that he is so tragic, and that is also part of the reason *Paradise Lost* is so moving.

Satan is of course wicked, and we must not lose sight of that fact. But he is not *simply* wicked. Perhaps we can say that he is not *starkly* or *sheerly* wicked, though *very* wicked he is indeed. He is surely a candidate for the status of *perversely* wicked, though he is not exactly what Professor Milo meant by that expressive label, as we shall see. Satan is also exceedingly odd, as indeed we might expect when we apply our human standards to a non-human, though humanoid, being. He may be odder even than Milo's conception of perverse wickedness requires.

In what way is Milton's Satan "perverse"? He has the sincere conviction that certain kinds of behavior are morally wrong. About this, he does not change his mind. Nevertheless, he makes no effort to renounce such actions in his own conduct, nor to oppose and disapprove of them generally. Instead he loves doing wrong and not for any reason other than that it *is* wrong. This, I submit, really is perverse—or worse. Some, perhaps most, moral philosophers recognize that this description of Satan flies in the face of their own view, often called "internalism," that it is a necessary condition of believing an act to be wrong that one have some con-attitude [unfavorable attitude] toward it.[18] But Milton's Satan, as I have interpreted him, is not particularly "connish" (negative) in his attitudes toward morally wrong acts. He loves moral wrongness, dedicates himself to it, because it is wrong, not for any incidental advantages it might have on a given occasion. So either internalism is mistaken or my interpretation of Milton's Satan is mistaken because it generates this incoherent picture. Perhaps I can be forgiven for preferring to believe that internalism is mistaken and that Milton's Satan is a very odd, but logically possible, sort of demon.

The word "perverse" seems so right in application to Satan that I hate to give it up. But Milo means something rather different when he uses the word. He contrasts two ways of deliberately doing what in fact is morally wrong without compunction or scruple: "(1) the agent himself believes that acts of this sort are right (either required or permitted morally), or (2) the actor believes that what he does is wrong, but does it nevertheless because he prefers the realization of some end to the avoidance of moral wrongdoing."[19] Milo calls the first of these "perverse wickedness" and the second "preferential wickedness." The second label fits well; I have no quarrel with it. But I would find a different label for the first of these, reserving "perverse wickedness" for a third way of being wicked, not considered by Milo. The perversely wicked person in my proposed terminology would be (3) the actor who believes that what he is doing is wrong but does it nevertheless, not because he prefers some end presently in conflict with moral rightness (like acquiring another person's money, for example) but simply because he wants to do what is wrong for no other reason than to glory in its wrongness. The person (or demon) who believes that the moral wrongness of an act is a good reason, or even the best reason, for doing it is about as perverse as one can be. Satan would be proud to have such a title!

The picture of Satan that emerges may just border on incoherence, or if it stays inside the coherence border, it may describe a person who, if her nature were entirely human biologically, would be impossible psychologically. It may be, for all I know, that Milton's Satan is too odd for words, even for Milton's words. In another word, impossible. But that picture is our quasi-official model of extreme wickedness, and given that role, it is not surprising that the purest evil of which a poet can conceive is so bizarre.

Could it be that the Devil is mentally ill? Could Jeffrey Dahmer be triple sick, and the Devil himself not sick at all? Is the pure glee that comes from torturing people in hellfire and maximizing their pain and suffering by keeping it at maximum intensity forever be less of a symptom of mental illness than skinning adolescent boys in the manner of Dahmer? Could a witness from earth observe the Devil's torture chambers in hell without muttering, sotto voce "That is sick"? Surely, no normal human being could enjoy the prospect as Satan is supposed to. If "normal" refers to all-human standards, then without question, Satan is abnormal. His human psyche, or some parts of it, is simply not functioning properly. His psyche is not in proper working order because some of its faculties, like defective parts in machinery, are broken. But why is it necessary that we use all-human standards to judge a fiend? Even a saint would do poorly if judged by the wrong norms. A juicy orange makes an "abnormal" apple.

While Satan smirks at his own criminal trial (we can imagine), his lawyer argues that his client was mentally ill, and that this is shown by the incoherent nuttiness of his conduct. When asked why he killed his victim, Satan replies: "Because I sincerely believed that it was morally wrong to do so."

"You killed him precisely because you thought it wrong to do so?"

"That is correct."

"Why do you want to do what is wrong?"

"I love doing what is wrong. In fact I have dedicated my life to it. Wrongness (what you call 'evil') is my good."

Satan's lawyer would then be able to argue that his client does not satisfy the cognitive prong of the insanity defense, being obviously incapable of understanding how evil is different from good or, as the M'Naughten Rules put it, what is the difference between right and wrong.

There are times when persons are prone to seek simple explanations. None of the usual accounts of our misfortunes seems applicable. It would be paranoid, at first, to assume that there must be some person or persons who have it in for us and are carrying on a vendetta without letting us know. It would be equally tempting for many to claim that there is nothing personal about the imposition of our misfortunes; it is *things* that have it in for us. We have no evidence of that either, except that things seems to be acting up, and we have no other explanation for it. Perhaps it is a poltergeist that is causing our canned jars of turnips to jump up and down in the night, not earthquakes as we previously thought. In any event there does seem to be something out there that threatens us with harm, maybe a kind of impersonal evil built into things and prone to strike us hard for no visible reason. In a candid moment, the Devil will say, "I did it only to produce bad results. That is evil, but I *love* evil."

Despite its recent comeback among historians and philosophers, the nominative "evil" is not a prominent word in ordinary speech. I think that is in part the influence of philosophers and theologians. As these scholars use the term, it is not merely a technical term in ethics. More fundamentally, it is a term in the metaphysic of morals. In the philosophy of religion, evil stands for a state of the universe as it must be described if it is not to be attributed to a deity. Philosophers have debated with one another over the "nature of evil." Is evil a positive thing or a negative "absence of being"? This and similar questions are as much questions of metaphysics, that is, questions about the nature of what ultimately exists, as questions calling for moral judgment.

Perhaps it is because of its association with such things as God and theology, cosmic ontology, and other great momentous themes that the concept of evil does not tempt many of us to a kind of relativism more widely invoked in theories of value (goodness and badness) and "oughtness." It is not open to us, for example, while agreeing on all the historical facts, as collected in official documents, to deny that the Holocaust was evil, that the mass murders ordered by Pol Pot were evil (not just "a bad thing" or something the perpetrators "ought not" to have done) or that, on a smaller scale, most instances of child abuse leading to rape, battery, and murder are evil. If we hesitate at all in making these judgments, it is only because we are not sure whether to classify these cases as examples of sheer evil or as examples of triple sickness.

What it is most implausible to say is that judgments of evil are "highly controversial" and that reasonable persons therefore can be expected to disagree over them. Some are tempted to the view that when we say that x is evil we are expressing our distaste for or rejection of x, so that we would be saying something conceptually incoherent, as well as diabolical, if we were to say that we "love evil" or that evil is to be "our good." If x is to be our good, then (these writers conclude) why do we call it "evil" in the first place? That is like giving with one hand and taking away with the other.

I am unpersuaded by that argument. The term "evil" may not be quite as clear and invariant as some other moral terminology (for example, "moral" and "immoral") but it is far from being a wild card in the deck that one can apply to anything at all that one rejects. However we define "evil," our definition must be consistent with the judgments that child abuse, mass murder, genocide, terroristic bombing, sadistic cruelty, ruthlessness, and the unscrupulous pursuit of worthwhile ends by use of cruel means, in the absence of some extraordinary complication, are all examples of evil doings. The actions themselves are evil; the voluntary doing of those acts precisely because they are seen to be evil reflects evil on the character of the doer; and insofar as the doer is disposed generally to act in similar ways from similar motives, he is an evil person.

Insofar as talk of pure evil emphasizes the unmixed and unattached, it suggests the Platonic formulas—"for its own sake" or "as an end in itself." The truly evil person then is she who glories in what is in fact something bad. A person like that is herself evil if she values things that are bad in themselves, and values them precisely because they are bad.

Other persons may also like to produce bad things but they are not evil persons unless they value those things for no other reasons than that they are bad. Another person might produce or promote the same bad thing, but not because it is bad, but rather because it is a useful means to something else that is bad in itself, or even to something that is good (perhaps) in itself. Whether these judgments are correct is not generally a topic of ordinary moral discourse. In that respect they are similar to judgments about morality. Reasonable persons do not differ over whether morality really forbids murder, battery, and rape, or whether it really condemns lying, cheating, and stealing. If we understand this part of our English vocabularies at all, we know what sorts of acts are disapproved of or commanded by morality. We may very well wish to profit by performing an act we know is immoral, but we do not do that by arguing that these things are not immoral after all, that they are "inherently controversial," and so on. Only the Devil can get away with that kind of talk.

Perverse Impishness (Edgar Allan Poe)

Perversity is a peculiarly irritating complex of character flaws. The original Latin from which the English word evolved was a kind of all-purpose directional term that combined readily with prefixes, which then served as turn indicators. See, for example, "inverse," "obverse," "reverse," and so on. The main job of "perverse" has been to indicate a wrong turn, and even in modern English it bears the sense of being turned away from what is right or good. If I am headed in the wrong direction because someone turned me in that direction, then I have been perverted or corrupted.

The perverse person is not only the person who is headed in the wrong direction, he is the person who heads off at a tangent in order to frustrate his associates. He defends positions that the others strongly believe to be false and mischievous, and they are likely to simmer in anger. They believe that he does not even hold the controversial opinions himself but voices them for the sole purpose of irritating or insulting the others. But there is nothing playful about his manner, which is often harsh and dogmatic. More exactly, he is "stubborn, obstinate, and persistent by temperament and disposition in opposing what is right, reasonable, correct or accepted."[20]

With these traits he does not make friends easily, and he does not really care. His wrongheadedness typically grows into peevishness or petulance, and he is often in a sulk. In summary, the perverse person is wrongheaded, obstinate, and persistent in his errors. Basically, there are two main flaws that come together in this person: wildly erroneous opinions and stubbornness. He *will not* change.

So far there is nothing in the perverse person to suggest sheer wickedness. A fortiori, there seems to be nothing in impishness that suggests pure evil. My model of the imp is the small child who loves to play by being naughty with adults, usually giggling and screaming all the while, as she uses grandpa's stomach as a trampoline.

In Edgar Allan Poe's short story "The Imp of the Perverse," these two very different notions, perversity and impishness, are brought together. The story has the form of a first-person narrative. The narrator is a convicted murderer awaiting his hanging for the crime he committed several years earlier. He thought that he had got away with "the perfect crime" and could never even be suspected, much less discovered and exposed. But that was before an "imp" from his own psyche began to give him away. He knew that to escape discovery there were certain things he must never do or say, else he would arouse suspicion. He suffered no intellectual confusion about this, nor was he subject to coercive pressure or trickery. His exposer was a kind of imp perversely goading him to do what he must not do if he were to escape hanging. Thus he did not escape hanging.

The prisoner's tone suggests that he has no doubts, or is aware of no doubts, that his original plan—to keep quiet, cover up evidence, and the like—

was the truly rational one, and that escaping detection was the proper goal for him to have. Thus he thinks of the imp as a kind of enemy within, perversely dedicated to his undoing. In this respect, he is unlike the professor in the Pan Dulce story and unlike other abjectly wicked persons who are nearly "done in" by their own consciences. The imp in Poe's story represents reason and decency. It upholds what is best in the person it undoes and directs the sacrifice of the elements of that self to the requirements of justice. These are important differences.

Yet Poe's account in only four short pages of "The Imp of the Perverse" has much to teach us. He gives other examples in which the internal imp really is working for the demise of its victim, and not merely in the sense in which conscience leads a guilty person to his punishment. Poe's imp leads the characters described in his narrator's other examples to act for no apparent reason:

> Through its promptings we act without comprehensible object; or if this shall be understood as a contradiction in terms, we may so far modify the proposition as to say that through its promptings we act, for the reason that we should not. In theory no reason can be more unreasonable, but in reality none so strong. I am not more sure that I breathe than that the conviction of the wrong or impolicy of an action is often the one unconquerable force which impels us. . . . Nor will this overwhelming tendency to do wrong for the wrong's sake, admit of analysis, or resolution into ulterior elements.

Poe's narrator then presents his own case as well as three other examples, none of which he says, are aimed at promoting the person's own well-being. First, "There lives no man who at some period has not been tormented, . . . by an earnest desire to tantalize a listener [whose good will he needs] by circumlocution." "A shadow seems to flit across the brain, accompanied by anger and a thought of how he might torment his listener." The impulse increases to a wish, the wish to a desire, the desire to an uncontrollable longing, and the longing, in defiance of all consequences, is indulged.

Poe anticipated me, for here is a similar example from my own experience:

> I had known Hal East [not his real name] for about a dozen years. He had received a Fulbright fellowship to study at Cambridge and was just leaving Great Britain when I arrived with funds from a Guggenheim fellowship. Hal was remarkably kind and helpful to me and my family, arranging housing, transportation, introductions, and so on. For years after that, I saw Hal every couple of years, usually at social functions during the annual meeting of the American Philosophical Association. In addition we corresponded irregularly about a text we were editing.
> One year I happened to meet Hal at one of the APA receptions. We were both mingling with numerous common friends. Suddenly I turned to Hal,

and in all seriousness proceeded to insult him in a gross and vulgar way. ("Hal, you are a stupid son of a bitch.") Hal was taken aback and puzzled. After a considerable pause he asked, "Are you serious?" There was nothing at all jocular in my manner. That gave me a chance to recover, and I did. "No," I said. We both withdrew in a state of puzzlement, I am sure, and relief. But will either of us ever understand what had happened?

Among other differences from the Pan Dulce case, there is this: The professor in the Pan Dulce case nearly committed murder. I merely came close to rupturing a valued friendship (which is bad enough), thus depriving myself of a benefit.

The second example is familiar in the lives of writers. Perhaps Poe himself had such an experience. Imagine that a professional writer has an unprecedented publishing opportunity:

> A task must be speedily performed. We know that it will be ruinous to make delay. We glow, we are consumed with eagerness to commence the work, and our whole souls are on fire with anticipation of the glorious result. It must, it shall, be undertaken today, and yet we put it off until tomorrow, and why? . . . There is no answer except that we feel perverse.

The third example is one that will be found in the experience of many who have climbed or hiked in the mountains. Poe writes at great length about this one, and with his greatest vividness: "There is no passion in nature of so demonic an impatience as the passion of him, who shuddering upon the edge of a precipice . . . meditates a plunge." Some climbers have reported a fearsome inclination to jump in such circumstances. But Poe's narrator insists that the impulse derives its whole force from the feeling that we ought not to do so. Therein lies its appeal: It is genuinely perverse.

The person whose actions are prompted by an internal "imp of the perverse" bears some close resemblance to the abjectly wicked person, but the differences between them are of considerable importance. The abjectly wicked person is abject because he suffers the agony of remorse conjoined with confusion and uncertainty over his own guilt. The perverse person defies his conscience and approves of his own wrongdoing. He loves doing what is wrong even though he must have some uncertainty how much "credit" he can take, given the decisive role of the impish whim in producing his conduct. We should note also that the imp of the perverse does not prompt the criminal into his crime. Rather, in Poe's famous short story, the imp of the perverse prompts the criminal into public behavior that leads to his capture and punishment for his crime.

More should be said also about that which can be called "perverse reasons." When a consideration is both a reason and perverse, we are led to distrust the apparent power of perversity to grow in importance at the expense of rationality generally. Poe's narrator would encourage us to say such things as "The absence of a reason for me to do x is itself a reason for my doing x" or "I desire x but only because I do not want x" or "Because x lacks attractiveness, and for that reason only, I find it attractive." Poe's narrator shows some reservation about what he calls "contradictoriness," and that is to Poe's credit. But the danger of conceptual anarchy is always present, and philosophy cannot flourish in its shadow.

Another lesson to be learned from a consideration of perversion is that wickedness achieves coherence through a rather extreme conception of the unity of the self. The imp of the perverse is, in one way of thinking, an essential constituent of the self. When it prompts a person to action, it is an "inside cause," not something exerting pressure from the outside. In another conception, the perverse imp is an outside cause, and its causal influence on the person it moves to action is something destructive of that person's freedom. A gang of imps might try to pull in opposite directions, or first in one direction, then in the other. Or the plurality of imps might be like a constituent assembly in government. Each might be the representative of a different part, phase, interest, or value of the complex whole.

The constituent assembly might be fairly unified and harmonious, or it may be constantly in civil war, or some strange position in between these extremes. When an imp acts by "prompting" the whole self, its choice of action may be wholehearted, or it may be less sure than that. I could be halfhearted or even, as David Lewis suggests, "quarter-hearted."[21] The latter act might yet be voluntary on the part of the whole self, but it will also be the reluctant decision of a house divided. A perverse imp then, sprouting up from the depths of my psyche, still speaks for me. And if *he* is wicked, then a part, at least, of *me* is wicked too. But the sheerest evil person would be a person with a deeply rooted impulsive disposition, without a trace of disharmony among its parts. Whether unification of the parts of the larger self in the face of a perverse imp mitigates or aggravates guilt is, as we shall see, one of the central problems of ethical theory.

The opinion has been attributed to Thomas Hobbes that a wicked man is nothing but the small child grown large. Imagine a genuine imp. It may or may not be a child. It could also be a genie out of the *Arabian Nights*. Common to all imps is a certain spirit of playful cockiness, a contact with secret powers. In the beginning, an imp was an evil or malicious child, but that sense has been archaic since Poe's time. A new sense evolved, borrowed from the remains of the original one: "a small demon, devil, or wicked spirit." Note that a small size is still part of the conception. Now in addition we have a third, closely related meaning: "a mischievous child, urchin." No longer is genuine wickedness or supernatural power a part of our impression. Mischief and spiteful playfulness replace them. When we describe a child these days as "impish," it is mostly in the same spirit as an ascription of "cuteness."

Most small children are naturally called imps. Imagine, as Hobbes did, that one of them, having been aided by a liberated genie, grows to a muscular seven feet tall, three-hundred pounds. But his nonphysical traits have not changed much. Perversity comes natural to him, and any circumstances that would lead a normal small child to a typical juvenile tantrum would do the same for him. Now, we would not call him "cute" or "naughty." He would be more like a fiend, as selfish but not as clever as Satan.

Further Studies in Evil

Psychopathy (Getting Along without a Conscience)

The disorder which for many years has been called "psychopathy" has been renamed and classified as one of the "personality disorders." A personality disorder is defined in turn as an enduring pattern of inner experience and behavior that deviates markedly from the expectations of the prevailing culture, is pervasive and inflexible, has an onset in adolescence or early adulthood, is stable over time, and leads to distress or impairment. If the impairment is appropriately severe, the disorder can also be called a mental illness, though my impression is that psychiatrists are now more comfortable with the "disorder" vocabulary.

There are ten basic personality disorders recognized in the official diagnostic manual:[22] paranoid personality disorder, schizotypal personality disorder, borderline personality disorder, histrionic personality disorder, narcissistic personality disorder, avoidant personality disorder, dependent personality disorder, obsessive-compulsive personality disorder, and personality disorder not otherwise specified. The classification no longer includes psychopathic personality disorder, which has been replaced by antisocial personality disorder and defined as "a pattern of disregard for, and violation of, the rights of others." Once more we encounter a kind of definitional blending of the psychiatric and the moral, the psychiatric disorder being defined in moral terms ("others' rights").

For all the merits these new definitions have, there are various ways in which they can confuse a moral philosopher. The philosopher will find it easy to distinguish a "personality disorder" from a "character flaw," but he may not understand how he is to interpret a "personality defect." In ordinary language, we usually assess the personalities of our friends not by applying basic moral terms to their dispositions, terms like honest-dishonest, cruel-kind, generous-mean, and so on, but rather we use such terms as nice guy, bore, lively, dull, witty, dour, pleasant, feisty, or sweet. We could then loan those personality-appraisal terms that are negative to the psychiatric classifiers. They are clear and familiar. The only trouble is that they are probably not what psychiatric classifiers have in mind.

Their intentions would be better fulfilled, I suspect, if they used the word "personal" where they now use the word "personality." A personal disorder could be understood to be a disorder of one's person, one's whole person, that is, and not just his arm or leg, his eating or sleeping. A personal disorder involves the whole human being; usually by impairing her capacity to act or to have feelings of a desired kind in the appropriately matching circumstances.

Some of the definitions of personality disorder listed in the psychiatric manual employ terms of moral condemnation, terms ascribing flaws of character (formerly called "vices") instead of defects of personality. In ordinary language, we would reserve such phrases as "defective personality" for people who are otherwise decent but obnoxious, unpleasant, humorless, boring, and the like. It might be taken as an interesting suggestion that psychiatrists should help people improve their sense of humor and call that "therapy." The descriptions in the psychiatric manual that seem to be morally condemnatory include "detachment from social relationships," "disregard for and violation of the rights of others," "instability in interpersonal relationships," "excessive emotionality and attention-seeking," "grandiosity, need for admiration, lack of empathy," "hypersensitivity to negative evaluation," "compulsive preoccupation with orderliness," and "need for control."

Some of these traits clearly are character flaws, and some of the character flaws are clearly moral faults. Some others are clearly just personality defects, ways of being unpleasant without necessarily leading to harm or doing anything immoral. Consider, for example, suspiciousness, eccentricities of behavior, excessive or deficient emotionality, need for admiration, feelings of inadequacy, hypersensitivity to negative evaluation, excessive need to be taken care of, clinging, preoccupation with orderliness, and perfectionism.

In fact, the defects of feeling and behavior that define the ten basic personality disorders are almost all personality defects as opposed to character flaws; those that are character flaws are almost all nonmoral flaws. A mentally disturbed person who is obsessed with orderliness and who suffers from feelings of inadequacy or an excessive need to be admired can be a pain in the neck to those who must be frequently in his company; that makes him a bore, not a brute. Almost all of the personality disorders are compatible with honorable behavior, including the keeping of promises, repayment of debts, and abstention from violence. The one big exception among the personality disorders is the one called antisocial personality disorder. That is a new name for a class of persons who used to be call psychopaths.

Clinical investigators have studied psychopathic behavior quite thoroughly in recent years. The picture of psychopathy that has emerged is an ugly one indeed. Most formal definitions of the psychopath have encountered some difficulties, but the thousands of profiles and anecdotes compiled since the 1930s have made a wonderfully precise picture, which we recognize immediately as a type all of us have encountered dozens of times, and not only in gutters, hospitals, and jails. Partly because psychopaths are often "masters of deceit," some of them have become quite successful in respectable professions. If we can believe Professor Robert Hare, some psychopaths have even entered, often with forged licenses and diplomas, the honorable profession of psychiatry itself.

The most skilled practitioner of the method of narrative description and anecdote was the Georgia medical doctor Hervey Cleckley[23] and, in our time, his follower Robert Hare.[24] In 1941 Cleckley published a book full of literary snapshots, word pictures of patients he had treated and diagnosed as "psychopaths," and also anecdotal accounts of episodes in which the psychopaths had been involved. After one has read a couple of hundred of these descriptions, she will be confident that she could spot a genuine psychopath any time she encountered one, say, on the streets. The images called up by Dr. Cleckley's words, and Dr. Hare's, are vivid and memorable. The reader could put down Dr. Cleckley's list and draw up a profile chart of her own, with six, eight, ten, or twelve especially salient traits selected from the rest to serve as essential features of psychopathy. Of course we can hardly expect each and every selected "defining trait" to belong to all psychopaths or only to psychopaths. All that could be said at that point is that the selected traits are generally characteristic of psychopaths, and more so than they are of any other defined group. Some people will be only borderline psychopaths since they seem to straddle the minimal line of entry. Others will rank very high on some traits, but inexplicably low on some others since many traits differ in degree. We do not, therefore, have an exact, generally accepted set of necessary and sufficient properties of psychopaths, but what we do have is remarkably abundant data, and a useful, tentative (ten-part!) definition. What is known about this strange aberration of behavior is largely due to the researches of Dr. Hare, who extracted from a rich database a test for diagnosing psychopathy. The test and instructions for its use are now called "the psychopathy checklist," a "twenty-item clinical rating scale completed on the basis of semi-structured interview and detailed collateral or file information." Answers to each question are scored on a three-point scale, and a final score will fall in the range of zero to forty, with the highest numbers (those closest to forty) the most likely to be those of the genuine psychopaths. Dr. Hare considered testees with scores above twenty-five to have at least psychopathic tendencies.

Dr. Hare used his checklist both for practical purposes (e.g., using the results to help lawyers and prosecutors prepare their cases) and to help his fellow psychological investigators to draw up a more formal definition of the psychopath, which in turn will be useful one day.

The degree of overlap both of method and result in the work of Cleckley and Hare is quite impressive. In effect, each makes the other more persuasive. Cleckley's basic position on the relation of moral and psychiatric judgments is revealed in his title, *The Mask of Sanity*. The psychopath, he insists, will seem to be much like us in many ways until one is able to look under his mask and see the morally incomplete person residing there. Here are some paraphrased passages from Cleckley's book, which convey the general spirit of that work.

The psychopathic personality, as that term is now most commonly understood, is a man or a woman with a clearly recognized pattern of traits that leads to a lifetime of almost continuous antisocial behavior. To those who examine and treat psychopaths, it seems quite impossible that people with their character dispositions could be anything other than chronic troublemakers and petty criminals, at best. A minority composed of the more extreme psychopaths commit serious crimes, although these are not properly called crimes of passion, since the psychopath never experiences genuine passion of any kind and, unlike the psychoneurotic, suffers no anxiety either. His characteristic behavior seems "free" enough, noncompulsive, nonobsessive, often stubbornly willful. Many but not all psychopaths are highly intelligent. Typically, they have learned how to be charming, witty, and shrewdly manipulative. These social skills enable them to win releases quickly from mental hospitals when they are transferred there by desperate prison authorities, who after are utterly frustrated by the psychopath's disruption of prison discipline and routine. Hospital authorities, especially after repeated experiences with the same person, are even more eager to have him discharged as soon as possible, lest the doctors are driven to changing places with the mental patients. As a consequence, in hundred of cases, the psychopath, over the course of his life's history, often has a record of more than a hundred convictions, incarcerations, and transfers to and quick releases from mental health facilities. The cycle goes on and on. It seems that the psychopath is not fit to be free and not fit to be tied.

Hare, having had the advantage of Cleckley's earlier stories, contributed many more in the same vein and also gave formal definition to the term "psychopath." Like most of the other psychologists studying psychopathy, he was fond of the number ten, listing ten important characteristics of the psychopathic personality disorder and including highly literary development of them and anecdotes to go with them. I will borrow Hare's ten characteristics here. They will be important in my own argument, for they are the only definition we will have of the subject of my remarks. Some of the characteristics listed by Hare are theoretically uninteresting since they attach to psychopaths only in an accidental way and are not causally related to the characteristics that are actually part of the explanation of psychopathic behavior. The nonexplanatory characteristics help us to identify the psychopath, not to understand him, just as, say, a set of fingerprints or a regional accent would.

The first characteristic is an almost infallible indicator. The psychopath is glib and superficial. She even has a certain amount of charm, acquired by imitation of others who use charm successfully. She then carefully cultivates these traits. Psychopaths have the gift of gab, and they use it to win their victims' trust. They are the world's most accomplished liars. When they are imprisoned, it is frequently for crimes of fraud. For the most part they win the confidence of others easily. There are some astute observers, however, who have the impression that psychopaths are play-acting, mechanically reading their lines.

Most psychopaths share the second characteristic too. They are egocentric and grandiose. Each sees himself as the center of the universe and has an exaggerated sense of his own entitlement.

Hare has a richly expressive enumeration of adjectives to describe the third characteristic. Psychopaths, he tells us, often come across as arrogant, shameless braggarts, self-assured, opinionated, domineering, and cocky. These traits, which the psychopath can assume or abandon whenever it suits his will, are not likely to make friends for him. They are in fact more likely to get him involved in street fights. Dr. Cleckley had hundreds of cases illustrating this. A psychopath, whom he calls Max, because of his characteristic egotism and dogmatism is led into quarrels and fisticuffs with strangers almost daily. However, he "always took care not to challenge an antagonist who might get the upper hand." In that way his behavior resembles that of the schoolyard bully. But some mornings he wakes up in a deserted alley or park, dirty, bloody, aching, and sore, after a late-night barroom quarrel with a better fighter. Of course, on other mornings, he wakes up in jail: "In his encounters with the law, he has usually appeared in the role of petty bully and braggart." Cleckley continues: "Some months later I . . . testified at court when efforts were being made to have Max committed by law as 'insane.' . . . In trying to explain briefly and comprehensibly that I believed that this man, while not suffering from a psychosis that could be named, or any of the technical symptoms of one, was entirely unsuited to be at large, my sense of futility was oppressive. Max, neat and well groomed, insouciant, witty, alert, and splendidly rational, rose beaming, to hear again the verdict of freedom." This passage is painfully ironic, for Max as a criminal defendant, under judgment by a court, got away with the same kind of mendacious trickery that had become part of his life, and for which he was being tried at the time.

The fourth characteristic is one of the more fundamental ones, a virtual sine qua non of psychopathy. The psychopath has a complete incapability of feeling remorse or guilt. She can cause devastating harm to others and then show a "stunning lack of concern" about it. She does not spend time or invest emotion pondering the suffering she has caused. It is quite unreal to her, not even there to be thought about; she experiences no remorse, does not feel even simple regret. Her attitude toward her own wrongdoing, I imagine, is much like that of the reader of these lines after swatting a fly, or deliberately though somewhat absentmindedly squashing a cockroach.

Perhaps the most basic of all the definitional elements is the fifth. It tells us that the psychopath is also incapable of experiencing empathy, the putting of oneself imaginatively into another person's shoes and thus coming to know how the other person feels (a prerequisite to *caring* how the other person feels). Dr. Hare expands on the point:

> Because of their inability to appreciate the feelings of others, some psychopaths are capable of behavior that normal people find not only horrific but baffling. For example, they can torture and mutilate their victims with about the same sense of concern that we feel when we carve turkey for Thanksgiving dinner.
>
> However, except in movies and books, very few psychopaths commit crimes of this extremely violent sort. Their callousness typically emerges in a less dramatic, though still devastating, way: parasitically bleeding other people of their possessions, savings, and dignity; aggressively doing and taking what they want; shamefully neglecting the physical and emotional welfare of their families; engaging in an unending series of casual, impersonal, and trivial sexual relationships; and so forth.[25]

Hare's comments help clarify one of the ambiguities in Cleckley's account. Cleckley, whether he so intended or not, managed to convey the impression that psychopaths committed only minor or trivial crimes, though over the course of their lifetimes, many hundreds of them. There are few Jeffrey Dahmers, John Gacys, or Ted Bundys among the cases Cleckley has so vividly cataloged. Popular journalism, on the other hand, hardly uses the word "psychopath" for anything other than triple-sick rapes and murders. Both usages are unfortunate. In fact, two distinctions cut across one another, that between major and minor crimes (felonies versus misdemeanors, violent versus nonviolent, triple-sick versus not sick) and that between psychopaths and nonpsychopaths. There are thousands of relatively minor crimes committed by psychopaths and well described by Cleckley. There is a much smaller number of especially revolting serial rapes and murders committed by psychopaths. Nonpsychopaths commit both major and minor crimes, but Hare estimates that only 10 percent of all criminals are psychopaths. I know of no studies, however, that try to determine the exact percentage of wrongdoers in each criminal category who are psychopathic. What is really at issue here is the percentage of murders that are done by conscienceless killers (psychopaths) and the number done against the killers' consciences (nonpsychopaths).

In his useful and deservedly popular book, Hare lists as an independent defining characteristic that the psychopath is deceitful and manipulative, traits at which we have already looked in connection with glibness and superficiality. Now he examines in greater detail the facility with which these accomplished liars do their damage. Some of them actually "seem proud of their ability to lie," and all of them are remarkably unfazed by the danger of being found out.

The next trait Hare considers is one that he calls "shallow emotions." When it comes to emotion, the psychopath "knows the words but not the music." He knows that emotional displays can be useful, and he has learned how to turn them on and off. Some sudden bursts of violent anger may be genuine for the brief period he feels them, but even they have the sound to the experienced ear of playacting, and for the more profound emotions, perhaps Cleckley has said it best. He speaks of "incapacity for love," "general poverty in major affective reactions," "sex life impersonal, trivial, and poorly integrated," and a "lack of ability to become aware of what the most important experiences in life mean to others."

Some of the remaining characteristics Hare groups together under the heading "Lifestyle." They include impulsiveness. Many have written that the psychopath is like an infant demanding instant gratification. Under this heading, as elsewhere, Hare notes that psychopaths "give little serious thought to the future and worry about it even less." And it is not only other people who are unreal to them. They care just as little about their own futures. They care neither about their neighbor's projects nor their own, indeed about anything that is scheduled for the future. They have no life plans. They exercise no prudence nor any virtue aimed at the future. Threats, therefore, do not move them, and that includes the sanctions of the criminal law.

The next section is labeled "Poor Behavior Controls." The reference here is to the psychopath's inability to inhibit antisocial responses. As Cleckley had put it, some of the psychopath's violence is "inadequately motivated," and Hare adds that they are aggressive over trivialities. Only those who do not know them will be misled by their "hair triggers," and when they have outbursts of temper it is only *as if* they were having a temper tantrum; they know exactly what they are doing. Further traits evolve out of those already mentioned. Lack of responsibility, a need for excitement—the picture is becoming complete. Cleckley adds a few details. The psychopath's inability to know deep and authentic passion applies to negative passions too. Hatred spurs normal people sometimes to violent crime, and some very bad people are being propelled by powerful hatred as they wreak their havoc. But this is not the psychopath's way.

There emerges from the Cleckley and Hare case studies and biographical descriptions a coherent picture of the psychopathic personality disorders. Collectively, they make a rogue's gallery of persons we have all known from the somewhat odd boy next door to the cantankerous problem child and the teenage mother. Chances are statistically remote that we have been acquainted during our lifetimes with rapists and murderers, though that is by no means impossible. Hare estimates that there are two million psychopaths in North America, only some of whom are in prison. He is confident that all of us have met psychopaths at one time or another and have been manipulated (or cheated) by them. They are often charming, he warns, and "their hallmark is a stunning lack of conscience; their game is self-gratification at the other person's expense."

These are not esoteric technical terms commonly employed by behavioral scientists. Rather they are terms drawn from our moral vocabularies, and strongly condemnatory. In fact, Hare's definitional essay reads more like a list of sins than a list of symptoms of some psychological disorder. The terms in Hare's checklist positively bristle and crackle:

> Psychopaths are social predators who charm, manipulate, and ruthlessly plow their way through life, leaving a broad trail of broken hearts, shattered expectations, and empty wallets. Completely lacking in conscience and in feelings for others, they selfishly take what they want and do as they please, violating social norms and expectations without the slightest sense of guilt or regret.[26]

These are bad people not just because they sometimes slip and do what violates their conscience to their later passionate regret, but rather they are bad people through and through without consciences to violate in the first place. When a psychopath steals cash from his employer's till or shoots the clerk in a convenience store hold-up, he is just acting naturally. His behavior is preceded by no serious deliberation, no anguished struggle with conscience. He just "does it," that is all. Why has he no scruples or self-restraints? That is just the way he is. We need not divide his soul into parts, as some Christian moralists do and as moral psychologists as otherwise diverse as Plato and Freud do. The psychopath's immoral behavior is not the result of a split vote in some internal constituent assembly. His decision is the full consensus of a unified self, an ego that need not effect a compromise between body and soul, between reason and appetites, between reason and the passions, or among ego, superego, and id. Rather, he is all of a piece. He sees what he wants, and takes what he sees, without anguish or self-doubt. As Aristotle put it, he is bad through and through.

We have here an example of the involvement of moral with psychiatric judgments. The psychiatric or clinical psychologist presents a full and detailed description of a type of mental disorder, the symptoms of which turn out to be almost entirely moral character flaws. The criteria for the very existence of the disorder then correspond with the moral criteria that condemn it. The checklist of behavioral dispositions that define a psychological disorder in this instance can also be said to be a catalog of immoralities, a kind of syndrome of character flaws.

Moral syndromes are not common in our modern age, and those compiled by psychologists in describing disorders in which symptom and sin are so easily interchanged are less common still. The ancient moral philosophers, however, were quite familiar with the profiles of types of flawed characters. The Greeks called these traits of character "characteristics" and used the word "character" for the whole collection of virtuous or vicious characteristics.[27] Aristotle, building on collections of character descriptions compiled by his students, analyzed moral virtues as settled dispositions to act or have feelings of certain sorts in certain sorts of circumstances. Among those people who are disposed to act or feel in praiseworthy ways, those whose dispositions are strongest or most "deeply rooted" are the best (certainly the most reliable) people. Those whose behavioral and emotional dispositions are evil but not quite as firmly fixed are not quite as evil.

Professor Hare's evil psychopaths exemplify a leading pattern of wickedness, but by no means the only pattern. The psychopath is just a natural wrongdoer. It is in his nature (as we sometimes say) to do wrong to others, and that is enough to establish him as wicked, no matter how his blameworthy dispositions were acquired in the first place.

His characteristic moral flaws are the incapacity to feel empathetically, to experience remorse or guilt, a complete indifference to the state of any other people. There are other patterns of wickedness, however. A nonpsychopath may inflict hardships on others in a way that is quite different. And nonpsychopaths, after all, constitute 90 percent of our prison population.

Consider three patterns of wrongdoing (corresponding in part to the list of culpability conditions in the Model Penal Code). First is "moral recklessness." A harms B recklessly when, even though it is not his conscious intention to harm B, he consciously (or willingly) runs the risk that B will be harmed by what he does. He could stop in time to prevent harm to B, but he just does not care that much.

The second is "evil purpose." The primary objective of A's voluntary behavior is to cause harm to B. He values that consequence as an end in itself. It is not true that he acts as he does despite his awareness of the danger that he will thereby harm B. Rather he acts as he does precisely because he believes that he will cause harm to B ("perversity").

Third is "unscrupulousness" (also called "ruthlessness"). A is unscrupulous (unrestrained by scruple) or ruthless (without mercy) in his pursuit of some gain for himself. That is, if it appears necessary that B get harmed in order for A to gain, A will produce harm to B, either as a means to his own primary objective or as a by-product of the pursuit of another end. In summary:

A is *reckless* when he is indifferent to the danger he knowingly causes another person, B.

A is *diabolical* (wanton, gratuitous) when he pursues harm to B as an end in itself (pure evil, sheer wickedness).

A is *ruthless* when he causes harm to B as a means to, or side effect of, the pursuit of something else.

The psychopath would perhaps be most likely to commit his crimes in a morally reckless manner, for the essence of his immoral character is his total indifference to the interests or feelings of other people. Other people hardly exist for him. He never wonders or worries about other people. If it is more convenient for him to do so, he will run down any person who happens to get in his way. But he is no Jeffrey Dahmer. There is no necessity that his crimes be triple-sick ones. If his sexual tastes run in a "sick direction," and running over a child is a means of getting to a rendezvous with his victim, he will not care that he is imposing heavy costs on the child he runs over in order that he enjoy his cannibalistic or necrophilic pleasure. But the fact that he derives pleasure from such weird activities is probably not a consequence of his psychopathy.

The psychopath is no Satan either. To be indifferent to the harms that might be suffered by another person is not the same as seeking people out, as Satan is alleged to do, for the purpose of, say, inflicting pain on them as an end in itself, and responding to that pain with joyous hilarity. The most characteristic of the psychopath's shortcomings is his lack of major goals, aims, and purposes. He lives in the present moment only and is without ambition or passion that links him to any distant future.

Crimes of ruthlessness are committed by people with ultimate aims, bad or good, but aims in either case. Good men go bad when they pursue commendable aims but with "dirty hands," producing bad means to good ends. I suppose there is no reason why a psychopath could not commit a crime or a "moral offense" of this kind, and clearly some do.

Why not treat psychopathy then as an excuse? The descriptions of psychopaths in the writings of Cleckley and Hare read like word portraits of a common kind of "plain bad" person, a selfish and nasty sort who does not care what happens to others (or indeed what happens to himself) as a consequence, of his behavior, who is utterly indifferent to the interests and sensibilities of others, and is a conscienceless, cold-blooded inflicter of harm on others. His own future is as unreal to him as that of other people. But how could his badness be so extreme that it actually excuses him from responsibility as if badness of character were itself a grounds for exoneration from blame? "I couldn't help it," he says in his own defense. "I'm just a plain bad guy, and the extremity of my badness reduces my guilt rather than magnifying it."

One way in which plain badness can mitigate (rather than aggravate) is for it to constitute a set of blameworthy traits that can be, or can be understood as, symptoms of functional impairment in the manner of illness, injury, or handicap. The reader will have noticed that the psychopaths described by Cleckley and Hare not only do not care; they do not and *cannot* care. They are not only insensitive; they are incapable of being anything else. Words like "inability," "incapacity," and the like suggest the impairment of organs in biological organisms and component parts in machines, for example, human livers and automobile carburetors, thus making it impossible for the larger body or machine of which it is a part to function properly. This is a characteristic cost of illness, injury, and breakdown. Given this account of sickness, our symptoms are always signs that "something is wrong" somewhere; some part is not doing the job it is supposed to be doing. Does this teleological concept of disease help us understand what writers are claiming when they say that psychopaths are victims of mental illness or disorder, which excuses or mitigates their wrongdoing (or what would otherwise have been wrongdoing)?

If Robert Hare is right, then psychopathic criminals commit more than their share of violent and triple-sick crimes. If, on the other hand, Cleckley was right, most of the crimes committed by psychopaths are relatively minor. Occasionally, however, a psychopath—on impulse or whim—might join a group of thieves, or beat and severely injure a weakling who dared impugn his manhood as part of some banal persiflage, or shoot and kill almost routinely, without giving it much thought or ever regretting it. A psychopathic woman might abandons a child born to her and do so almost casually. When the crime is serious, and the perpetrator's motivation so trivial, then he can seem either more blameworthy than ordinary criminals or less blameworthy, depending on how we look at him. On the one hand, he is the model of a cold-blooded, conscienceless criminal (killer, mugger, burglar, defrauder). On the relatively rare occasions when he kills, he acts not from anger, hate, or zeal (all states of mind foreign to him). He knows no guilt feelings, although he may feel something akin to shame if he should happen to kill awkwardly, unintelligently, or "unnecessarily." Only in this sense is there anything like honor among psychopaths. He is totally incapable of feeling remorse, which is a blend of regret, self-loathing, guilt, and concern for one's victim, all saturated with intense affect. In short, those respects in which the psychopath differs from other wrongdoers generally make him a morally worse person.

On the other hand, the psychopath's crimes seem rarely to produce any benefit for himself; they proceed from no long-range scheme, no premeditated strategy for gaining profit or advantage for himself. He is not the rational, calculating egoist traditionally assumed by the criminal law. He seems as much beyond the reach of the law, however, as any criminal in the other categories. Most important, like someone who suffers from a severe mental illness, he seems immensely handicapped. He seems doomed to the pointless, self-defeating life he usually leads.

Indeed, in the most common understanding of the concept of an illness, psychopaths *are* ill. In that conception, an illness in the generic sense is the impaired functioning of some necessary element of an organic system. An organic system in turn, whether it be like a machine, say, an automobile, or a living thing, say, an animal or vegetable (and of course only the animal organisms are ever *literally* sick), is a complex of component parts related in such a way that the macroscopic functioning of the whole assemblage depends on the microscopic functioning of its parts and, to an important extent, vice versa. Thus the health of a human being's body depends on each component part—each gland, organ, and nerve doing its job—but on the other side, each component part, if *it* is to be healthy and function properly, requires the general good health of the body as a whole.

Diagnoses of health and sickness, it is interesting to note, though they may seem to be entirely factual matters, have in reality a certain irreducibly normative aspect. This is shown by the inescapability in all functional analyses of such terms as "doing its job," "functioning properly," "adequate, effective, or proper working order,"[28] and so on.

If mental illness shares the generic character of sickness, it must then consist in the disabling impairment of some vital *mental* function, such as reasoning, remembering, feeling, or imagining. The most conspicuous mental illnesses are those that involve impairment of the cognitive faculties and consequent chronic irrationality of one kind or another. Most forms of proper functioning are quite impossible for a person whose memory has totally failed, or who is incapable of drawing inferences or of distinguishing fact from fantasy. There is a general agreement among us that the sorts of incapacities directly consequent upon these functional failures constitute being out of proper working order and, therefore, being sick.

Much more difficult questions are posed by the mental dysfunctions that are noncognitive. Persons are now commonly called mentally ill when their affective, emotional, or volitional faculties are awry, even when there is no attendant cognitive dysfunction. If one's superego is a mental faculty, and it fails to instruct or restrain, is its possessor mentally ill? Surely, there is one obvious sense in which no person can function "properly" if he has no conscience. And one might argue that any person who commits criminal batteries, thefts, and murders is not "in good working order" and that certain moral norms, therefore, must be included among the criteria for proper functioning. If failure to act in accordance with the norms of a rational morality is the necessary consequence of some misfunction of a mental faculty—such as failure of memory, deformity of conscience, caprice of will, hollowness of affect, perhaps even persistent antisocial desires—then such immoral acts are, by definition, "sick." Indeed, how can any organic system be out of proper working order unless there is some component that is misfiring? If an automobile will not run or runs only with great difficulty, it cannot possibly be that all of its parts and component systems are in good working order. By this mode of argument, inclusion of noncognitive faculties among the components whose failure can cause overall malfunction leads us to the brink of the theory that all patently immoral behavior is sick and, therefore, excused.

An athlete whose liver is not in good working order will not be able to perform well in the 10,000-meter run. A researcher whose brain is not functioning properly will not be able to do her work as a scholar. A laborer with a broken arm will be unable to perform his proper job (function) so long as his "component part" cannot do its task of lifting and pushing. If we can say these things, why can we not, by parity of reasoning, say that the psychopath cannot be expected to behave properly so long as his vitally necessary component part—his superego, or conscience—is not functioning properly? But once we say that, are we not committed to the belief that the entire distinction between sickness and sin must break down? Perhaps that is too strong. But if we subtract from the ranks of those who are fully responsible for what they do, not only the insane psychotics but the hordes of psychopaths, we seem to be left primarily with those rational, calculating wrongdoers whose super-egos are still more or less intact and functioning properly and who, never-theless, choose voluntarily to act contrary to the dictates of their consciences. Perhaps *these* are the criminals who are the most wicked, since they appreciate the wrongfulness of what they plan to do, and then, in defiance of internal-ized moral authority, they do it anyway. But then again, this group contains mostly individuals who know what guilt feelings are and are capable of suf-fering remorse for what they have done. Perhaps, then, an intact conscience, instead of aggravating the wrongfulness of its possessor's crime, is actually a mitigation, making it possible for her to deserve forgiveness and redemption. There seem to be arguments both ways. Perhaps that shows that there is something wrong with our conception of moral blameworthiness, illness, and the way they fit together. The problem will rise again in our discussion of Eichmann.

The intelligent psychopath, having followed this long and inconclusive dis-cussion of his character, might show his truly psychopathic indifference to the outcome by quoting the duke of Coffin Castle in James Thurber's *The Thirteen Clocks*: "We all have our flaws, and mine is being wicked."[29] The psychopath does seem to have a point there. His severely flawed character is "just there," a part of his original nature, an essential component of his identity. He is wicked just as the rest of us are flawed in one way or another (I am a flawed swimmer), and there is nothing for him to do but accept that fact about himself, for nothing can be done about it, any more than something can be done for the person born without some essential organ. (Perhaps that is so, though it is self-serving and unseemly for *him* to say so.)

It is a function of psychiatric judgments to undermine the differing judg-ments of character made about the same people by moralists, judges, attor-neys, philosophers, and ordinary persons. Suppose we judge a man as having a habit or other behavioral disposition to act in a morally flawed manner. Perhaps he has a standardly recurring fault, which seems to entitle us to judge him harshly. Like the ancient Greeks, we may slide him into a category of people who manifest that flaw regularly and predictably. His dominant flaw, we might say, is arrogance, or conceit, or tactlessness. Only some defects of character included on lists of this kind are *moral* flaws in a properly narrow, modern sense. Garrulity, pretentiousness, buffoonery, and glumness we would call personality flaws. These make a person "no fun" to be with, whereas cruelty, cowardice, meanness, and unconscionableness might make him dan-gerous and untrustworthy.

Imagine that the evidence supports a moral judgment that a particular person is cruel. This judgment, let us suppose, would be concurred in by most ordinary folk. At this point we receive a detailed analysis of that person from a forensic psychiatrist or a clinical psychologist. We may well conclude, despite the formerly convincing evidence of cruelty, that he has a "syndrome" or a "disorder" of a special kind, namely, a disposition to behave in ways that strike ordinary persons as mean or cruel. Here we have yet another strange mode of mutual involvement between the technical language of the psychiatrist and the moral vocabulary of ordinary folk.

At this point our language gives us a valuable choice. We can say that we used to think that Joe Doakes was cruel, but now that we have read the psychiatric report, we see that our former view was mistaken. He is not cruel; rather, he has a personality disorder that leads him to behave in ways that we judge cruel. But if we *truly* judge him cruel, then it follows that he *is* cruel, and placing the proper psychiatric label on him does not undermine our original judgment.

A second option is to say that Joe Doakes is indeed cruel, whether or not there is a psychiatric explanation for that fact. Psychiatric judgments do not undermine commonsense judgments so easily. Often the two types of judgment are reconcilable. A person can be cruel (a genuinely moral flaw) and schizophrenic simultaneously, or obnoxious and boring at the same time. Sometimes, one word is a member of both vocabulary groupings. Indeed "narcissism" is now a technical psychiatric term and is also a term in general usage (meant mainly for moral appraisal). In some cases, the psychiatric term came first and then was absorbed into the general vocabulary (e.g., "paranoid"). In other cases, the word was first in the moral vocabulary and then was preempted by the diagnostic manual (e.g., "anxiety," "depression"). It is understandable why a judgment from one list does not regularly undermine a judgment from another list when their key terms have roughly the same meanings.

One apparent use of psychiatric language is simply to undermine judgments made in moralistic terms. Sometimes the moral judgment gets upgraded, as when we are said to "forgive" what we have come better to understand. "He is cruel," some say. "Not cruel, just neurotic, poor guy," comes the response. On other occasions, the psychiatric judgment, while not explicitly rebutting favorable moral judgment, effectively leads us to withdraw our favorable moral judgment from the person that judgment is about. "She is a saint," we say at first. "She is no saint," we say after reading the psychiatric account of how her extremely "benevolent" dispositions were formed and strengthened. Thus the psychiatric diagnostician becomes an arbiter between conflicting moral judgments.

The use of psychiatric judgments to undermine moral judgments, whether by upgrading negative judgments ("He is a crook") or downgrading positive ones ("She is a saint"), raises subtle difficulties about the role of evidence and argument in the appraisals we make of other people. We might learn, for example, that a military disciplinarian (call him Sergeant Hoodock) does not enjoy witnessing the pain he inflicts inevitably on the military recruits under his training. He makes them suffer by his command in order to toughen and discipline them. He tells them this at every opportunity, but never quite convinces them. What he does enjoy is the satisfaction of doing an important and difficult job well. He has been raised to seek honor above all, and honor, as his teachers have instructed him, consists in the reliable discharge of his duty. If that incidentally causes some tears somewhere, all the better. That is visible evidence of his dutiful effectiveness. The psychiatrist may actually disclose that Sergeant Hoodock has a heart of gold, a tender regard for the feelings of those under his command, and that some of the tears he causes through his words are his own. The concept of one's duty, of course, has always been a favorite masquerade for the truly cruel person. "How I suffered to perform my terrible duties," complained Adolf Eichmann to his unsympathetic captors at the time of his trial. If the psychiatrist convincingly reveals the many ways in which Hoodock and Eichmann derived pleasure from their difficult labors, we might begin to suspect that satisfaction at their duty well done was not entirely disinterested and professional.

Let us return, however, to the case in which psychiatric testimony has the effect of upgrading a person's moral status. "He is not *really* cruel," we are led to say. It is only in virtue of some superficial aspects of his behavior and his motivation that he shares anything in common with the ordinary person's conception of what cruelty is.

It is not that the psychiatrists' judgments provide us with *evidence* that we can all use to guide our inferences nor do they *prove* that the person who stands before us for judgment deserves to be upgraded morally. Rather, it is that we understand that what is at issue when we decide whether a given set of moral dispositions should be thought of as symptoms, or as mental disorder, is whether it is appropriate for us to hold him in high (or better) regard. If we believe the psychiatric appraisal of Sergeant Hoodock, we will find ourselves feeling better disposed toward the sergeant than before, and more respectful. That is what general moral appraisal normally produces.

Unsavory Emotions

Up to now I have assumed that it is actors and their actions that make appropriate candidates for pure evil. But there may be another way in which people can be evil. As Bernard Williams put it, there may be standards

> about what a man [or woman] ought or ought not to *feel* in certain circumstances, or more broadly, about the way in which various emotions may be considered as hateful, while others appear as creative, generous, admirable, or—merely—such as one would hope for from a decent human being. Considerations like these certainly play a large part in moral thought, except perhaps in that of the most restrictive and legalistic kind. (Italics added)[30]

Williams here follows Aristotle, who, as we have seen, defined "virtue" (personal excellence) as a disposition to act in certain ways or to have feelings of a certain kind in certain circumstances (details to be filled in later). There is little doubt that the general assessment we make of a person will include our evaluation of his propensities to feel, as well as to act, and that one's actions can be impeccable even though one's feelings ill fit the circumstances of one's life. In such cases, we cannot say that the person acts wrongly or that he is to blame for harmful conduct. But we can say that his inappropriate feelings are, in a way, *ugly* to behold, and that it is their *moral* flaws that are repugnant. Furthermore, these flaws reveal that he is not, on balance, a very good person.

Several decades ago, the custom grew on college campuses for student groups organized by fraternity boys to visit the sites of the executions of convicted murderers at the scheduled time of the administering of the death penalty. Let us imagine that these visitors to prisons recited derisive chants and slogans, obscene verses, and drinking songs with lyrics especially composed for the occasion. "Burn, baby, burn!" might have been a typical line. The fraternity boys gathered outside the murderer's cell, well within hearing range, and got noisier and rowdier as the night wore on.

The idea for such a fiesta would probably have occurred to the pro–capital punishment demonstrators when they watched the videotaped demonstrations of a quite different kind, which might have occurred at an earlier time on the occasion of the electrocution of another convicted murderer. Indeed, the two sets of demonstrators can be imagined to have made a striking contrast. The earlier group was somber in demeanor and quiet almost to the point of inaudibility. They made music only with their voices and a single guitar (no trumpets or kettle drums). The sounds were not shrill. The lyrics came from prayers and church hymns. "We Shall Overcome" was sung frequently. Several faces glistened with tears. At the moment the death occurred, the fraternity group clapped and whistled, thus making a sound of continuous applause that lasted for several minutes. And then the singing and dancing began in earnest.

The basis of the flaws I attribute to the celebrants is not simply that they are vulgar. Rather, it is that they are uncaring. A man is being prepared to die, and these people are celebrating. Their very presence is a staged part of it. It is a kind of collective ceremony meant to produce a death. Victims of the prisoner's earlier killing are still weeping, and more weeping will come from this new killing. The demonstrators are not all necessarily vengeful or consumed by hate. It is bad enough simply not to care. And they do not care.

We can imagine also that there were similarities between the two groups of demonstrators. Both believed that the prisoner was guilty of murder, that he was a thoroughly wicked person for his indefensible behavior, that he had no excuse or justification for killing a human being, that he had received a fair trial according to due process, that he probably deserved to die (even), and that he was himself a human being (anyway). The church group would no doubt have thought that the behavior of the fraternity group was tasteless and unseemly. The fraternity group would think that the church group was sentimental and overly sensitive. Conclusive reasons for resolving a disagreement of this sort are hard to find, and I shall not try to do so here. Instead, I shall register my own judgment and explain how it comes to seem plausible to me.

I have a strong conviction that the feelings vented by the fraternity demonstrators (even had they not been vented) were vulgar, disgusting, and obscene. Gathered to celebrate a climactic event in the moving transition of human life from birth to death, they refused to pay respect to the gravity of the occasion. The result is moral ugliness, perhaps most of which attaches to the boisterous behavior of the demonstrators but some of which is attached to their vindictive, hateful, and contemptuous feelings, whether given voice or not.

My sentiments, as I understand them, are very Greek. Socrates and Plato were dedicated to the achievement of moral beauty. I have quoted elsewhere the line from Epictetus that the wicked person is sufficiently punished just to be the sort of person he is (that is, a morally ugly person.)[31] Surely, other things being equal, most of us would be unwilling to exchange our normal moral good looks for grotesque and distorted features. Feel sorry for the morally ugly person, but do not evade the proper appraisal of his feelings and the way they reflect on his character.

At five in the morning, our collegiate celebrants are found, still dancing and singing outside the prison gates. They are all having fun still, though they may no longer be thinking of the prisoner who was only recently executed. If I quickly pass them by, it is not because I disapprove of dancing and singing, but rather because I disapprove of an inappropriate jubilation that can coexist with such horrors.

For another example of virtuous action conjoined with inappropriate feelings, imagine a woman who puts her duty, as she and Immanuel Kant understand it, above everything else. Her husband has long suffered from an incurable chronic disease. Nursing him properly is her one major goal in life. She helps him in and out of bed, bathes him, administers his medication. She also provides him with tender loving care, not because she feels any genuine affection for him (she does not), but only because he needs, for his therapy, to believe that she cares. Then one night she discovers that he is dying. Her immediate reaction is to kick up her heels and dance with joy at the thought of her husband's agonized death. She is happy and exuberant. Now at last, she believes, she can pursue her own interests, free of the onerous duties that have ruled her and the miserable old man whose needs have governed her. Her conduct remains as it has been all along, morally impeccable, yet her joy at her husband's painful (let us suppose) death would not reveal the model of a morally excellent human being.

A third example is that of a morally sensitive political liberal who contributes time and effort to a large number of groups dedicated to the cause of racial equality and human rights. He is a boxing fan too, frequently watching boxing matches on television. Many of these pit African Americans against whites. In time, his fellow liberals discover that whenever a white fights a black, this man roots for the white, cheering when the white lands a blow, showing a pained anxiety when the black scores.

These are attitudes typical of white racists, not of white liberals. But he is unapologetic. He is a forceful and articulate advocate, in other contexts, of black rights, and he insists that blacks deserve a fair chance in their various competitions for jobs and careers. When he has had occasion to hire a person for a job, or promote him to a higher responsibility and salary, he never fails to treat applicants fairly and equally, regardless of race. Any lesser treatment would violate his sensitive sense of justice. When he serves as a referee in amateur boxing matches, he always enforces the rules impartially. He is an honorable man, who always upholds justice when he can. He simply favors whites, perhaps because he is himself a white, just as he always favors the Boston Red Sox in baseball for no better reason than that they are his hometown team. Kant, I think, would have no complaint against him. He is not a "behavior bigot" and not a "feeling bigot" either, since these two words do not really fit together.

The fourth example is that which Herbert Morris calls "nonmoral guilt." The nonmorally guilty person acts to harm someone, and does so with full justification. The example that illustrates this possibility was invented by Phillipa Foot, for another purpose, and was used effectively by Michael Moore, whom I quote:

> A railroad switchman can only turn a moving trolley car onto one line or another, but he cannot stop it. He chooses to turn the car onto the line where only one trapped workman would be killed. On the other line, five workmen were trapped and would have been killed had the trolley car gone their way. The switchman is not morally culpable for directing the trolley on to the line where only one workman would be killed, since the alternative would be even worse, thus he was justified in doing what he did, but still *the switchman should feel regret*, remorse and even guilt at killing the one workman. The switchman who experiences such emotions is a more virtuous person than one who has a "Don't cry over what can't be helped" attitude toward the whole affair.[32]

Moore's judgment is somewhat extreme. It is going too far, I think, to feel "remorse and even guilt" for something one was fully justified in doing. Mere regret, however, is another story. The switchman who does not even regret the tragic consequences of his innocent act is insensitive in a way that suggests a flawed character. What kind of man is this? He has just aimed a lethal object (the two-ton trolley car) at another human being and deliberately caused his death. Would not we expect that he would find the experience a little unsettling? His equanimity in the aftermath of his life-and-death decision implies an indifferent disregard or lack of care that ill fits the situation. Another switchman in the circumstances might have been haunted for years by the image of the switchman who was killed, his face stricken with terror. But the innocent killer in the story does not care about that. It is not his business. If he were justified in his actual conduct, and can do nothing to recover the loss, then put it out of mind. To a cold-blooded, "rational" person, the death is just "spilt milk."

It is not likely that any of the central characters in the stories just discussed—the hecklers of the murderer, the conscientious nurse, the antiracist boxing fan, or the trolley switchman—are plausible candidates for the status of pure evil. What these hypothetical examples do show is that the type and strength of the feelings to which one is disposed can, quite apart from one's actions, help determine how good a person one is. Inappropriate feelings are like discordant musical scores, ugly to listen to, or like fingernails scratching a slate board.

The fraternity brothers are glorying in the suffering of someone who may well deserve to suffer anyway. The nursing wife in her private life is full of bottled-up hatred and resentments. The boxing fan perhaps is the one who least closely approaches wickedness in his private states of mind, though it might be replied that his arbitrary favoritism even on the level of private mental states is at least a wicked preference. Perhaps the most that can be said in criticism of the boxing fan is that he has an evil mental state, but in the sense of the word "evil" that it bears in the expression "an evil smell."[33]

In any case, as we have seen, the concepts of "evil" and "wicked" build on more ordinary ethical terms. To determine whether a person's action, for example, is wicked (or evil), we must first determine whether it was wrong, blameworthy, or bad and then whether it carries the distinctive mysteriousness of evil. None of the fictitious characters in the previous stories satisfies all of these foundational conditions.

The "Banality" of Eichmann's Evil as Described by Hannah Arendt

During the twentieth century, mass murders and politically organized attempts at genocide occurred in countries on every continent. But the Holocaust conducted by German officials in Germany and Eastern Europe was in a number of ways unique. In retrospect, it amazes and horrifies historians as it did contemporary observers, and it deserves our special attention here for a number of reasons. The first is its massive scale. The most commonly used estimate of the number of Jewish victims alone is six million. Second is the precise identification in advance of the victims. There was less secrecy and less mendacity than usually accompanies mass killings. The chief targets were, and were known to be, the Jewish populations of Europe, but various Slavic peoples too, notably Poles and Russians, were targeted though not totally eradicated. Poles were not killed as quickly and efficiently as Jews, because the chief mode of their extermination was for them to be worked to death as slave laborers. On the other hand, Hitler wanted the Jews and various other "inferior" groups quickly and totally destroyed.

The third reason is racism. Why did Hitler have this ambition? Because he thought the groups he targeted for destruction were inherently inferior, and thus posed a threat to the genetic purity of the master race. Hitler claimed to be doing a favor to the rest of the world by protecting it from contamination. But the whole "reason" for the Holocaust was that Hitler and his close associates did not like Jews; he did not like their looks; he did not like their songs; he did not like their prayers; and above all, he did not like their frequent successes in competition with their alleged superiors. What then is the "solution"? Why obviously, chant the racists, the solution is to murder six million people! And they did.

Fourth is its unprecedented efficiency. The designer of the weapons of mass obliteration operated within budgetary constraints. They applied the latest technology and employed skilled engineers. They actually learned from their research on bodies, living and dead, about how the human body reacts to various toxins. Never before in history had such huge populations been moved and manipulated so efficiently.

Fifth is the appeal to duty. Although difficult to believe, the Nazis, who were treating their prisoners as if they were subhuman animals devoid of any rights, were fond of a kind of moralistic rhetoric. Their philosophers claimed that a higher duty prescribed a kind of collectivism, and they condemned all forms of individualism as mere self-indulgence. Social reality was the group, and individuals counted in their moral deliberations only insofar as they were members of a group. Nazi youths thrilled as they marched in perfect lockstep, and in immense numbers. In the meantime, lesser peoples were murdered with a gruesome efficiency sufficient to win the admiration of the directors of animal slaughterhouses. How could this possibly have happened in one of the world's most advanced countries? Or anywhere else, for that matter? What was the rest of the world doing? Did the murderers have any reason for killing six million people apart from the fact that Hitler did not like them? Was it "fun"? If ever we had a case of pure evil or wickedness, this must be it.

In our effort to understand pure evil, we naturally begin by analyzing Adolf Eichmann, who was appointed by Hitler to be the director of the "final solution." But we will be disappointed if we expect to find evidence of the Devil incarnate there. Eichmann had a good reputation among the Nazi bigwigs because he was loyal, industrious, respectful of his bosses, and efficient. Ideological questions bored him. He was quite ordinary looking, calm, and soft-spoken. He could be relied upon to "get the job done." But he had never had a job like this one.

Eichmann, if we can believe Arendt's persuasive account, in committing his most heinous offenses, did not act against his conscience. The very idea of mass killings was at first as repugnant to him as to most normal human beings. But Eichmann was above all a respectable, ambitious, middle-class functionary. According to Arendt:

> What he fervently believed in up to the end was the virtue of success—the chief value of "good society" as he knew it. . . . His conscience was set at rest when he saw the eagerness and zeal with which "good society" every-where reacted to the Nazi genocidal program. What was being laid down at the Wannese Conference [where the original plan was developed] was done by the elite—the popes, as it were—of the state, said Eichmann [at his trial] in Jerusalem. . . . He had seen with his own eyes, and heard with his own ears that not just Hitler, Heydrich . . . and Muller, not just the S.S. and the party, but the elite of the good old Civil Service were there vying with one another to take the lead. . . . "At that moment I sensed a kind of Pontius Pilate feeling, for I felt free of all guilt."[34]

Who was he to judge? Who was he, as he expressed it, to have his own feelings in the matter? Well, Arendt comments, "Eichmann was neither the first man nor the last to be ruined by modesty."[35]

Eichmann's normal civilized conscience, Arendt estimates, lasted about three weeks after the brutal shippings and killings began. But then the "new German values" took over and, fortified by a renewed sense of duty, he over-came his natural repugnance and threw himself into his work. Sympathy for fellow creatures was now turned around and directed at the self, which was suffering in its faithful obedience to duty: "Instead of saying, 'What horrible things I did to people!' the murderers would be able to say, 'What horrible things I had to watch in the pursuance of my duties! How heavily the task weighed upon my shoulders!' "[36]

As for the enthusiastic ideological anti-Semites, Eichmann had for them supreme contempt. In Jerusalem, at his trial, he frequently denounced Karl Hermann Frank as "a low type," a "Jew-hater of the Streicher kind." Such men are vulgar and obscene, bestial sadists who made the respectable and proper people (with whom Eichmann like to place himself) hold their sensitive noses.

There were then at least three types of Nazi criminal. First, those like Julius Streicher and probably Hitler himself were righteously corrupt from the be-ginning and unrepentant at the end. Second, there were those like Otto Brad-fisch and Artur Greiser, who allegedly kept their civilized consciences unim-paired while deliberately acting contrary to them. Finally, there was the much larger and more troublesome class that contains Arendt's Eichmann and thousands of other "respectable people," who in an important way are like people all of us know. These Nazis found it remarkably easy, whether through the contagion of example or subtler self-deception, to shed their consciences and assume other prefabricated ones. At first these people acted against their consciences but felt guiltless because they were only imitating their moral betters, but then they came positively to approve of what they were doing, while both pitying and congratulating themselves for the suffering they caused others "in the line of duty." The third kind of evil is the more "banal," but which is the more wicked?

No one has ever caused as much harm to others by a single act as Adolf Hitler did by his order to put the final solution program into operation. More than six million people lost their lives. Of course at the moment of the pre-cipitating command the stage was already set, and the German population more than ready. But much of the prior setting of the stage was itself the work of Hitler and his Nazi party confederates.

If harmfulness were the sole criterion of evil, then we could say that the more harm caused by an act, the more wicked the act is. But this would be to condemn acts that are harmful only by accident or innocent mistake. They might be both extremely harmful and quite innocent. So we would be wise to say only that the more harm intended, the more wicked the intent.

Nevertheless, when philosophical moralists have ranked and cataloged the forms of moral goodness and badness, they have tended to rank what they call "disinterested malevolence" below "interested" (hence, intelligible) malev-olence, thus preserving a kind of symmetry with benevolence on the virtuous side of the ledger. For just as disinterested benevolence is supposed to be the highest kind of moral goodness, consisting of an overflowing of kindness from the sheer abundance of one's good heart above and beyond anything objec-tively called for by the situation, so wanton or gratuitous cruelty, serving no intelligible interest of anyone is supposed also to be a kind of extra outpouring of evil from an abandoned and malignant heart, and ranks below even the most flagrantly self-serving and intelligible kind of cruelty. But to the modern mind, this is the plainest inversion of values, and motiveless wrongdoing is the leading candidate for the sort of mental illness that is beyond good and evil.

There remain to be considered various scales for ranking degrees of blame-worthiness as the "sole criteria" of wickedness. The most interesting of these we can call the "scale of moral discredit." Applying this scale, we are allowed to consider how likely the person's evil acts were, given his background and upbringing. Then the more natural and probable his wrongdoing seems against this causal background (which includes his character as so far formed), the less wicked he is. It follows that a given evil act would be more to the discredit of a good man acting out of character than to the discredit of a rogue of hardened evil character doing what comes naturally. That this way of judging has some support in common sense is shown, I think, by the familiarity of the mode of argument employed by James Fitzjames Stephen in the following passage:

> A judge has before him two criminals, one of whom appears from the circumstances of the case to be ignorant and depraved, and to have given way to a very strong temptation under the influence of the other, who is a man of rank and education, and who committed the offense of which both are convicted [say, burglary] under comparatively slight temptation. I will venture to say that if he made any difference between them at all every judge on the English bench would give the first man a lighter sentence than the second.[37]

The context from which this passage is drawn indicates that it was apparently Stephen's intent to show that not only factual ignorance, temptation, and provocation but also a morally flawed character mitigate the "degree of moral wickedness involved in the crime." Defect of character then, especially if it is ineradicable, is a kind of excuse, whereas "knowing better" is an aggravation. The incorrigibly ill-disposed person may, in virtue of his defective character, be called extremely flawed, but perhaps by the time he is entirely defective, it is too late for him to be wicked, just as a person in total derangement can no longer be scorned as stupid or silly; just as a paralyzed man is beyond the slur of mere clumsiness; and just as a mute can no longer be criticized as inarticulate. Perhaps the incorrigible man is a moral cripple grown firm along his crooked bent and no longer able to stand straight. If so, wickedness *is* a kind of excuse!

Wickedness, according to this line of thinking, is apparently found at its maximum in the person of mixed character, generally good, but inclined from time to time to slip into evil in perverse defiance of his own better self. Wickedness so conceived is the supremely tragic flaw, the undoing of a person of substantial merit. Indeed, wickedness at its worst cannot exist without substantial merit upon which to feed. So another strand of moral common sense leads directly into a paradox, namely, that mixed evil is worse than pure evil. It seems to imply that there must be some point in the moral degeneration of a good man when he is just as wicked as he can be, so that as he becomes more and more abandoned to his evil bent from that point on, he becomes less and less wicked, until at the limit of near-depravity, he is not wicked at all. Wickedness, in short, has a critical point of diminishing return.

There is of course a quite different way of interpreting the scale of moral discredit, but it leads straight to its own equally curious consequences. A good conscience, however egregiously violated by its possessor, is at least a redeeming trait in the wicked man, it might be argued against Stephen. An evil man's better nature is at least *something* to his credit, it might be said, whereas the totally depraved or conscienceless evildoer has nothing at all to be said for him, and therefore is a more plausible nominee for extreme wickedness.

Something in common sense reverberates to this round of argument to—at first. But not for long. For a bizarre instance of its use, consider the defenses advanced by certain Nazi war criminals at their trials after World War II. Some S.S. men, according to Hannah Arendt, invoked in their defense what they called the "doctrine of inner emigration":

> The sinister Dr. Otto Bradfisch, who as an *Einsatzgruppen* commander had presided over the shooting of at least fifteen thousand people, . . . told a West German court that he had always been "inwardly opposed" to what he was doing. . . . the same argument was used, though with considerably less success, in a Polish court by former Gauleiter Artur Greiser. . . . only his "official soul" had carried out the crimes for which he was hanged in 1946; his "private soul" had always been against them.[38]

One does a double take at these arguments. At first, they seem at least relevant even if unconvincing, but at second sight they appear quite astonishing. The defendants argue in mitigation not that they acted conscientiously, following their genuine moral convictions in good faith for better or worse, but precisely the opposite, that they are to be relieved from much of their guilt because they acted *against* their consciences in one sense at least, in bad faith.

How could an S.S. man regard these facts as mitigating? Presumably, the reasoning is as follows: "Internal opposition" to his own actions is cited to show that he is not one of those detestable psychopathic beasts, one of those self-righteous sadists who thought they had a solemn mission to rid the world of inferior races. No wild beast or misguided fanatic he! On the contrary, he has a civilized conscience just as you and I do, and surely that much is to his credit. Once more then, we can ask, who is the more wicked man, he who acts against his civilized conscience or he who remains loyal to his depraved convictions and shows a certain "sincerity" and unrepentant righteousness? If the question asks, who is the more guilty, we can reply that they are equally guilty if they have intentionally committed the same prohibited acts. If the question asks, who is the more punishable, then perhaps we can appeal to familiar standards of social utility and retributive justice, and settle the issue no doubt as Bentham directed, to the disadvantage of the righteously corrupt man who "must be restrained by greater terrors." But if the question is simply, who is worse all told, quite independent of our practical purposes in assessing guilt, blaming, or punishing, then I see no way in which it can be made subject to any exact judgment at all. The corrupt man is, as Aristotle said, vicious through and through, unredeemed, and incorrigible (like a victim of a chronic disease), whereas the uncorrupt offender bears a heavier load of discredit and shame, having had a greater distance to fall. If these are the relevant criteria of wickedness, however, then they work necessarily against one another.

What then of the criterion of motivational uncertainty (unintelligibility)?

Was Eichmann's wrongful, blameworthy, and harmful behavior also unintelligible in the manner characteristic of wicked and evil people? The answer is clear. Eichmann's behavior was not "mysterious" enough to be pure evil. His reasons for doing what he did were commonplace. He wanted to secure a higher social status and respectability for himself among the right people. And if these objectives, achieved at such great cost, seem insufficient to move any normal person to action, we should correct our vision and direct it at the many bourgeois societies, including our own, where social respectability is pursued and cherished. I must admit, however, that the depressing saga of the aspiring bureaucrat is an extreme case. It is not often the situation that a kind of snobbery is the motive for mass murder.

Consider, nevertheless, the view that wickedness is to be identified with the intent to do harm (with or without its fulfillment in actually harmful conduct), and that the more harm intended, the more wicked the intent. Thus, we might say that the intent to injure a man's person is worse than the intent to steal or injure his property, but not yet as bad as the intent to kill ten persons, and that the worse a killer's intention on some such scale, the more wicked a man he is. By these criteria, Richard Speck would surely qualify as wicked for his deliberate murder of eight student nurses in their Chicago apartment, but he would not rate as evil as Charles Whitman, whose well-aimed rifle fire from the University of Texas tower wounded thirty-one and killed fifteen and whose intention (to judge from his ammunition supply) was to kill many more. Adolf Hitler would win honors, hands down, as the most evil man who ever lived, and the ultimate model of human wickedness would be the person (some "mad scientist" or "evil genius") whose intention was to destroy the whole human race.

One rather curious consequence of this criterion is that ordinary people of only moderate influence and power can hardly aspire to really monumental wickedness, however dark and twisted their motives may be. In order for a person to have an intention to bring about a result, he must believe that he can at least exercise some influence over the intended course of events. When I flip an unbiased nickel in an honest way, for example, I can wish or hope that it comes down heads, but unless I believe that I have some minimal control over it once it has left my hand, I can hardly *intend* that it do so. What I believe to be totally beyond my control *is* totally beyond my intention. If, indeed, a desired result is not only beyond my power to influence, but also (unlike the coin flip) extremely unlikely to occur whatever I do, then it may even be beyond my power to *hope* for, since hope is blended of desire and expectation, and one cannot even minimally expect what is believed to be totally unlikely. A misanthrope who is rational in at least the Humean sense may therefore *wish* the imminent and painful destruction of the whole human race, but it would tax his psychic powers to *hope* for it, and it would certainly exceed his capacity to intend it. If wickedness then is a function of *intended* harm, the poor and the weak of the world would have little opportunity to qualify. Equal justice for the laboring classes, therefore, requires a different criterion.

Evil as Bestiality

There is a view, widely held by the public though not popular with philosophers, according to which genuinely evil persons are like wild beasts or mad dogs. (A similar view stresses the analogy to rotten apples.) Sheerly wicked criminals who have lost their essential humanity are said to be like hungry tigers at loose in an Indian village, the inhabitants must destroy the animals if the village is to survive.

If a marauding grizzly bear is seen in our town, her claws already bloody with the flesh of half-consumed children and other miscellaneous fauna, what must we do? I should think we must form a posse of hunters to track the beast down and shoot her. We need not hate the bear, nor waste our moral judgment on her. There is just one thing to do. Shoot her and get it over with, in the same spirit as that in which we would cope with other natural calamities—fires, storms, slides, quakes, and floods.

There is surprisingly much to be said for this analogy. Granted, it does not apply to relatively minor and nonviolent crimes nor to repentant criminals and those with intelligible and self-regarding motives. One does not acquire similarity to a wild beast by petty thievery (though one can come to resemble raccoons and campground blue jays). But there is no doubting the resemblance between the triple-sick serial killer and the bear who ravages whole neighborhoods protecting her cubs.

The attitude of the innkeeper in Robert Louis Stevenson's "The Devil and the Inn-Keeper" would be exactly the appropriate attitude toward sheerly wicked criminals if we accepted the wild beast or mad dog models. The innkeeper has discovered among his guests a man who resembles the Devil. Somehow he captures him and puts him into confinement.

> "Now I am going to thrash you," said the innkeeper.
> "You have no right to be angry with me," said the Devil. "I am only the Devil and it is in my nature to do wrong."
> "Is that so," said the innkeeper.
> "Fact I assure you," said the Devil.
> "You really cannot help doing ill?" asked the innkeeper.
> "Not in the smallest," said the Devil. "It would be useless cruelty to thrash a thing like me."
> "It would indeed," said the innkeeper. And he made a noose and hanged the Devil.
> "There," said the innkeeper.

This Stevensonian parable is one of my favorites. Stevenson, I suspect, would have agreed with philosophers who think of triple sick-serial murderers

as no different from wild beasts. But he did not therefore advocate hunting
them down without mercy and venting hatred against them. Nor did he mor-
alize in the Kantian manner and urge that wickedness receive the comeup-
pance it deserves. Rather his attitude was that of a hunter or worker, perhaps
a carpenter or craftsman. The job is there to be done, so in an unemotional,
workmanlike manner he does it. "And he made a noose and hanged the Devil." No prayers, no curses. Just "There." What a beautifully expressive word!

When a criminal acts from intelligible and familiar motives, we can think
of ways to anticipate, threaten, bribe, or cajole him. But if his motives are
wholly unintelligible to us, not only do we seem defenseless before him, but
he is likely to seem weird and sinister and thus is able to evoke in us ancestral
and superstitious anxieties. Hence, we reserve for the unintelligibly nasty person our strongest epithets—ghoul, ogre, and fiend—and our more sober moralists speak of "senseless brutality" and "sheer wanton barbarity." That a
cruel crime seemed motiveless makes the harm it caused seem in the most
absolute sense unnecessary, and that rubs salt in our psychic wounds, as if
an intelligible motive would make our wounds any less injurious or the woun-
der any less blamable. Since we are unable to cope with irrationality in the
criminal, we are urged to abandon methods of response appropriate to human
beings and adopt instead attitudes appropriate to mad dogs or wild beasts.

At this point, attitudinal inconsistency becomes manifest, for whatever be
the attitudes we can appropriately hold toward real mad dogs, moral loathing
is not one of them. Hunger and protection of children are not plausible models for wickedness whether in the animal or the human world. Moreover, if
unintelligibility of motive argues irrationality in the actor, then, one might
claim, there is no further room for wickedness.

Subhuman irrationality has for a thousand years been not only a standard
of wickedness for some but at the same time a definition of exculpating "insanity." One of the leading tests of mental incompetence before the
M'Naghten rule was adopted held that a man is not responsible for his acts
"if he doth not know what he is doing no more than an infant, nor a brute,
nor a wild beast."

Is a wicked human at all like a wild beast or a mad dog? Well, of course.
Any two things are alike in some respects but not in others. The question is
whether human wickedness is similar in some significant or illuminating way
to the undiscriminating use of lethal violence characteristic of some wild
animals.

Pure evil is a notion designed to distinguish human actions from the wider
genus of actions that are subject to negative appraisal. Wickedness is a species
of that wider genus. Purely evil actions are, like the other members of the
wider class, actions that are morally wrong and extremely harmful or dangerous to others, behaviors for which the actor, lacking excuse, is blameworthy.

In addition to the characteristics listed above, some wrongful actions are also wicked or evil. Which are they? Surely not the actions of grizzly bears or of brain-damaged sufferers of rabies, conditions that are not even subject to the ordinary terms of negative appraisal. Lacking even these bare minimal qualifications, they hardly fit the definition. It is a waste of breath to call a hungry tiger "blameworthy." In that case, a fortiori, a tiger cannot be "wicked."

A rotten apple rarely has even this much in common with a wicked man. As it sits in the innocent comfort of the bottom of its barrel, it poses little threat to anyone. If the harvesting farmer sees its soft and mushy spot, a bruise beyond repair, he will of course throw it away in the same spirit as that in which R. L. Stevenson's innkeeper disposed of the Devil.

There.

7

FUSION

The Blending of Moral and Psychiatric Judgments

Sickness as Mitigation

Philosophical perplexity about atrocious criminals begins when a person notices that the more bizarre the crime, the stronger one's inclination to think of the criminal as sick. When an armed robber holds up a convenience store, we find that our moral vocabulary is quite adequate for expressing a suitable judgment about his behavior. If the robber goes on to shoot the grocery clerk, quite "unnecessarily," that is more troublesome. If he then uses an automatic weapon to shoot an entire kindergarten class of small children as they cluster in a school playground, that is "sick." If he drags the still-breathing bodies into his apartment and, in the manner of Jeffrey Dahmer, boils, skins, and eats them, that is sick! sick! sick! As the behavior of the criminal in these examples gets worse and worse, it seems in parallel fashion to get sicker and sicker.

What makes this situation especially disturbing is the fact that sickness (at least, mental sickness) is a traditional ground, both in law and morality, for the mitigation of culpability. We are now far beyond the day when (mental) illness was really taken seriously as a criminal defense. To think of a person's conduct as a product of mental illness was once to ease up on him and urge that he be at least partially exonerated. What is new, however, is a development in the opposite direction. We have now grown accustomed to the use of the idea of sickness to condemn behavior and to aggravate (the opposite of "mitigate") wrongdoing.

A survey of call-in talk shows and other news and opinion media will provide numerous surprising examples. One of the clearest is the remark spoken by a listener to a radio talk show. The New York City police had tortured a suspected criminal by jamming objects up his rectum, damaging internal organs most painfully. The caller spoke with great anger, much more anger than one would normally feel toward a person whom one regards as sick: "Whoever did this thing is sick and psychotic," she said, "and ought to be punished."

This usage, however familiar it has now become, breeds paradox, for if the most immoral crimes are also the most sick, and the sickest crimes are those for which there is substantial mitigation, then it seems to follow that the worse the crime, the more forgiving we should be of the criminal. And if a person with serious mental illness could on that ground gain acquittal, then at least some of the time, we would have to turn the most horrifyingly violent criminals free to roam the streets.

To avoid these unacceptable conclusions, we must reexamine the relation between wickedness (for example, the crimes of Jeffrey Dahmer) and mental illness (for an example once more, the crimes of Dahmer). If it should turn out that we cannot explain the relation between sickness and wickedness, we fall short not only of the conceptual clarity we seek as an end in itself, but we are left also with unsolved problems for moral judgment. Is the triple-sick criminal who puzzles us, for example, the typical serial murderer, more sick or more wicked? And how, if at all, does his degree of sickness affect his degree of guilt?

I wish that I had a simple and general answer to these interrelated questions, but I am afraid that I do not. The best I can do is offer a slightly unusual explanation of why problems of this sort are so difficult. The answer is that the concepts in which the dispute is formulated are themselves blurred from the start. Both basic concepts—sickness and wickedness—are complex mixtures, each containing essential elements of the other. They are strings that need to be disentangled, elements that have not remained distinct, having fused or blended, one into the other. (The reader is invited to select her own metaphor.)

It can be unsettling to a theorist who is trying to determine how psychiatry and morality can interact, or indeed whether they should interact, to learn that they are already so intimately related at the level of basic definition that it is difficult to pull them apart. And, given the uses to which they have been put over the centuries, it is no accident that each bears the mark of the other.

The most promising method for sorting out the relations among these various elements, I think, is historical. By identifying the elements that have in the past entered the developing, now-fused concept and strengthened the bonding of its components, we can hope to learn how moral and psychiatric concepts have come so close together.

A great variety of philosophical theories and therapeutic practices, beginning with the immense influence of Plato's philosophy, have contributed to this condition. I have counted as many as two dozen contributing factors. Some of these factors are changes in the meaning of words, a process that is continuous and usually incomplete, as earlier meanings continue to exercise some influence into the present. J. L. Austin was recommending this methodology when he wrote that "a word never entirely forgets its past."[1]

Plato: Illness as Internal Usurpation

The concepts of mental illness and immorality first began their promiscuous intermingling in Athens in the fourth century B.C. The very idea of mental illness was Plato's invention.[2] Plato had analyzed injustice, both unjust societies and unjust individuals, in terms of the internal discord that occurs when organic parts and subsystems usurp one another's natural functions, that is to say, when they usurp a function for which they are not well suited by their natures.

When reason, the part of the soul meant by one's nature to govern all of the other elements, is overcome by the relatively lowly "appetites," or when that which Plato called "the spirited element" in the soul does not do its proper job, the soul is wracked by conflict and confusion, just as a political state would suffer if its social classes were riven by hostility. When square pegs are forced into round holes, as we say, they suffer the spiritual equivalent of a headache. Injustice in the soul throws the whole organism out of kilter, which is exactly what it is to be mentally ill. One can appreciate then how mental illness, according to Plato, cannot possibly be in a person's self-interest. Even a crime that is successfully executed and clearly self-serving does not "pay." To be in that manner out of kilter, Plato insists, is to be mentally ill, and that is no fun.

To be mentally ill, then, is to be in a condition not easily distinguished from morally bad character. The mark of both (poor mental health and poor character) is a kind of out-of-kilterness, which also results when parts of a whole stand in relations to one another similar to those in a community most of whose members are thieves or burglars.

Fundamental to this picture is the concept of usurpation which, in its application to the human mind, is a political metaphor. Badness of character, according to Plato, is just one kind of out-of-kilterness, and it is subject to the same kind of analysis whether applied to human character or to machines and organisms.

Usurpation, as Plato understands it, can be external or internal, or typically both. If I act wrongfully in a social context, violating the rights of other people or preempting the prerogatives of another person's office, I throw the relations among the involved parties out of kilter. But in so doing, the element of my soul whose natural function is to govern me (reason) is itself usurped, internally. External usurpation is a relation between me and other persons. Internal usurpation is a relation among the parts of myself.

Usurpation exhibits a number of familiar patterns. Sometimes an element with authority is overruled by a subordinate, as when a mere appetite overturns reason, or a subject defies a legitimate ruler. Sometimes the usurper is one individual element wronging another element at the same level, as when alcohol robs one's body of the nutrition it needs, and it is a case of one appetite (psychological craving) against another (physical hunger).

Obviously, Plato's political philosophy gives emphasis to the analogy between the state and a biological organism. Thus, when something is out of kilter in the state, the statesman's job is to set it right, just as a physician corrects biological processes that have gone awry. Plato's medical analysis, applied to individuals, serves him in the same way as his legal or political analysis, applied to the state. To be mentally ill is to be in the grip of the same sort of impairment as that which afflicts organic complexes (organisms or machines) when a component part or subsystem fails to do its natural job. So in a way, a mental illness is to a human being what a flat tire is to an automobile.

To be inclined generally to act in a way that is unjust to others is to be disposed to a kind of illness in which one's major "parts" fly off in different directions and lodge where they do not fit. When such usurpation occurs internally, the soul is wracked by conflict and confusion, and it suffers, just as a political state would in comparable circumstances.

There can be more than one usurper in a group, but clearly if almost everybody is after something that belongs to someone else, there can be no smoothly functioning community. This truism holds not only of groups of individuals but also of the constitutive elements within persons, lungs and livers, for example. If one's liver is not working well, then one's self cannot be working well either.

Legal punishment raised a moral problem for Plato that led him to formulate a theory that blended wickedness with sickness. It was his firm conviction that it is always morally wrong deliberately to inflict harm on another human being for any reason whatever. But if we think of punishment as therapeutic treatment by a moral practitioner who presumably is intent on benefiting (not harming) the person he punishes, we can appreciate how punishments can be a morally acceptable way of treating people, initial appearances to the contrary.

If punishment can restore a patient's soul to harmony, then by punishing him, we may positively benefit him. If Plato were alive today he might be directing a mental health facility, and if harsh language or painful treatment were ever imposed on the patients/prisoners in Plato's hospital, it would be because it was thought to be an effective therapeutic strategy to convince them of their own depraved conduct in the past, and then proceed from there, as when Plato's descendants today try to induce remorse in an unrepentant prisoner (or patient). Platonic therapists would describe their patients to third parties as "sick but not wicked," but they might choose to tell their patients that they are "wicked but not sick," because immoral people have to accept the truth of their own depravity if therapy (moral regeneration) is to have any chance of success.

The task of replying to Plato falls most heavily on supporters of the deserved harm theory. For these writers, punishment is justified if, but only if, it is deserved. It can be morally permissible actually to harm a wrongdoer if that is what she deserves. Desert is the gist of the new, post-Kantian, retributivist rejection of the old retributivism. The old retributivists cultivated their anger, resentment, or hate, preserving and enhancing it. Their anger was righteous indignation, not self-centered rage. But we should not think better of a man if we learn that he is obsessed with the infliction of suffering even on one who deserves it.

Plato's philosophy of punishment is a long way from any form of retributivism. The retributivists struggle to find a rationale for inflicting what they often admit to be harm on wrongdoers. The Platonists, on the other hand, do not have to make a case for deliberately inflicting harm, since punishment construed as therapy is not, or need not be, harmful in the first place.

Other Historic Influences

The science of medicine, of which psychiatry is a branch, has its own norms. Some of these stipulate what it is to be healthy as opposed to sick, and others what it is to be normal as opposed to being abnormal or deviant. Sometimes medical writers apply medical norms in their definitions of what it is to act properly. Sometimes moralists apply norms of moral propriety in their accounts of what it is to be normal or healthy. There are dangers, however, in both of these practices. Medical writers have always had to resist the temptation to infer from the fact that some behavior is morally suspect that it is also medically deviant or abnormal. Similarly, because a given kind of conduct is held to be medically abnormal, or sick, there have always been those who would infer, for that reason only, that it is also morally improper.

An example of the inference from morally improper to medically abnormal is reported by Tristram Englehardt and his colleagues in an interesting article. They describe the process by which the lists of official sicknesses in various European and North American countries came to include such behavior as masturbation.

At the dawn of the twentieth century, the list of recognized medical illnesses in various European and North American countries was extended substantially by medical societies in those countries, and the list of new diseases included examples of "victimless illnesses." In political democracies, a list of *crimes* is created by the enactments of democratically elected legislatures. Lists of official illnesses, on the other hand, are determined by an independent medical authority. That some common forms of conduct would be stigmatized, and retroactively at that, as newly created "abnormalities" must have come as a shock to many. Englehardt describes how such "morally suspect" conduct as cocaine addiction, homosexuality, and even masturbation were reclassified as sicknesses on the implicit ground that they were disapproved of morally.

Masturbation had been thought to be, from the medical point of view, at most a naughty peccadillo. It could hardly have been a disease, it was thought, unless its moral condemnation were more serious than that.

The medical writers of a century and a half ago seem likely to have argued as follows: They began by describing a set of autoerotic practices known to be frowned upon by many people, and then proceeded to transform those habits and practices into a "disease" with somatic, not just psychological, dimensions. This involved searching empirically for correlations between the regular practice of masturbation and such bodily disorders as migraine headaches and dyspepsia.

What we find when we look at a range of psychiatric and moral/legal judgments is that it is difficult to make the distinction clearly between the psychiatric realm ("He suffers from narcissistic personality disorder") and the moral realm ("He is a selfish and cruel person"). And when selfishness and cruelty are enshrined as part of the official definitions of psychiatric syndromes, the process is furthered and strengthened.

This is not the only place in our study where the reader, after pondering a particular mode of involvement between moralists and psychiatrists, would naturally wonder, What is the difference between them, if any?

How does a professor or a textbook writer turn a morally disapproved activity into an official sickness by simple decree? The simpler the process and the greater the invasion of privacy it makes possible, the more puzzling it is. In the case of masturbation, the historical process was clear, evident, and showed how "activities disapproved of within certain social or moral viewpoints [can] become transformed into diseases by changing what is understood as morally or socially improper into what is viewed as physiologically or psychologically abnormal."[3] The practice, moreover, of including moral criteria in the very definition of mental illnesses is, as we have seen, another factor in the fusion of formerly distinct elements.

At the turn of the twentieth century, psychiatric writers in effect produced a merging of moral and psychiatric vocabularies. This in turn produced a blending of moral and psychiatric subject matters. These effects were produced, in part, by the simple device of adding the adjective "moral" to a number of psychiatric nouns. Thus we have "moral weakness," "moral dementia," "moral imbecile." These ways of talking were early attempts to have one's cake and eat it too. In particular, they were used in the interpretation of so-called moral imbeciles, who were said to be cognitively "impaired" and morally blameworthy at the same time. They were said by those who talked in this fashion to be suffering from chronic learning disorders, which prevented them from "getting the point" when it came to understanding moral judgments. Thus moral imbecility was regarded as a kind of retardation, a form of incapacity. Those who were labeled moral imbeciles were now simply people who were stupid about morality. They did not know the difference between right and wrong, and their inability probably prevented them from ever learning it.

It is surely not impossible for some of one's behavioral or emotional dispositions to be *both* blamable morally and symptomatic of mental illness. It may even be that the criteria for some particular syndrome and some complex moral failing coincide exactly, so that the same litmus test applies to both. Indeed, as we have seen, the leading checklist for psychopathy purports to be a set of criteria for identifying people who have this psychiatric disorder and also a mental failing virtually identical in its symptoms to a set of moral character flaws.

In various other places, we see the use of moral character flaws as names of "mental" disorders. These terms are then liberally distributed among the technical terms in the definitions. So, for example, "narcissistic personality disorder" is defined in the lexicon of the American Psychiatric Association as "a pattern of grandiosity, [excessive] need for admiration, and lack of empathy." Thus if you have an acquaintance who has these moral flaws in a recognizable pattern, you need not only judge him to be morally flawed (and perhaps obnoxious), you can also judge him to be mentally disordered or neurotic (and perhaps excused).

It takes no particularly great insight to see how intertwined in complicated definitions these propositions are. Moral evaluations affect diagnoses, diagnoses affect moral judgments, and the very traits that give a person low grades morally can assign him serious illness medically.

The fusion of the normative and the psychiatric seems both acknowledged and reinforced by the psychiatric profession itself. Its official definitions of psychiatric disorders in many cases include reference to important and substantial moral flaws. One of these cites the propensity to disregard the rights of innocent people. If we see Mr. Jones deliberately disregarding the rights of innocent Mr. Smith, that becomes, ipso facto, evidence that Mr. Jones has a medical problem. His moral flaws are symptoms of his mental illness. The concept of a right thus becomes part of the framework of psychiatric theory and practice.

NOTES

Chapter 1

1. Aristotle, *Nicomachean Ethics*, 1131a32–33 (paraphrased).

2. Some purists might insist that Shakespeare's *Othello* requires that Desdemona be white and Othello black and that a black actress and a white actor in those roles would distract an audience into missing a good deal of the dramatic clash that Shakespeare was trying to exploit. A more reasonable view now, however, is that audiences can be expected not to be distracted by so irrelevant a thing as skin color and therefore can be relied upon to provide their own appropriate projections of historic setting. One must admit, however, that a switch in gender might overtax an audience's imaginative resources.

3. *People v. Johnson* (1967) 52 Misc 2d 1086, 278 NYS 2d 80.

4. The quotation is from Lynn C. Cobb, "Annotation: Validity of State or Local Regulation Dealing with Resale of Tickets to Theatrical or Sporting Events," American Law Reports, *Cases and Annotations*, 3d ed. (1977), 81:672.4.

5. Ronald Dworkin, "Hard Cases," in his *Taking Rights Seriously* (Cambridge, Mass.: Harvard University Press, 1971).

6. Compare John Rawls, *A Theory of Justice* (Cambridge, Mass.: Harvard University Press, 1971), pp. 54–117, with J. S. Mill, *Utilitarianism* (1861), chap. 1.

7. Sir William Blackstone, *Commentaries on the Laws of England*, (Chicago, Ill.: University of Chicago Press, 1979).

8. See Joel Feinberg, *Harm to Self* (New York: Oxford University Press, 1986), pp. 87–94, on the differences between privacy, in the ordinary sense, and autonomy, or self-determination.

9. That occasions for "Solomonic wisdom" still exist is shown by recent well-publicized cases in the United States of hospital-switched babies later suing for "divorce" from their biological parents.

10. William Blackstone, *Commentaries on the Laws of England*.

11. See Robert M. Cover, *Justice Accused: Antislavery and the Judicial Process* (New Haven, Conn.: Yale University Press, 1975): "The court can assert a sort of bend-over-backward principle by which there is an obligation to achieve a profreedom

(antislavery) result unless there is a very specific, concrete positive law that prevents it" (p. 62).

12. Ronald Dworkin, "The Model of Rules," in *Taking Rights Seriously*. In his interesting discussion of the distinction between legal rules and legal principles, Dworkin treats *stare decisis* (a legal doctrine requiring fidelity to precedents) as an example of a conservative principle.

13. Lon L. Fuller, *The Morality of Law* (New Haven, Conn.: Yale University Press, 1964), pp. 33–38.

14. Lloyd L. Weinreb, *Natural Law and Justice* (Cambridge, Mass.: Harvard University Press, 1987), p. 4.

15. Cover, *Justice Accused*, pp. 151ff.

16. Ibid., p. 161.

17. Ibid., p. 6.

18. Ibid.

19. Francis Lieber, *Political Ethics*, 2d ed. (Philadelphia, Pa.: Lippincott, 1874), 1:344, quoted in Cover, *Justice Accused*, p. 147.

20. Cover, *Justice Accused*, p. 62.

21. Wendell Phillips, *The Constitution: A Pro-Slavery Compact*, quoted in Cover, *Justice Accused*, pp. 153, 178.

22. Cover, *Justice Accused*, p. 158.

23. Lysander Spooner, *The Unconstitutionality of Slavery*, quoted in Cover, *Justice Accused*, p. 158.

24. William James, "What Pragmatism Means," in his *Essays in Pragmatism* (New York: Hafner, 1948), p. 144.

25. Joseph Butler, bishop of Durham, 1662–1752. I do not know the exact source.

26. Cover, *Justice Accused*, p. 156.

Chapter 2

1. *Griswold v. Connecticut*, 381 US 479 (1965).

2. *Loving v. Virginia*, 388 US 1 (1967).

3. "A historian who said the British Agricultural laborer of 1810 had no right to organize in trade unions, would seem to be making a statement about actual conditions which could be judged true or false as it accorded with the facts" (S. I. Benn and R. S. Peters, *Social Principles and the Democratic State* [London: Allen and Unwin, 1959], p. 92).

4. The example is from R. B. Brandt, "The Concept of a Moral Right and Its Function," *Journal of Philosophy* 29 (1983).

5. A special issue of *Time*, dated Fall 1990, describes the practice: "A rite undergone by more than 80 million African women. Female circumcision—the mutilation of the external genital organs—is a centuries-old rite of passage, intended to ensure that young women become desirable wives [by eliminating a presumed motive to infidelity]. It frequently causes life-threatening blood loss and infection. It can also lead to painful intercourse, infertility and difficult childbirth. While often erroneously linked to Islamic scripture, it is not mandated by any religion and is practiced by people of many faiths in some two dozen black nations [as well as] Egypt and the Sudan. [It is the traditional practice of the lowly caste of Egyptian Arabs who collect the waste of the city of Cairo.] . . .

"Midwives, village healers and elderly female relatives perform the ritual without anesthesia, using unsterilized razor blades. Parents look upon it favorably on the grounds that removing the clitoris purifies their daughters and deadens their interest in sexual pleasure. Ironically, the frigidity or infertility caused by the mutilation leads many husbands to shun their brides.

"Doctors throughout Africa recognize the harmful effects of female circumcision but feel powerless to stop a practice so entrenched in custom and tradition. Many organizations are campaigning against it, and the new African Charter on the Rights of Children includes items condemning circumcision. Governments in Sudan and elsewhere have passed laws against it, but they are seldom enforced.

"It will take education, not just laws, to halt what Africans view as a symbol of their culture. Asks Birhane RasWork, president of the Inter-African Committee on Traditional Practices: 'How do you eradicate a tradition that is more powerful than a legal system?' " (p. 39).

6. "The practice of killing a favorite wife on her husband's grave has been found in many parts of the world . . . [among] the Thracians, the Scythians, the ancient Egyptians, the Scandinavians, the Chinese, and people of Oceana and Africa. Suttee was probably taken over by Hinduism from a more ancient source. Its stated purpose was to expiate the sins of both husband and wife and to ensure the couple's reunion beyond the grave, but it was encouraged by the low regard in which widows were held. . . . Isolated cases of voluntary suttee have occurred into the 20th century." (*The New Columbia Encyclopedia* [New York: Columbia University Press, 1975], p. 2662).

7. R. G. Frey, *Interests and Rights: The Case against Animals* (Oxford: Clarendon, 1980), p. 7.

8. Still another sense of "natural rights," usually left implicit, refers to rights based on natural *needs*, a conception that arouses the suspicions of some philosophers of libertarian persuasion. Other philosophers distrust the "natural law" all of whose moral requirements ("natural duties") reduce to acting in accordance with one's own natural inclinations, and all of whose defined sins reduce to acting contrary to the way we are actually inclined by our human natures to act.

9. E.g., W. D. Ross, *The Right and the Good* (Oxford: Clarendon, 1930), Appendix I, "Rights," pp. 48–55.

10. E.g., Richard B. Brandt, *Ethical Theory* (Englewood Cliffs, N.J.: Prentice-Hall, 1959), pp. 17, 433–54.

11. Howard Warrender, for example, writes that "A 'right,' as the term is generally used in moral and political philosophy . . . is . . . a comprehensive description of the *duties* of other people toward oneself in some particular respect . . . In this sense, the term 'right' has a rhetorical rather than a philosophical value. . . . the rights formula . . . is a loose, summarizing expression that would be useful in an argument where others are denying this right, or where long windedness is to be avoided, or where its emotional and personal reference is to be emphasized, but as a vehicle of philosophical inquiry, it is insignificant" (*The Political Philosophy of Hobbes* [Oxford: Clarendon, 1957], p. 18).

12. Frey, *Interests and Rights*, p. 12.

13. H. L. A. Hart, "Bentham on Legal Rights," in *Oxford Essays in Jurisprudence*, 2d ser. A. W. B. Simpson (Oxford: Clarendon, 1973), esp. pp. 179–80, and Carl Wellman, *A Theory of Rights* (Totowa, N.J.: Rowman and Allanheld, 1985), pp. 91–94, and passim.

14. Wellman, *Theory of Rights*, pp. 42–51, 66–68, 147–57.

15. The same kind of point can be made, *mutatis mutandis*, about respect for

others. In the relevant sense of self-respect, we respect ourselves when we think of ourselves as potential makers of claims in our own behalves. Similarly, to respect others is to think of them as potential makers of claims against us and against other parties. It is useful for a rights theorist to remind himself from time to time that rights possession is attributed not only in the first person singular, but in the first person plural, and the second and third persons too. That reminder would save him and his readers from the mistake of taking rights to be essentially the contrivances of selfishness.

16. United Nations Universal Declaration of Human Rights (1948), Article 24.

17. Rights and duties are names of moral positions. Sometimes a person is in a position to make a claim, but because of shortages or other incapacities, no one else is in the corresponding position to which attaches the duty. See the discussion of manifesto rights in Joel Feinberg, *Social Philosophy* (Englewood Cliffs, N.J.: Prentice-Hall, 1973), pp. 67, 110. We can say that when or if someone ever comes to occupy that position, then the claim of the other party, which is directed at the occupant(s) of that hitherto empty position, will generate a duty. The duty comes with the position and is merely latent until the position is occupied.

18. Robert Cover, *Justice Accused: Antislavery and the Judicial Process* (New Haven, Conn.: Yale University Press, 1975), p. 105.

19. Jeremy Bentham, conclusion to *Anarchical Fallacies* (1789), quoted in Jeremy Waldron, *Nonsense upon Stilts* (London: Methuen, 1987), p. 68.

20. There are no doubt some harmless principles that escape these strictures. It may be salutary to be reminded from time to time by official state declarations that it is rightful to rebel against a government that is itself the product of a wrongful rebellion, and that it is justified even in law to use force to remove one who has himself unlawfully seized power, whether by military means or by electoral irregularities like forged ballots. When a supreme court in a democracy rules that election results are invalid, and a corrupt usurper refuses to give up his office or the support of the military that maintains him in office, then there would be a point in declaring or redeclaring the legality of an armed rebellion. But wrongful occupancy and refusal to relinquish office are the only examples of this kind that I can find, while there are many examples of principles that ought not be included in a legal system because of their incoherence, their pointlessness, or their mischievousness.

21. A less common but equally effective example of an undoubted moral right not adequately analyzed in terms of the suitability to be a legal right is held against legislators. I refer to the moral right of American women before 1920 to vote. That moral right, we have seen, can be understood as the ground or title for a legal right, which the women "had coming" as their due. But on the "there ought to be a law" theory, for a pre-1920 woman to say, "We have a moral right to the enactment of a legal right to vote" would amount to no more than "We ought to have a legal right to the enactment of a legal right to vote," an absurd redundancy. Since the statement to be analyzed made perfectly good sense, the analysis of the statement, which converts it to nonsense, must be mistaken.

22. Yale Kamisar, "Euthanasia Legislation: Some Non-Religious Objections," in *Euthanasia and the Right to Death*, ed. A. B. Downing (London: Owen, 1969), pp. 85–133. I attempt a reply to Kamisar in my paper "On Overlooking the Merits of the Individual Case: An Unpromising Approach to the Right to Die," *Ratio Juris* 4, no. 2 (July 1991): pp. 131–51.

23. Professor Kamisar does not actually use the term "moral right," but he

does clearly accept the view that some suffering terminal patients have an impressive moral case and apparently full moral justification for arranging their own deaths if there is someone with whom to make the arrangements. In conversation with me, he appeared to have no objection to speaking of "moral rights" in this connection.

24. "If I say that a man has a natural right to [this] land—all that it can mean, if it mean anything and mean true, is that I am of opinion he ought to have a political right to it" (*The Works of Jeremy Bentham*, ed. John Bowring, [Edinburgh: Tate, 1843], 3: 218).

25. *Jeremy Bentham's Economic Writings*, ed. W. Stark (London: Allen and Unwin, 1952), 1:333.

26. Quoted in Jeremy Waldron, *Nonsense upon Stilts: Bentham, Burke, and Marx on the Rights of Man* (London: Methuen, 1987), p. 37, from Bentham's *Anarchical Fallacies*, in *Works of Jeremy Bentham*, vol. 2. These remarks of Bentham's suggest an optative theory of moral rights: "I have a moral right to X" means "Would that this were a legal right!"

27. Paraphrasing Bentham, *Works*, 2:501, 3:221.

28. L. W. Sumner, *The Moral Foundation of Rights* (Oxford: Clarendon, 1987), p. 199.

29. Ibid., p. 163. The primary application of the word "conventional" for Sumner is to the wide class of rules that are products of human design, or if not conscious design then mutual acceptance, recognition, efficacy, or enforcement. Some conventional rules are institutional rules. Some institutional rules are legal rules. All conventional rules, insofar as they confer rights, confer "conventional rights."

30. For a more exact formulation, see Sumner, *Moral Foundation of Rights*, p. 145.

31. Ibid., pp. 143–44.

32. Ibid., p. 136.

33. Ibid., p. 147. This is a strong point in Sumner's theory which my own quite different theory should be required to accommodate. Clearly, moral rights, however analyzed, must be understood as changing their content as the relevant historical circumstances change. I deny that moral rights, except in their most abstract formulations, are "eternal" or "immutable." Neither eternity nor immutability follow from their being *actual* as opposed to suppositional.

34. Gilbert Ryle, *The Concept of Mind* (New York: Barnes and Noble, 1949), p. 20.

35. Ibid., p. 19.

36. But I do not advocate the image of reason as a homeless pauper or wandering vagabond. Needless to say, those images are misleading too.

Chapter 3

1. See Joel Feinberg, *Harm to Self* (New York: Oxford University Press, 1986), pp. 269–316.

2. *Sorrells v. United States* 287 US 435 (1930).

3. Justice Owen G. Roberts, as quoted in W. R. LaFave and A. W. Scott, *Criminal Law*, 2nd ed. (St. Paul, Minn.: West, 1986), p. 421.

4. Leo Katz, *Bad Acts and Guilty Minds* (Chicago, Ill.: University of Chicago Press, 1987), p. 155.

5. For a discussion of this metaphor, see "Causing Voluntary Actions," in Joel Feinberg, *Doing and Deserving* (Princeton, N.J.: Princeton University Press, 1970), pp. 152–86.

6. *United States v. Kelly* (1984) 748 F. 2d 691.

7. Katz, *Bad Acts and Guilty Minds*, pp. 157–58.

8. Ibid., p. 158.

9. Gerald Dworkin, "The Serpent Beguiled Me and I Did Eat: Entrapment and the Creation of Crime," *Law and Philosophy* 4 (1985): 33.

10. We can be speaking now of strong dispositions not to commit a crime or, equivalently, of weak dispositions to commit the crime.

11. Discovering our formed dispositions may come as a surprise to us at any time of life. Self-knowledge may require self-discovery even of those aspects of our character that we have ourselves created by our voluntary actions and omissions. Cf. the following sentence in Lewisohn's novel: "Then a strange thing happened. Herbert, who didn't know he was irascible, felt a wave of violent irritation rise up in him" (p. 78).

12. Bernard Williams, "Moral Luck," *Proceedings of the Aristotelian Society*, suppl, 50 (1976): 115–35, and Thomas Nagel, "Moral Luck," in his *Mortal Questions* (Cambridge: Cambridge University Press, 1979), pp. 24–38.

13. Justices Rehnquist and Scalia apparently regard such stories of bad luck in the criminal law not as "moral paradoxes," but as the plain deliverances of common sense. See Scalia's opinions in *Booth v. Maryland* 482 US 496 (1987) and *South Carolina v. Gathers* 490 US 805 (1989), and Rehnquist's opinion in *Payne v. Tennessee* 11 S.Ct. 2597 (1991). In *Payne*, Justice Rehnquist quotes the example (from Scalia) of the two identical bank robbers and adds, with hearty approval, that "under the facts of *Tison v. Arizona*, a bank robber who acts recklessly and kills someone can be put to death while a bank robber who acts recklessly and kills no one cannot." Quoted from David Dow, "When the Law Bows to Politics: Explaining *Payne v. Tennessee*," *University of California at Davis Law Review* 26 (1992): 165.

14. Nagel, "Moral Luck," pp. 29–30.

15. Ibid., p. 30.

16. Ibid., pp. 30–31.

17. The preposition "for" seems to have a different sense in the judgment that a person is responsible for the harm he has caused than it bears in the charge that a person is responsible for his wrongful actions. We can detach actions from their results so that it makes sense to say that one is the cause of the other, but we cannot detach the actor from his actions, so he cannot be labeled the cause of those actions. We do not cause our actions; we just do them.

18. Nagel, "Moral Luck," pp. 33–34.

19. Michael Dummitt, *Truth and Other Enigmas* (Cambridge, Mass.: Harvard University Press, 1978), pp. 14–16.

20. Nagel, "Moral Luck," p. 34.

21. Ibid.

22. Thomas Gray, "Elegy Written in a Country Churchyard," quoted in Nagel, "Moral Luck," p. 34n. The lines in question are "Some mute inglorious Milton here may rest. / Some Cromwell, guiltless of his country's blood."

23. Hannah Arendt, *Eichmann in Jerusalem: A Report on the Banality of Evil* (New York: Viking, 1963).

24. I do not mean to deny that there might be an element of luck in the

development of one's moral dispositions, as also of one's abilities, capacities, and the like. The usual argument for moral luck in this dispositional sense, however, is that our dispositions come to us already determined, for better or worse, and are not the products of our own efforts and deserts. That is a complex argument that I have prudently avoided considering here, concentrating instead on Nagel's account of two other types of moral luck (see Nagel, "Moral Luck," pp. 29–30). There is enough stimulation in Nagel's other categories fully to occupy an essay of this length. To take a further stand on the question of antecedent determination of dispositions would involve us in the complex of puzzles about free will, the analysis of the concept of luck, Rawls's natural lottery theory, and Aristotle's and Sartre's divergent accounts of how it is that we can "choose our own characters."

25. The word refers to the old common law crime of wrongly influencing juries in certain specific ways.

Chapter 4

1. The earliest reference to the problem is in Plato's last dialogue, *The Laws* 9.876. Plato was so concerned with the various combinations of perpetrators and victims, particularly the possible combinations of family statuses—father-son, son-father, husband-wife, sister-brother, slavemaster–his own slave, householder–neighbor's slave, and so on—and also with the combinations of intended and actually resultant harm involving that cast of players—intended killing, actual maiming, intended minor physical injury, actual killing, intended injury, actual absence of harm altogether, and so on—that he has little time for a detailed discussion of the combination that concerns us here, namely, the intended killing by anyone at all of anyone at all, resulting by a fluke in a failure to do any harm at all. Plato devotes only a couple of sentences to that kind of case, but the tone of his remarks suggests that he would concur with the position taken in this chapter. He writes of the unsuccessful homicidal attempter: "He is not to be pitied. He deserves no consideration but should be regarded as a murderer and tried for murder" (*The Dialogues of Plato*, 4th ed., trans. B. Jowett [1953], p. 4). Plato's Model Penal Code has only one other requirement pertaining to this kind of case, and clearly it is a response to the intended victim's good luck: The luckily escaped would-be victim, lest his apparent ingratitude should tax the patience of the deity, must make an offering of thanksgiving.

2. Yoram Shachar uses an especially felicitous name for our problem: "the problem of the fortuitous gap." See his interesting study in moral psychology, "The Fortuitous Gap in Law and Morality," *Criminal Justice Ethics* (1987): 12–36.

3. In California, wherever a sentence to a term of imprisonment with a fixed upper limit is specified in the sentencing code, it is stipulated that the penalty for the corresponding unsuccessful attempt will be exactly half as long as the specified maximum (*Califorina Penal Code* S 664 [West 1994]). In Great Britain, some jurisdictions permit the sentencing judge to fix her own discount rate. See, e.g., *R. v. Clfaver*, 13 Cr. App. R(S) 449 (1991).

4. A combination of factors, including the traditional Anglo-American reluctance to be impressed by the moral seriousness claimed for crimes that cause no harm (in the common law, mere attempts were classified as misdemeanors only) and our current crisis of prison overcrowding, explains why in some states it is now common for prisoners who have been convicted of attempted murder to be released on parole in only a few months.

5. To those who respond to this point by saying that "all life is an uncertain risk" and "luck is ineliminable from human affairs," Richard Parker has the right answer: "Fortune may make us healthy, wealthy, or wise but it ought not to determine whether we go to prison" ("Blame, Punishment and the Role of Result," *American Philosophical Quarterly* 21 (1984): 269, 273).

6. There is at least one kind of exception to this sweeping denunciation. When there is a reason against resorting to reasons, then random decisions and selections, ordinarily called "arbitrary," are perfectly appropriate. Thus random procedures for conducting lotteries to raise funds or to raise troops in a wartime conscription are meant to assure impartiality by excluding bias and favoritism. One can defend these techniques in context either by saying that they are not really arbitrary since they have a reason, or by saying that they are instances of justified arbitrariness. Which terms are preferable for putting this point is itself an arbitrary question with no clear answer and no importance.

7. It is interesting to note, incidentally, that this "very odd thing" is precisely what Plato says about the unsuccessful attempted killer: "He should be tried for murder," and his failure actually to kill his enemy is no reason for giving him any special "consideration" (*Dialogues of Plato*, S876.445).

8. In this opinion, I seem to differ from Chief Justice Rehnquist in *Rummel v. Estelle* 445 US 263, 281–84 (1980), who writes: "[Yet] rational people could disagree as to which criminal merits harsher punishment. . . . Once the death penalty and other punishments different in kind from fine or imprisonment have been put to one side there remains little in the way of objective standards for judging." Two questions, at least, are involved here: (1) whether judgments of the comparative moral gravity of offenses and the comparative severity of different criminal penalties are subjective (as Rehnquist says) or objective (say, in the manner of scientific reports), and (2) whether these judgments, if subjective, must therefore be arbitrary, or beyond reasoning altogether.

9. W. R. LaFave and A. W. Scott, *Criminal Law*, vol. 9 (St. Paul, Minn.: West, 1972).

10. Ibid., p. 7.

11. Ibid.

12. Joel Feinberg, "Harm to Others," in his *The Moral Limits of the Criminal Law* (New York: Oxford University Press, (1984), p. 1.

13. A philosopher should tread with caution if she uses the phrases "for their actions" or "for the consequences." Quite apart from their moderate infelicity in some contexts, especially when they are used with the word "guilty," these phrases are conceptual booby traps. Perhaps they are used most commonly with the word "responsible" since that term has a legitimate role in moral discourse as well as in all branches of the law. Even the idiom "responsible for," however, tends to cause mischief when used in a criminal context, and "guilty for" is even worse. The danger in complacent use of the phrase "responsible for" in criminal law, when what follows the preposition is some state of affairs—a presumably harmful state of affairs—is that it suggests a relation between a harm causer and his harm, with the implied question of whether he should be made to compensate a harmed person for her loss. That, of course, is the model of the tort situation. It is no better when we speak of a person being responsible not for a state of affairs that is the result of her conduct, but for her own actions themselves. That is rather clearly another sense of "responsible for," functioning in most of its uses simply

to identify the agent of a given action, and in other uses it may serve to identify the party who is answerable.

The preposition "for" brings to mind the standard case of producing results and suggests to the unwary that in ordinary action we stand in a relation to our own actions analogous to the relation between an action and its consequences, or between those immediate consequences and more remote results or effects. The preposition "for" suggests a causal relation, leading philosophers in earlier times to say that when we are responsible for our acts, our contribution to their coming about must have been to do something in our heads that caused our bodies to move in a certain manner. But in that case, either we should use a different prepositional construction and speak, say, of being guilty of an act of disobedience or being guilty by doing or in doing something prohibited, or else we should stipulate that we are using the preposition "for" in a sense different from its customary (causal) one in which it stands for some linkage between act and consequence. When you say that you are guilty for some state of affairs, you suggest that criminal guilt is determined in the same way as tort liability for harm sometimes is, by measuring the extent of the harms to be compensated, so that the more the harm, the more the liability.

When people talk of being guilty for their actions, they inadvertently invite even greater confusion. Since the preposition "for" often stands for a causal relation, it seems that when we are responsible for a result, we must have done something to produce it. Thus, when a person is said to be "guilty for" his actions, the implication is that he did something first (something prohibited) in his head to produce a volition, or in his body to produce a muscle contraction in his trigger finger, in order to cause his action to come about. After that, his contribution to the whole sequence blends with contributions from the outer world to produce the effects of his minimal action, some harmful, some not. (Sometimes the whole sequence of linked phases is itself called an action—his action—perhaps because it began in his head and was initially under his control. In that case, no distinction is made explicitly between acting, doing, and causing, and instead of saying he pulled the trigger and thereby propelled a bullet irretrievably in the direction of the victim, people say simply, "He killed him" or "He did it."

But if a person cannot properly be said to be guilty either for her action or for a state of affairs, then how can we mention the ground for holding her guilty at all? It would be much less misleading to leave the preposition "for" over in the land of torts and speak of a person's being guilty of murder, or say that in killing the victim she violated the law, or by killing him, she incurred great guilt. Finally, there is still one clear and legitimate use of the phrase "responsible for some action," namely, "being properly identifiable as the doer of the deed." See Joel Feinberg, "Action and Responsibility," in *Doing and Deserving*, ed. Joel Feinberg (Princeton, N.J.: Princeton University Press, 1970), pp. 119–51.

14. Everyone is familiar with the contention that criminals ought to "pay their debts to society" and that wrongdoers are made to "pay for their sins" when they are punished, as if one could buy a license to sin, then pay first, and sin afterward. Kadish and Schulhofer tell us that there is a simple theory "that it is perfectly legitimate . . . to grade punishment according to the amount of harm actually done, whether this was intended or not" (Sanford Kadish and Stephen Schulhofer, *Criminal Law and Its Processes*, 5th ed. [Chicago: University of Chicago Press, 1989], p. 624). They go on to nominate the following sentence for our list of commercial

metaphors: "If he has done the harm he must pay for it, but if he has not done it, he should pay less." From this kind of mixed metaphor one gets a picture of a clumsy chap accidentally breaking a dish in a china shop and then taking out his wallet to pay the debt thereby incurred. There is very little properly called "punitive" about that, especially if the owner of the shop remains polite and sympathetic.

15. Oliver Wendell Holmes, Jr., "The Path of the Law," in his *Collected Legal Papers* (Bedford, Mass.: Applewood, 1996), pp. 167–70.

16. George Fletcher, *A Crime of Self-Defense: Bernard Goetz and the Law on Trial* (New York: Free Press, 1988), pp. 63–83; and George Fletcher, *Rethinking Criminal Law* (Boston, Mass.: Little, Brown, 1978), 472–83.

17. Judith J. Thomson, "The Decline of Cause," *Georgetown Law Journal* 76 (1987): 137.

18. Fletcher, *Crime of Self-Defense*, p. 83.

19. It is interesting how many philosophers have resorted to terms like "elitism" in their attempts to explain either why the arguments of philosophers often fail to convince ordinary people or vice versa. Michael Moore, who defends what he called (in private conversation, with a twinkle in his eye) "the blue-collar view," refers to the view that is more popular with philosophers (like me) as "the standard educated view," thus associating it with the educated class, even though he, a leading member of that class, rejects the view. Michael Moore, "The Independent Moral Significance of Wrongdoing," *Journal of Contemporary Legal Issues* 5 (1994): 237. Jeffrie Murphy refers to the preferred positions of the majority being condemned by "a refined and condescending elite" (Jeffrie G. Murphy, "Getting Even: The Role of the Victim," *Social Philosophy and Policy* 7 [1990]: 209, 212). Murphy is speaking here of the attitude of "retributive hatred," common among ordinary folk, but ill-regarded by professors. Judith Thomson, in her article about the causal requirement in the definition of torts and some crimes, refers to those who, like the present writer, would downplay actually caused harms, as "moral sophisticates," who regard the majority view as a "vulgar error" (Thomson, "Decline of Cause," pp. 137, 139).

20. Fletcher, *Crime of Self-Defense*, p. 83.

21. The reference in brackets is to Joel Feinberg.

22. Kadish here refers to himself.

23. Peter Winch, *Ethics and Action* (London: Routledge and Kegan Paul, 1972), pp. 141–50.

24. See Herbert Morris's helpful essay in this area: Herbert Morris, "Nonmoral Guilt," in *Responsibility, Character and the Emotions*, ed. F. Schoeman (New York: Cambridge University Press, 1988), pp. 220–40. Morris distinguishes two or more basic types of guilt—moral guilt (the most familiar kind, based on legal models) and nonmoral guilt. The latter category includes as guilt feelings "anomalous cases" that are likely to seem confused, morbid, or neurotic to those who have been excessively concerned with "moral guilt" on the legal model. The anomalies include guilt for states of mind only, guilt for unjust enrichment, survivor's guilt, and vicarious guilt.

25. I include in this the element of intense anxiety over being caught, if only to bring into the boundaries of relevance Dostoevsky's Raskolnikov, who is also considered a paradigmatic study. In Dostoevsky's novel *Crime and Punishment*, Raskolnikov lives in nearly constant terror of being caught. It seems that the only

thoughts capable of deflecting this anxiety are those that drown him in moral guilt.

26. Fletcher, *Rethinking Criminal Law*, p. 483.

27. W. E. H. Lecky, *History of European Morals*, vol. 2 (New York: George Braziller, 1955).

28. C. D. Broad, *The Mind and Its Place in Nature* (London: Routledge and Kegan Paul, 1980).

29. Adam Smith, *The Theory of the Moral Sentiments*, part III, section II, chap. 2, paragraph 4 (1759).

30. Very likely, he meant by "atrocity" what could just as well be expressed by "atrociousness."

Chapter 5

1. The local representative, of course, can hope to succeed only by promising to vote in the committee for much more expensive projects in the chair's home state, thereby adding to the chair's already considerable clout. This is the process that brought us a $40 million museum of the steam locomotive in Pennsylvania and an "authentic Bavarian resort" in the Idaho mountains, neither of which was much appreciated by the National Park Service. Leaders of both parties have condemned the pork system, and some have estimated that it wastes billions of dollars annually, but its momentum in Congress shows no sign of slowing.

2. Brian Kelly, *Adventures in Porkland: How Washington Wastes Your Money and Why They Won't Stop* (New York: Villard, 1992), pp. 15ff.

3. A clearly written critical summary of these and other leading theories can be found in Noël Carroll's "Can Government Funding of the Arts Be Justified Theoretically?" in *Public Policy and the Aesthetic Interest*, ed. Ralph A. Smith and Ronald Berman (Champagne-Urbana, Ill.: University of Illinois Press, 1992), pp. 68–82. It is a natural starting place for this whole subject.

4. The preceding three paragraphs are drawn from Joel Feinberg, *Harmless Wrongdoing* (New York: Oxford University Press, 1988), pp. 314–15. The treatment of rotational justice in the book is more detailed than it is here.

5. Ibid., pp. xxvii–xxix, 20–32, 125.

6. Thomas Nagel, "Symposium on the Public Benefits of the Arts and Humanities," *Columbia Journal of Art and the Law* 9 (1984): 236.

7. Ibid., p. 237.

8. *Newsweek*, Oct. 12, 1992, 67.

9. Nagel, "Symposium," p. 231.

10. G. E. Moore, *Principia Ethica* (Cambridge: Cambridge University Press, 1903), pp. 83–84.

11. Bartlett's *Familiar Quotations* attributes this familiar line to two sources: Lew Wallace in *The Prince of India* (1893) and Margaret Wolfe Hungerford in *Molly Brown* (1878). The word "altogether" appears in the Wallace but not the Hungerford quotation.

12. George Santayana, "The Philosophy of Mr. Bertrand Russell," in *Winds of Doctrine* (London: Dent, and New York: Scribner, 1913), p. 146.

13. Nagel, "Symposium," p. 237.

14. The NEA, I believe, devotes 3 percent of its graphic arts budget to projects in this category.

15. *Arizona Daily Star*, May 13, 1992.

16. The sadomasochistic Mapplethorpe photographs, I think, are a different matter. Depictions of unlikely objects jammed painfully into unlikely orifices are not exactly "playful." If the victim of this photographed abuse had been a woman rather than a homosexual man, Robert Hughes suggests, the Mapplethorpe show would never have gotten off the ground. See Robert Hughes, "Art, Morals, and Politics," *New York Review of Books*, Apr. 23, 1992, p. 24.

17. Note that an object or facility can be worthy (deserving) of support, and yet there might be overriding reasons, in the present circumstances, for not giving that support. The money might better be used to support AIDS research, to end homelessness, to confront genuine military danger, to reduce gigantic government deficits, and so on. It is no contradiction to say that *x* is worthy of support (because worthy of being admired and cherished) and yet we ought to withhold support so as to reduce or prevent harms.

18. Noël Carroll's similar concern, however, is quite explicitly about justification: "It may be true, though one has one's doubts, that art is intrinsically good. But even if the production of art is intrinsically good, that in and of itself, would not warrant state funding of the arts. For the state does not, and in some cases should not, be taken to have a role in the production of whatever we conceive to be an intrinsic good (if there are such things). State intervention in these matters calls for justification." See Carroll, "Can Government Funding of the Arts Be Justified Theoretically?" p. 80.

19. One final, ironic footnote. I have learned, since completing this essay, that Congress did acquire the Manassas battlefield from various private owners (developers) for $250,000 an acre for a 542-acre site. Many more old battlefields remain vulnerable, so Congress, unable to afford any more direct purchases, set up a fifteen-member advisory commission to cooperate with a new nonprofit Civil War foundation to raise private money for future purchases and maintenance. Projects whose costs are totally beyond private support remain "the exceptional case."

Chapter 6

1. Even in relatively trivial matters, there is a deep social inertia inhibiting change. Often resentment of new trends and fads manifests itself in overt hostility and even violence. A recent magazine article (Julie Raskin and Carolyn Males, "Some Joggers Run a Gauntlet of Fear," *Parade*, July 15, 1979) gives graphic accounts of the widespread harassment of joggers in the period during which that new practice was establishing itself as a prominent feature of American life. Joggers reported that their attackers were "out to get them solely because they were runners." "While injuries as severe as David Gottlieb's are rare, other runners throughout the country have reported being punched, shouted at, thrown at (bottles, cans, cherry bombs, rotten apples, eggs, milkshakes, coat hangers), or having drivers deliberately intimidate them with their cars." The motivations for these attacks were probably mixed, but there seems little doubt that some expressed a natural resentment against fancied exclusiveness, cultish trendiness, and the like, taking it somehow to be threatening to the attacker's own self-confidence or self-esteem. To many people, anything new is *eo ipso* something alien, menacing, and contemptible. This mindless conservative inertia is a social tendency equal and opposite to bandwagon jumping and faddishness, which are, of course, equally mindless. In less injurious forms, it has a valuable function of regulating social

change, quickly deflating fads, and providing a test that new practices must pass if they are to become entrenched (as jogging apparently has) in our way of life. It is the nature of mere trendy fads to come and then (partly under conservative pressure) to go. Those that have some useful basis (like jogging), and perhaps only those, catch hold in some firm and permanent fashion.

2. See André Gide's conception of the purely "gratuitous act" as a model of perfect freedom. This conception is defended by a character in the novel, not by Gide himself. See *Lafcadio's Adventures*, trans. Dorothy Bussy (Garden City, N.Y.: Doubleday, 1953). The protagonist pushes a stranger out of a speeding train as a wholly "gratuitous act."

3. Curtis Bok, *Star Wormwood* (New York: Knopf, 1959), pp. 138–40.

4. Robert Schopp was a student of mine at the University of Arizona, where he earned a Ph.D. in philosophy and a law degree. He already had a Ph.D. in psychology. He is now a professor of law at the University of Nebraska. I had many fruitful discussions with him and an exchange of letters, which are the sources of this discussion.

5. See, for example, Andrew Delbanco, *The Death of Satan* (New York: Farrar, Straus and Giroux, 1955), and Tzvetan Todorov, *Facing the Extreme*, trans. Arthur Pollack and Abagail Pollack (New York: Holt, 1996).

6. Many triple-sick crimes of violence—assault, battery, rape, homicide—are *not* undertaken to produce benefits or harms for anyone, and thus they satisfy at least part of the definition of "pure evil" or "sheer wickedness": They are done "for no reason." But the nonhomicidal serial rapist may be an exception to this description. One might interpret sexual gratification, for example, to be a "benefit" for the rapist or, more plausibly, the "benefit" might be the pain and humiliation (harms) of his victim.

After telling the story of the wanton killing of the boy on the bridge, Stephen provides a second example: "A man makes advances to a girl who repels him. He deliberately but instantly cuts her throat. In neither of these stories is there premeditation, but each represents even more barbaric cruelty than that involved in the natural sense of the word" (J. F. Stephen, *A History of the Criminal Law of England* [London, 1883], 3:94).

7. Carl Goldberg, *Speaking with the Devil* (New York: Viking, 1996), p. 1.

8. Ibid.

9. Perhaps Satan's favorite moral theory then is that which requires us to maximize pain for others while exempting ourselves.

10. See John Stuart Mill, *Utilitarianism* (Oxford: Blackwell, 1949), chap. 5, for a discussion of the origin and interpretation of this famous slogan.

11. Ronald Milo, *Immorality* (Princeton, N.J.: Princeton University Press, 1984), p. 8.

12. Ibid., p. 236.

13. Ibid.

14. G. Rostrevor Hamilton, *Hero or Fool? A Study of Milton's Satan* (Oxford: Oxford University Press, 1940), p. 30.

15. C. S. Lewis, *A Preface to Paradise Lost* (Oxford: Oxford University Press, 1941).

16. Charles Williams, *Introduction to the English Poems of John Milton* (Oxford: Oxford University Press, 1940).

17. Albert Camus, *The Myth of Sisyphus*, trans. J. O. O'Brien (New York: Random House, 1955), p. 91.

18. Milo, *Immorality*, p. 29.

19. Ibid.

20. *Webster's Unabridged Dictionary*, 3d ed. (Springfield, Mass.: Merriam-Webster, 1986), p. 1688.

21. David Lewis, "The Punishment That Leaves Something to Chance," *Philosophy and Public Affairs* 18 (1989): 53–67.

22. *Diagnostic and Statistical Manual of Mental Disorders*, 4th ed. (Washington, D.C.: American Psychiatric Association, 1994).

23. Hervey Cleckley, *The Mask of Sanity*, 5th ed. (Augusta, Ga.: Cleckley, 1988).

24. Robert D. Hare, *Without Conscience: The Disturbing World of the Psychopaths among Us* (New York: Simon and Schuster, 1993).

25. Ibid., p. 45.

26. Ibid., p. xi.

27. See, e.g., Theophrastus, *Characters*, trans. J. J. Edmonds (Cambridge, Mass.: Harvard University Press, 1952).

28. Carl Hempel, "The Logic of Functional Analysis," in *Symposium on Sociological Theory*, ed. Llewelyn Gross (New York: Harper and Row, 1959), p. 99.

29. James Thurber, *The Thirteen Clocks* (New York: Simon and Schuster, 1950), p. 114.

30. Bernard Williams, "Problems of the Self," in *Moral Luck: Philosophical Papers* (Cambridge: Cambridge University Press, 1981).

31. Joel Feinberg, *Harm to Others* (New York: Oxford University Press, 1984), p. 68.

32. Michael Moore, "The Moral Worth of Retribution" in *Responsibility, Character, and the Emotions*, ed. Ferdinand Schoeman (New York: Cambridge University Press, 1988), p. 99.

33. In American English, evil now seems to go naturally with smell, so that a really disagreeable smell will be said to be "downright evil." Delbanco thinks this has the effect of downgrading the significance or impact of evil generally. An English-language speaker, on the other hand, might judge that using the word "evil" to refer, say, to an "evil-smelling" cheese has the effect of elevating, not diminishing, the expressive power of the word "evil." See Andrew Delbanco's sensitive discussion of the distinction in German between *ubel* and *böse*, in *The Death of Satan*, pp. 5ff.

34. Hannah Arendt, *Eichmann in Jerusalem: A Report on the Banality of Evil* (New York: Penguin, 1944), p. 114.

35. Ibid.

36. Ibid., p. 106.

37. James Fitzjames Stephen, *Liberty, Equality, Fraternity* (London, 1878), pp. 149–50.

38. Arendt, *Eichmann in Jerusalem*, p. 127.

Chapter 7

1. J. L. Austin, "A Plea for Excuses," in *Freedom and Responsibility*, ed. Herbert Morris (Stanford, Calif.: Stanford University Press, 1956), p. 6.

2. See A. J. P. Kenny, "Mental Health in Plato's Republic," *Proceedings of the British Academy* (1969): "The concept of mental health was Plato's invention. Metaphors drawn from sickness are no doubt as old as metaphor itself and the first recorded application of the Greek word for healthy was to a sound argument

rather than to a sound body (*Iliad*, p. 524). But nothing in Greek thought before Plato suggests that the notion of a healthy mind was more than a metaphor, and nowhere in the Old Testament is sin represented as a sickness of the soul. It was Plato who in the *Gorgias* developed the metaphor in unprecedented detail, and in the *Republic* crossed the boundary between metaphor and philosophical theory" (pp. 229–53).

3. Tristram Englehardt, A. L. Caplan, and J. J. McCartney, eds., *Concepts of Health and Disease* (New York: Addison-Wesley, 1981), introduction. In the case of the disease of masturbation, the authors illustrate how "moral suspicions can lead to certain activities being identified as the cause of illness states." Citing American and British textbooks and journal articles published between 1866 and 1895, they find the following illnesses attributed to masturbation: dyspepsia, constriction of the urethra, epilepsia [*sic*], blindness, vertigo, loss of hearing, headache, loss of memory, irregular heartbeat, rickets, leukorrhea, conjunctivitis, and nymphomania.

INDEX

abolitionist, 19
ABSCAM, 61, 66
ameliorist, 19
American Psychiatric Association, 199
anger, natural, 91–95, 97
animals, punishing, 93
appropriations, tax supported, 106
Aquinas, 32
arbitrariness, 78, 99
Arecibo, radio signal from, 109, 113
Arendt, Hannah, 183, 185, 214 n.34
Aristotle, 4, 86, 111–12, 172, 201 n.1
Article IV, 32
arts, government funding of, 211 n.3, 212 n.18
attachment, cultural, 85
Augustine, 9
Austin, J. L., 194

Bahai, 38
benefit principle, 104–5
Benn, S. I., 202 n.3
Bentham, Jeremy, 43, 48, 49, 53–54, 149, 188
Blackstone, William, 32, 201 n.10
blameworthiness, 78, 100–102, 128–29, 131, 186, 198
"bloody cause," the, 18, 32
Bok, Curtin, 213 n.3
Bradfisch, Otto, 185
Brandt, Richard D., 202 n.4, 203 n.10

Broad, C. D., 139
Budd, Grace, 133
Butler, Joseph, 27

Camden, Lord, 31
Camus, Albert, 155
candor, merit of, 24
capital offense, stealing a turnip, 21
Carroll, Noël, 211 n.3, 212 n.18
charities, 104
Christians, early, on slavery, 18
Cicero, 9, 32
Civil War, battlefield of the, 122
Cleckley, Hervey, 167–71, 174–75
clitorectomy, 38, 202 n.5
Cobb, Lynn, 201 n.4
Commentaries on the Constitution, 45
compulsion, 57
conservative principle, 85
Cover, Robert, 19, 45, 201 n.11
cowardice, 69
Crime and Punishment, 201 n.25

Dahmer, Jeffrey, 127, 130, 132, 147, 158, 170, 174, 193–94
Davis, Michael, 81
defilement, 86
Delbance, Andrew, 213 n.5, 214 n.33
deodand, 94
Descartes, René, 53
deterrence, 100